P9-DDB-626

The Interpretation of French Song

The
Interpretation
of
French Song

BY

PIERRE BERNAC

TRANSLATIONS OF SONG TEXTS

BY

WINIFRED RADFORD

784.93
B45612

W · W · NORTON & COMPANY

New York · London

Barton College Library
Wilson, N.C. 27893

W. W. Norton & Company, Inc., 500 Fifth Avenue, New York, NY 10110
W. W. Norton & Company Ltd, 10 Coptic Street, London WC1A 1PU

© Pierre Bernac 1970. All translations © Winifred Radford 1970. © Pierre Bernac 1976. © Winifred Radford 1976.   Printed in the United States of America. All Rights Reserved.

First published in the Norton Library 1978 by arrangement with Victor Gollancz, Ltd.

Books That Live
The Norton imprint on a book means that in the publisher's
estimation it is a book not for a single season but for the years.
W. W. Norton & Company, Inc.

Library of Congress Cataloging in Publication Data
Bernac, Pierre.
   The interpretation of French song.
   (The Norton Library)
   Includes index.
   1. Singing—Interpretation (Phrasing, dynamics, etc.)
2. Songs, French—History and criticism. I. Title.
[MT892.B4   1978]   784.9'34   77-17160

ISBN 0-393-00878-9

4567890

To Winifred Radford

11.70

Fine Arts

MAR 3 0 1995

Contents

Foreword

This book does not claim to be anything more than a guide for English-speaking singers, who wish to study a repertoire which may not be very familiar to them, and which, judging by my experience as a teacher, presents problems which are not easy for them to solve. The repertoire of the French mélodie, though it is far from being as vast as that of the German Lied, contains some of the most genuine masterpieces ever written in music.

The Lied began to develop in Germany at the end of the eighteenth century, reaching its zenith early in the nineteenth century with the Lieder of Schubert. In France, however, it was almost the middle of the nineteenth century before the first mélodies were composed. They were in no way derived from the Germanic Lied, but stemmed directly from the 'romance' which had reigned in France since the middle of the eighteenth century. This art of the 'romance', which may lack substance, but is not without charm, remained popular up to the middle of the nineteenth century, and profoundly influenced the first mélodies written during this period by Berlioz and Gounod.

*

Berlioz was the first to use the word 'mélodie' as a title for his compositions for one voice with piano accompaniment. *Mélodie* is the term always used in France for this musical form, and is therefore employed throughout this book to designate the French song (called in the United States the French Art Song). There is, in French, a very sharp difference between 'mélodie' and 'chanson'. 'Mélodie', which is the French equivalent of 'Lied', denotes serious song, concert song; whereas 'chanson' refers to a folk song, a popular song or night-club song. If some composers of mélodies occasionally use the word 'chanson' in the title of their songs, it is to suggest that they are intentionally in a very simple style, or in folk-song style: i.e. Poulenc: 'Chansons Villageoises'. It may also be because the word 'chanson' has been used in the title of the poem: Duparc: 'Chanson Triste'.

*

In the first chapter of this book, the problems inherent in the interpretation of vocal music are briefly considered, and I will express my own views on the subject, and give my ideas on the method of approach to the repertoire here studied.

The second chapter includes the phonetic principles, and contains some very important notes on peculiarities of the French language. This knowledge is absolutely essential as a solid basis for the performance of French vocal music.

A short chapter follows which contains a few general remarks on the style of interpretation of the mélodie.

In the chapters devoted to the study of the repertoire it is, of course, impossible to discuss all the composers of mélodies. Only the most outstanding are considered, and from among their songs, the choice is limited to some of those which are the most beautiful and most typical of their individual genius. Living composers have unfortunately had to be excluded.

Where the key of a song is not mentioned it is either not of importance or the song is at present published in only one key.

For each of the chosen songs, the text of the poem is first printed, giving indications of the liaisons, the elisions, the breaths, etc., of the particular setting to be studied. With this text will be found a literal line-by-line translation. Suggestions are given for the interpretation and performance of each mélodie. All ideas of interpretation are of necessity personal and therefore open to disagreement. In writing this book, I realize the difficulty of conveying these ideas without the actual presence of the performer. How is it possible to describe a certain phrasing, a subtle nuance, a stress, a *rubato*, a vocal colour? An attempt has been made tò solve this problem as simply as possible, avoiding at all costs unnecessary verbosity.

This book is not written by a musicologist, and indeed it is not from the angle of musicology or musical analysis that the study of the interpretation of the French mélodie is here approached, or should be approached! It is written by an interpreter, whose only wish is to offer the benefit of his experience to those singers who wish to explore an enchanting realm of song.

Acknowledgements

My thanks are due to the following for permission to quote copyright song texts. It has not always been possible to quote the titles of the actual poems from which the song texts are taken since in some cases these are fragments from longer poems or appeared originally under a different title.

All possible efforts have been made to reach copyright owners but in some cases these have been of no avail. The publishers would be glad to hear from any person(s) who can assist in tracing poems that are in copyright but are not acknowledged.

Librairie Ernest Flammarion—Paul Fort: 'Cloche d'Aube', 'La Ronde', 'L'Adieu en Barque'

Éditions Gallimard—Louise de Vilmorin: poems from *Fiançailles pour Rire, Le Sable du Sablier*; Paul Eluard: poems from *Les Yeux Fertiles, Chansons Complètes, Le Livre Ouvert*; Léon-Paul Fargue: poems from *Tancrède, Ludions* © Éditions Gallimard

Éditions Messein—Guillaume Apollinaire: poems from *Il y a*

Mercure de France—Tristan Klingsor: *Shéhérazade*

Éditions Albin Michel—Pierre Louÿs: poems from *Chansons de Bilitis*

Société des Gens de Lettres—Jean Richepin: 'Au Cimetière'

Académie Française and the Société des Gens de Lettres—Henri de Régnier: 'Le Jardin mouillé'

Éditions Bernard Grasset—Jean de la Ville de Mirmont: *L'Horizon Chimérique*

Jean Rostand—Rosemonde Gérard: 'Villanelle des Petits Canards', 'Les Cigales'

Paul Morand for 'Don Quichotte à Dulcinée'

For permission to quote 'Cinq Mélodies Populaires Grecques' by Maurice Ravel I have to thank Durand & Cie, Éditeurs-propriétaires, Paris.

KEY TO THE SIGNS IN THE FRENCH TEXTS

✓	breath
(✓)	breath, if unavoidable
|	break or no liaison
⌒	at the end of a line: no breath
‿	liaison or elision
s̲	consonant which should be pronounced
¢	consonant which should not be pronounced
m̲m̲	double consonant sounded
e̲nnui	expressive stress

1 | The Performance and Interpretation of Vocal Music

A work of music—which is a creation in time, as opposed to a work of plastic art, which is a creation in space—comes into actual existence through the performance of the interpretative artist; but unless the work is an improvisation of this artist, it is necessarily the performance of a work already conceived by the composer and notated on paper. The signs penned on paper, however, are mere symbols; the actuality of the sound is totally absent from them. In the art of music, it is the interpreter's performance which we come to regard as the work itself.

The great French poet and philosopher, Paul Valéry, puts this in an apt and humorous way: 'A work of music, which is only a piece of writing, is a cheque drawn on the fund of talent of a possible performer.' A painter or a sculptor, who conceives his work and realizes it completely, may indeed pity a musician for having to trust his work to an interpreter. How is the 'intimate correspondence' (in the words of Gisèle Brelet) between invention and execution to be ensured? This is the whole problem of musical interpretation.

*

What exactly is involved for the performer? Something quite other than simply giving sonority to signs set down on paper. And yet, this is the first thing that is involved. It is by means of these signs that the performer comes to know musical works. As Furtwängler has said, he follows the composer's path in the opposite direction. The composer creates his music by giving it its living meaning, before writing it down, or while doing so. Whereas for the performer, the work is presented as the very opposite of an improvisation: as a thing noted down, with fixed signs and of immutable form, the enigma and meaning of which are to be divined and spelled out afterwards.

The performer's first task is therefore to decipher this notation and embody it in sound, with the utmost care and scrupulous accuracy. This is his only possible means of divining the enigma. As Stravinsky puts it: 'The sin against the spirit of the work always begins with a sin against its letter.'

Those who are not themselves performers may think that it should not be very difficult to observe this scrupulous accuracy, this precision. But conscientious performers know well how difficult it is. There are so many things to be observed: indications of tempi, precision of rhythm, of values (values of the notes, values of the rests), the accents, the dynamics, the phrasing, the nuances, etc. It can be said that one never reads the score with sufficient care.

This is enough to underline that, in this book, the precision of the performance will be the first concern and requirement.

*

Despite the fact that a composer may carry about in his head the ideal interpretation of his work, he will be powerless to indicate it by means of signs set down on paper. It is quite true that when the text is compared to the performance, it can be seen how ill-defined are its indications with regard to all that is required beyond the exact precision of the musical notation. Obviously the written text, however fully annotated, cannot contain the actual reality of the performance. Liszt, the very model of the composer-performer, said: 'It would be an illusion to think that one can set down on paper the things that constitute the beauty of the performance.' And Gustav Mahler went as far as to say that the essential elements of his music were not to be found in his scores.

To treat the work with respect it is, therefore, necessary to go beyond the text. 'Musical performance', says Gisèle Brelet, 'is not material realization, but rather the spiritual function that this realization exercises.' All the interest of the performance lies in the fact that, to be faithful to the work he performs, the interpreter has to give his personal vision of it. Only the performer's *presence* can give *expression* to his rendering.

In instrumental music, when the composer indicates on his score: *espressivo* (with expression), he cannot specify the kind of expression he means. He therefore relies on the emotion that his music arouses in the interpreter; but in vocal music the expression is clarified by specific poetic texts.

*

The performance and interpretation of vocal music raise problems of a particular kind: two elements—a musical text and a literary text— must be analysed and then synthesized.

Obviously the literary text deserves the same care, the same scrupulous accuracy, in short the same respect that is demanded by the musical text. This respect will be manifested in the first place on the purely technical level, by means of the concern with articulation and pronunciation. In so far as the vocal difficulties and the tessitura permit, the poetic text must be perfectly intelligible. This is a matter of elementary politeness to the listener, and of fundamental honesty to the poet.

*

In vocal music, the sonority and the rhythm of the words are an integral part of the music itself. The word is itself a musical sound. The sonority and stress and rhythm of words inspire music no less, and at times even more, than the emotion they express. (Except for certain composers, in whose works the vocal line is purely instrumental, and in which the same words are repeated over and over again: Bach arias, for example.) In the case of most composers of songs and operas, it is apparent that the primary impulse to melodic inspiration comes from the sonority and rhythm of the literary phrase, its inflections, its stresses, its own and proper music.

In order to do full justice to vocal music, each sound must have its value, not only in pitch and rhythm, but also in colour and verbal stress. If the singer ought to make an effort to sing each work of music in its original language, the reason is that the music *of* the poem is as important as the music set *to* the poem. The music of the words and the music itself are one and the same; they should not be disassociated.

*

The musicologist Gisèle Brelet says that fundamental musical expression lies in what is rightly called the singing line, the 'cantabile', the melody that is born of the vocal gesture. Every instrument obeys the 'phrasing', this original rhythm of the voice; and for any instrument, the ideal of expressive playing is to imitate the sound, the melody, the life of the voice, the suppleness of its impulses, punctuated by breaths and silences. Expression is always an imitation of the singing voice.

If, then, the obvious model for the instrumentalist is the human voice, and if he constantly derives from it a lesson for his 'cantabile', it goes to prove that the finest quality of singing is its legato, its phrasing, its human rhythm. *Thus it is the musical line, above all, that the singer must serve and respect.* There can be no question of sacrificing it for the benefit of the words.

But the true beauty, the true value of singing is the combination, the mixture, the indissoluble union, the mysterious alloy of melody and words.

How is this to be achieved? How is one to guarantee both the integrity of the music and that of the words? This is the problem that the singer must solve technically, but, above all, spiritually. Advice on the technique of singing the French language is given in the following chapter. Put briefly, the main problem lies in achieving the perfection of the vocal line and of the musical phrase, despite the change of shading of the various vowel sounds; and in achieving the continuity of the sound, despite the occlusion of the consonants. If this is done, the music will probably be fairly well phrased and the instrumental aspect of the singing preserved; but justice will not have been done to the poem, the phrase, the word.

The sung text must preserve the inflexions, modulations, stresses and rhythmic subtleties that are found in a good spoken monologue, but the person reciting creates his own verbal melody, his own range of sound and rhythm. He thus manifests his sensitivity, not only to the idea of the poem, but also to the music of its words.

The singer enjoys none of these freedoms. His verbal melody, range of sound and rhythm, are determined in advance and set down by the composer. It is the composer's vision, or rather audition, of the poem that must seem to rise spontaneously from the singer's lips.

Even if the prosody is bad, even if the rhythm or the inflexions of the poem are not respected by the composer, the singer has to make the verbal and expressive shortcomings appear natural, intentional. This is inevitable in strophic songs, in which the different stanzas of the poem are sung to the same music. Indeed, to put it mildly, a great flexibility is often demanded of the singer, in order that the spoken phrase and the melodic phrase may be superimposed upon each other, and may move forward hand in hand without any verbal or musical distortion. The poetic comparison of the writer Yassu Gauclère can be paraphrased: Just as a fresco can be adapted to the curve of an arch, without the actual distortion causing any apparent distortion in the figures, so the literary phrase must take the exact shape of the line of sound. But whereas for the painter there is a solid architecture on which to lean, for the singer, verbal design and vocal curve must rise simultaneously from one and the same effort, and the balance of this perilous construction can be maintained only by the constant awareness of its two aspects.

*

The constant awareness of these two aspects of vocal music, verbal design and vocal curve, implies not only the achieving of the mysterious blending of words and music, but above all, the synthesis of the poetic idea and the musical idea.

When a composer sets a literary text to music, he has his personal conception of the feeling expressed in the text, and it is this feeling that he attempts to express in his music. It may happen that the interpreter has quite a different view of this text, and thus finds himself torn between the two feelings he is required to express: that of the poet and that of the musician. Once again it is the musical feeling that must be given priority, since it is the musician who gives his personal interpretation of the poetic text, and it is essentially *this* interpretation that the performer is required to bring alive. He must therefore attempt to bring his own conception of the poem into line with the composer's, without of course losing any of his own personality.

A striking example of the necessity for this submission to the musician is offered by the fact that certain poems have been set to music by various composers, for instance: Goethe's 'Harfner Gesänge' have been set to music by Schubert, Schumann, Liszt and Hugo Wolf; the same poems of Verlaine have been set to music by Fauré, Debussy, Reynaldo Hahn, etc. In the face of these at times very different interpretations of the poet's feelings by the musician, the performer must be totally submissive to the musician's idea, which he must adopt in order to express it with utter sincerity, lacking which, he is unworthy of the title of interpreter.

Fortunately, this inevitable split in the personality of the performer is not often carried to painful extremes. In operatic works, the conception of the character is generally obvious, and the singer manages to don the feelings of his role along with his costume. But far more subtle is the task of the concert singer who, in the course of an evening, must be not one but twenty different characters, who, at times within the compass of just a few measures and without any visual aid, must succeed in creating an atmosphere, evoking an entire poetic world, suggesting a drama—that is more often than not an inner one—expressing one after the other the most varied feelings: sadness and joy, quietness and passion, tenderness, irony, faith, casualness, sensuousness, serenity, and so on. He must from moment to moment, from one work to the next, completely alter his inner attitude, his mind, and, in some mysterious way, even the timbre of his voice.

*

All this of course is carefully thought out in advance, carefully calculated, worked at, clarified and perfected, and . . . finally surrendered to the improvisation of the moment. For, although a performance must in no way be a material improvisation, it will always be essentially a spiritual one.

However carefully prepared and minutely worked out a musical performance may be, it will never be the same twice, even if the performer lives to the age of a hundred and plays or sings the same work a thousand times. There will always be an element of improvisation, of inspiration, of the unforeseen. A performance is always an adventure. One runs a risk at each and every performance, which leaves its future uncertain until the moment it ends. This is sufficient to indicate how necessary it is that there be a firm basis, a solid framework of technical security and of created automatism, to ensure the security of the performance, despite the influences that will inevitably operate at the last moment, mental and material influences that will modify the physical and spiritual behaviour of the performer.

*

A few practical recommendations can be given concerning the performance of all vocal music, but more particularly the performance of the concert repertoire.

When a singer has the support of an orchestra, he may at times find this helpful in concealing certain vocal shortcomings; moreover, the conductor takes the responsibility for the musical performance. But a singer, alone on a platform with his pianist, takes the entire responsibility for the concert, even for the pianist who is playing for him, whom he has chosen himself and to whom he is supposed to have transmitted all his musicality. (Even though it is, at times, the exact opposite . . . occasionally to the music's advantage.) This singer cannot hope that any flaw in his voice, his singing, his musicality, his interpretation, will pass unnoticed by his audience.

*

In my opinion there is nothing to be feared more than the supposedly 'intelligent' singer, who more or less 'speaks' a poem, more or less on the notes of the composer.

The concert repertoire, which is the subject of this book, does not perhaps require the same volume of voice as the operatic repertoire, but it certainly requires a still more refined art of singing. It is completely wrong to imagine that one can interpret a French mélodie (or a German

Lied), if one is not capable, first of all, of doing justice to an aria by Mozart or by Bellini. This is to say that one must have acquired a perfect mastery of the breath, of legato, of phrasing, etc. Besides, a concert singer must be able to sing *fortissimo* as well as *pianissimo* over the whole range of his voice.

Vocal problems are not the subject of this study, but there are some musical shortcomings that can be brought to the attention of singers.

*

For instance, singers too often make what I call *involuntary nuances*, generally due to technical difficulties, and which are made for no musical or expressive reasons whatsoever; nuances that an instrumentalist playing the same phrase would never make. Why should a singer do this ? He must be careful, for example, not always to make a crescendo when the voice goes up and a diminuendo when it goes down. It is so beautiful to be able to sing a whole page, whatever the vocal problems may be, without any change of dynamics, and it can prepare the following contrasts so well. This is true mastery.

*

Too often also one hears singers who are careless about the sustaining of *each note* of their vocal line. Each note must always be 'sung', that is to say the sound of its vowel should be sustained as long as possible, even on short notes. This fault occurs frequently on the weak syllables of the words, and also on notes which are not on the beats, particularly in phrases where the notes have even values. The upbeats must be sung too, especially when the musical phrase begins on an anacrusis. How can a beautiful line be achieved if this is not observed ?

*

The values of the rests, of the 'silences', indicated by the composer, are as important as the values of the notes. Too often, for instance, a singer is careless about the duration of the last note of a musical phrase, making it too short or too long, thus disturbing the harmony with the piano part; by unduly prolonging the last note of a phrase, the singer is often late in his preparation to attack the following phrase.

Of course the 'rhythmic value' of a rest, in the vocal line, does not always have the same 'expressive value'. This is specially obvious in recitatives, but is true also in arias and songs. There, the manner of taking the breath is of predominant importance. Breaths can be made expressive and can add to the interpretation, both of the music and of the literary text. For example: breaths which have no musical or literary reasons are sometimes required by the length of the vocal line. By making them intentional, expressive, they can add intensity to the phrase.

In the vocal line of a song there are often silences, while the piano part goes its way. These silences, more or less long, may occur in the middle of a literary phrase, or of a musical idea; they should not be 'dead' silences, and the singer with his 'presence' must succeed in 'making a bridge' between the two fragments of the phrase. The best way to achieve this linking of the musical and literary idea is to take a breath immediately and slowly at the end of the first fragment, and to hold it until one resumes singing, instead of waiting until just before singing to take the breath. Thus the tension is held; it makes a great difference.

*

The indications of dynamics can never be taken in an absolute sense. A *mf* may be quite loud enough to be the climax of a soft song, in spite perhaps of an indication of *f* by the composer. Equally a *pp* may be too soft in a broad song. A certain scale of dynamics should be chosen for each different song, as well as a certain scale of vocal colours.

*

There are songs which have no piano introduction to help the singer to capture the appropriate mood and colour of timbre from the beginning. He must nevertheless succeed in establishing this mood and colour from the very first note. To achieve this demands great concentration. Singers must use a different voice for each different song.

One can be expressive without being sad and, above all, without being sentimental.

*

It is important, from the very beginning, to eliminate the idea of the pianist 'following' his singer; except, of course, on certain occasions when the singer must lead the way, or, let it be admitted, in order to facilitate particular vocal difficulties. There are, in fact, times when the singer has to 'follow' the pianist, either for technical or musical reasons. But in general this conception of following each other often produces the worst possible musical results. It is of paramount importance for the pianist to give his singer a firm basis of flawlessly musical and rhythmical support, which should not yield leniently. Upon this support the singer will be able to give flexibility to his vocal line and correct and expressive accentuation to the literary text.

*

In a song cycle, the duration of the silences between the songs is very important and should not always be the same. This must be carefully planned in advance.

*

Choosing a recital programme is always very difficult. It is rather like hanging pictures in the right place in a painting exhibition. Even the same songs can be successful or not, according to the order in which they are arranged. The contrasts must be carefully foreseen and calculated: contrasts between the styles of the different composers, contrasts between the songs of the same composer, contrasts of tempi, of keys (never two songs in the same key one after the other), contrasts of rhythmic patterns in the piano part, contrasts of mood, of expression, etc. In my opinion it is of no importance to observe the chronological order.

2 | On Singing French

'Conductors, singers, pianists, all virtuosos should know, or recall that the first condition that must be fulfilled by anyone who aspires to the imposing title of interpreter, is that he be first of all a flawless executant,' says Stravinsky, and it could not possibly be better expressed.

In order to be a 'flawless executant' one must first, as already stated, have complete respect for the written work, but one must also have mastered a technique that makes it possible to do full justice to this work. For the interpreter's conception of the work remains visionary until the technique of the performance makes it a reality.

It is by overcoming technical problems that the singer succeeds in performing the musical line correctly. There is no reason why the technical performance of the literary text should not be as perfect as that of the music. One must, however, admit that singers all too often do not take as much care, do not make as much effort, to perform the literary text correctly, even in their own language.

However, if singers wish to have a comprehensive repertoire, they must be able to sing correctly in at least four or five different languages. Happy is the instrumentalist who can play Scarlatti, Purcell, Schubert, Debussy or de Falla in the same musical language.

One is not obliged to speak a language fluently in order to sing it correctly. Of course it is preferable that the singer should have a good knowledge of the language he is singing, but it is more important for him to have clear diction and a good accent than to know rules of grammar or have a large vocabulary. Obviously he must understand exactly the meaning of each phrase, of each word that he sings, other-wise how could he hope to interpret a text with sincerity? But to achieve this understanding he can study a good translation or, better still, make his own translation. A singer can give the impression of having a good knowledge of the foreign language he is singing if he works carefully on his articulation and his pronunciation.

*

Well-founded and precise principles of phonetics provide the first step in overcoming the difficulties of words in a foreign language. The use of the International Phonetic Alphabet is the basis of the following short study of the French language.

First of all the *vowel sounds* must be studied, because the primary consideration if one wishes to sing correctly in any language is the exact awareness of its different vowel sounds: they are the musical sounds.

This awareness is particularly important for English-speaking singers who are unaccustomed to pure vowel sounds in their own language.

In French (as in German, Italian, etc.), each vowel represents a *single sound*, a pure and definite sound, and in singing, it must be main-tained *unaltered during the whole duration of the musical sound*. This cannot be sufficiently emphasized, as there is nothing more disturbing than the intrusion of English diphthongs or triphthongs into any other language.

The following chart indicates for each vowel sound: first a number (which is convenient for reference); secondly, the phonetic symbol; and finally a few examples of words using the vowel sound with *different spellings*. These examples are given in French and in German, as many singers are more familiar with the German vowel sounds, and even if the equivalence may not always be total, it is near enough to be used as a basis.

French	German

1. [i] midi, il lit — Liebe
   [ɪ] (short) — bitte
2. [e] été, aimer, et, nez, j'ai — gehen, lesen, See, schwer
3. [ɛ] mère, mer, belle, lait, mais — wenn, helfen, Bächlein
4. [a] la table, art — alle
5. [ɑ] âme, passe — Vater, Bahn
6. [ɔ] mort, comme, sonne, dort — Sonne, dort
7. [o] mot, eau, au, dos — wohl, Sohn, Rose
8. [u] ou, doux, sous, tout — du, Schuh
   [ʊ] (short) — Mutter
9. [y] dur, nu, lune — grün, über, süss
   [ʏ] (short) — Hütte
10. [ø] deux, feu, peu — schön, König
11. [œ] le, je, jeune, cœur, seul — können, Götter
    [ə] lune — gehen
12. [ɑ̃] enfant, lent, quand, tremble
13. [õ] bon, mon, non, tombe
14. [ɛ̃] fin, pain, sein, simple, rien
15. [œ̃] un, humble, parfum

As can be seen on this chart, there are in French fifteen vowel sounds, including the four nasal sounds. Some phoneticians use sixteen sounds, and this chart does in fact indicate sixteen phonetic symbols: for the sound 11 there is [œ] and [ə] which indicates the final [ə]: lune, but these two sounds [œ] and [ə] are so close in singing that we can simplify.

As can be seen, also, there are three sounds, numbers 1, 8 and 9, which exist—long and short—in German. This difference does not exist in French.

*

It is not at all easy to indicate in a book the precise shading and colour of these different vowel sounds without the advantage of live demonstration. However, by explaining *how* they are formed—the actual position of the tongue and lips during articulation—the correct sounds can be produced.

On the following diagram the different vowel sounds (excluding the nasal sounds) are again indicated by their numbers and their phonetic symbols:

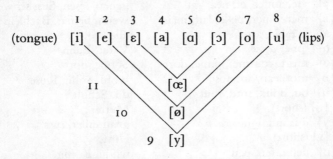

On the horizontal line will be found the first eight sounds. If, singing on one note, one begins with an ideally produced [a] and if, with a completely opened and supple throat, one wishes to produce the sounds [ɑ] [ɔ] [o] [u], it will be noticed that, without altering one's voice production, one gradually closes one's lips; they are already in a rounder shape on [ɔ], more on [o] and still more on [u]; this without changing the throat or moving the tongue. If one now begins again from the ideally produced [a] and wishes to form the sounds [ɛ] [e] [i], it will be noticed that, without the voice production being altered, the tongue is gradually lifted. It is already higher on [ɛ], more on [e] and still more on [i], without the throat being changed or the lips being moved.

It can now be remarked that by moving either lips or tongue, the first eight vowel sounds have been formed. But there are still three more sounds. These are formed by the combination of the preceding movements of the lips *and* of the tongue simultaneously.

If the tongue is placed in the position of [i], and if, *without changing* at all this position, the lips are moved to the position of [u], one gets the sound [y]. If the tongue is placed in the position of [e], and if, without changing at all this position, the lips are moved to the position of [o], one gets the sound [ø]. And if the tongue is placed in the position of [ɛ] and again without changing at all this position, the lips are moved to the position of [ɔ], one gets the sound [œ].

This is the phonetical theory for the formation of the vowel sounds.

When I speak of these movements of the lips and of the tongue, I am not, of course, unaware of the fact that the position of the larynx, for instance, varies according to the vowel sung. But if in singing [i] the larynx has a tendency to go up, it is not by thinking of lifting the larynx that the vowel [i] is made. This movement is a consequence, not a cause.

(It can be remarked, in passing, that English-speaking singers tend to use their lips and tongues less actively—to muscle them less—in forming both their vowels and their consonants, than German, Italian, and French singers.)

*

A few comments can be made on these different vowel sounds:

1: [i] is not a problem for English-speaking singers, as they have this sound in their own language. English has both the long and the short vowel as in German (liebe—sweet, bitte—little).

2: [e] is much more difficult. In the mouth of an English-speaking singer it always has a tendency to be too open, near the [ɛ], and it should be very sharp, nearer the [i]. It is also (with [o]) the most difficult sound to avoid diphthongizing, that is, to avoid closing it with a little [i] before pronouncing the following consonant or vowel. For instance 'aimée' must sound [e]m[e][ə] and not [e]m[e][i][ə].

3: [ɛ] is easier. The vowel in the English words 'care', 'fair' (without the diphthong at the end) is not unlike it. A consciously loose jaw and tongue is necessary to pronounce this vowel correctly. These two sounds 2 and 3 should be clearly differentiated. *Note*: The spelling 'ai' has the sound [e] and the spellings 'ais', 'ait', 'aid', 'air', 'aix' have the sound [ɛ]. This has to be carefully observed, especially in verb endings: the ending 'ai' is the future; the endings 'ais', 'ait' are the conditional.

(The English vowel sound in cat [æ] comes between [ɛ] and [a].)

4: [a] is the Italian 'a' and is the most frequent in French.

5: [ɑ] is much rarer. It is the [ɑ] for 'father'. *Note*: The letter 'a', when followed by an 'r', always sounds [a] in French, never [ɑ], and the English singer has the tendency, which is normal in his own language, to sing a long [ɑ] before an 'r'.

6: [ɔ] and 7: [o] should be well differentiated; the first one being bright and open, the second dark and round. It is very difficult for an English singer to avoid the diphthong in this last sound—[o][u] (low) —but it must be completely avoided. *Note*: In French the letter 'o' followed by an 'r' or a double consonant always sounds [ɔ] and not [o].
8: [u] is no problem. It exists in English (too, loose).
9: [y] is more difficult. It is the German long 'u' with 'umlaut'.
10: [ø] is the German long 'ö'.
11: [œ] or [ə] should be well differentiated from the [ø]. It is a really open sound. *Note*: The spelling 'eu' sounds generally [ø] (deux, Dieu), but when it is followed by an 'r' or by a consonant that is sounded, it always sounds [œ] (coeur, seul, jeune). When this spelling 'eu' is the past of the verb 'avoir' it sounds [y]: j'ai eu, j'eus, il eut, etc.

*

The four nasal sounds of the French language must now be considered. Their phonetic symbols are quite revealing. One sees four symbols which are familiar: [ɑ], [o], [ɛ], [œ], but they are surmounted by a 'tilde', which indicates that these sounds should have a nasal resonance. Thus one knows that:

12: [ɑ̃] (an, en, am, em) is formed with the broad [ɑ] with added nasal resonance.
13: [õ] (on, om) is formed with the round [o] with added nasal resonance. (Some phoneticians indicate [õ] with an open [ɔ], but in singing it produces a sound which is too near the [ɑ̃].)
14: [ɛ̃] (ain, aim, in, im, rarely en) is formed with the open [ɛ].
15: [œ̃] (un, um) with the open [œ]. These last two sounds should be well differentiated. It is vulgar, for instance, to pronounce the word: 'lundi' (Monday) l[ɛ̃]d[i] instead of l[œ̃]d[i].

One should not be afraid of these four nasal sounds. They are not at all unfavourable for singing, when the right production has been established. (Lilli Lehmann said: 'I cannot emphasize enough the importance of studying and utilizing nasalization.') It is not for a moment a question of singing into the nose, or through the nose, but simply of exaggerating to a slight degree the nasal resonance of certain vowel sounds. Singers who are not French often have a tendency to overdo this resonance. The sounds should be rich and full, and carefully blended with the sound of the pure vowel.

The following is extremely important: In a nasal sound, *followed by a consonant*, one must never sound the 'n' or the 'm'. In other words: at the end of the sound, the tongue must in no way come into contact with the palate to make an audible 'n'. Likewise, the lips must never meet to form an audible 'm'.

English-speaking singers too often have a tendency to pronounce 'n', 'm', or 'ng' (as in the English 'sing'), at the end of the nasal sound. For instance: 'entendre' should be [ã]t[ã]dr[ə] and not [ã]nt[ã]ndr[ə]; 'simple' should be s[ɛ̃]pl[ə] and not s[ɛ̃]mpl[ə]; 'ange' should be [ã]g[ə] and not [ã]ng[ə]. One must understand that, in French, the 'n' or the 'm' are simply a matter of spelling to indicate a nasal vowel.

(To have the right conception of this fact, alternate such words as 'penser' and 'passer'.)

It must be remarked that the letters 'a', 'e', 'o' when they are followed by a *double* 'nn' or 'mm' are *not* nasals. For example 'année' is pronounced: [a]n[e][ə] and not [ã]n[e][ə]. 'Comme' is pronounced c[ɔ]m[ə] and not c[õ]m[ə].

*

After speaking of the fifteen vowel sounds it must be added that there are, in French, what are called 'semi-vowels'. There are only three, and two of them are not a problem for an English singer, for he has them in his own language:

[j]: yeux [jø], lieu [ljø], bien [bjɛ̃]—as in English: yet, you.
[w]: oui [wi], ouest [wɛst], moi [mwa]—as in English: will, walk.

But the third 'semi-vowel' does not exist in English and is sometimes difficult:

[ɥ]: nuit [nɥi], lui [lɥi], juin [ʒɥɛ̃]. Generally speaking English-speaking singers have a tendency to sing: 'la nouit' [nui] instead of 'la nuit' [nɥi], 'je souis' [sui] instead of 'je suis' [sɥi].

In practice one can consider the semi-vowels [j], [w], [ɥ] as being the vowels [i], [u], [y] pronounced very quickly.

Note: The spelling 'oi' (moi, voix, soir, <u>oi</u>seau) is the compound sound semi-vowel–vowel: [wa]. That is to say that one has to pass rapidly over the [w] and sing on the [a]. The spelling 'oin' (loin, moins) is the compound sound [wɛ̃]. Short [w] and sing on the [ɛ̃].

The spelling 'ill' (fille, famille, billet, brillant, etc.) is the compound sound vowel–semi-vowel [ij], that is to say that one has to sing on the [i] with a short [j] at the end of the value of the note.

There are exceptions to this pronunciation, where the double 'll' is pronounced like one 'l', for example: 'ville', 'village', 'mille' or 'million, milliard', 'tranquille' or the words starting with 'il': 'illustre', 'illusion', etc.

'ail' (travail, médaille, etc.) sounds [aj].
'eil' (soleil, sommeil, oreille, etc.) sounds [ɛj].
'euil' (fauteuil, feuille, feuillage, etc.) sounds [œj].
'ouille' (grenouille, mouiller, etc.) sounds [uj].

In all these compound sounds one has to sing on the first vowel sound, putting a short [j] at the end of the value of the note.

One more remark about vowel sounds:

When the letter 'y' comes between two vowels it should generally be pronounced (there are a few exceptions) as if the spelling were 'ii', and the two 'i's' did not belong to the same syllable. The first syllable ends with the first 'i', and the second syllable begins with the second 'i'. For example: 'voyage' is the equivalent of 'voi-iage' so it sounds v[wa]-[ja]g[ə], and not v[ɔja]g[ə]. 'Rayon' is the equivalent of 'rai-ion' so it sounds r[e]-[jõ] and not r[eõ].

*

The French language has seventeen consonants and these are not a problem for English-speaking singers for they have them in their own language (plus a few others). Only one does not exist in English: this is the [ɲ] as in 'agneau', 'seigneur', 'cygne' or in Italian: 'agnello', 'ogni'. The French [ʒ] is represented by the 'j' (jour, juin), or the 'g' (age, sage, page), and this consonant exists in English—for example in the word 'mea<u>s</u>ure'.

But a few observations should be made about some of the consonants:
One 's' between two vowels always sounds 'z': 'poison' (poison).
A double 's' is pronounced as a hard 's': 'poisson' (fish), but of course without doubling this consonant.

English-speaking singers should watch their 'l's, which are pronounced much further back in English than in Italian, German, and French; and they have a tendency to anticipate them.

There is sometimes a misconception of the French 'r' in singing. In *speaking* French we use the so-called uvula 'r', and night-club singers or folk singers use it in their popular songs. But it should never be used in serious music, as it gives the diction a great vulgarity. Of course, one should not overdo the rolling of the 'r', generally one flip is enough, but it must be clearly pronounced with the tip of the tongue only. It is, in fact, rolled in exactly the same way as in well-sung English, but in English it is permissible to exaggerate the rolling at times—to sing on the consonant—which is not allowed in French. Of course the unrolled 'r' used in English speech, and the 'r' far back in the mouth as in American speech, are out of place in singing any language—even English. But whereas in English it is a question of taste as to whether the 'r' should be rolled when followed by another consonant in the middle of words such as 'charm', 'firm', 'curl', in French it must always be rolled—'charme', 'arbre'.

English-speaking singers should also be careful about their 't', 'p', and 'k' (hard 'c'). They generally surround these consonants with air, as if they were followed by an aspirate 'h': 'a c'hup of t'hea'; this is 't'hotally imp'hossible' in any other language. These three consonants must be produced by a precise movement of the tongue ('t' and 'k') or the lips ('p'), without any breath escape. The vocal cords should close *before* the release of the consonant. Observe that the aspiration (one should say 'expiration') is produced in 'pin', 'take', 'cool' but not generally in 'spin', 'steak', 'school'. Comparing these two groups of words one can realize the different acoustic that should be achieved.

*

From the foregoing remarks about the vowel sounds, a careful reader will already have noticed that I have insisted several times not only on the necessity of remaining on these vowel sounds, without altering their colour (avoiding diphthongs), but also without anticipating the following consonant or semi-vowel.

There is in French speech, and in French singing, a clear-cut effect which is extremely characteristic and which is the result of syllable division differing in many respects from the English, and two fundamental rules can be set down:

1. *In French every syllable must contain one and only one vowel sound.*
2. *In French every syllable begins with a consonant and ends with a vowel.*

There are only two exceptions to this second rule:

(a) When the word begins with a vowel sound. Then, obviously the first syllable begins with this vowel: 'enfant' en-fant, 'éléphant' é-lé-phant, 'adorer' a-do-rer. But it can be seen further that in a group of words this exception no longer exists.
(b) When the vowel sounds are not separated by any consonant: 'anéantir' a-né-an-tir, 'cruel' cru-el—here Rule No. 1 applies: only one vowel sound in each syllable. The above phonetic division corresponds to the written syllable division, as can be seen on the music score.

French diction is entirely based on these two fundamental rules, and it is the very opposite of English diction, where one tends to close all syllables with a diphthong or with a consonant. (For example, in the phrase 'an egg at eight' spoken by an Englishman, each syllable ends with a consonant. But spoken by a Frenchman—and even more in singing—it will sound: a-ne-ga-teight.)

English speakers and singers are often at a loss with regard to the division of words in syllables and accordingly make many mistakes. If they follow the two rules that have been given here, they will have no more problems. The contrast between the English and French principle of syllable division may be seen by the comparison:

English	*French*
cap-able	ca-pa-ble
amus-ing	a-mu-sant

By virtue of the fundamental rule, the following words are obviously divided thus: 'inutile' i-nu-ti-le, 'honorer' ho-no-rer, etc. and also, the 'h' being mute: 'malheur' ma-lheur, 'bonheur' bo-nheur, and words with groups of consonants: 'agrément' a-gré-ment, 'confluent' con-flu-ent. This corresponds to the syllable division printed on the music score.

But also, and this is very important for singers: in words having a written double consonant, syllables are divided before this double consonant, which is in fact pronounced as only one consonant: 'aller' a-ller, 'année' a-nnée, 'terrain' te-rrain. This phonetic division does *not* correspond to the written division, as printed on the music score.

Therefore the rule can be formulated: *In French one should never double audibly the double consonants.*

It must be admitted that there are a few exceptions to this rule: mostly in words beginning with the prefixes 'il' or 'im', such as:

illusion	immense
illustre	immortel
illogique	immobile

and other very rare words (curiously similar words exist in English):

syllabe	intelligent
collègue	grammaire

and also a few verbs, the spelling of which, and the pronunciation, is the only indication of the different tenses:

je courais (imperfect)	je courrais (conditional)
je mourais (imperfect)	je mourrais (conditional)

The fundamental rule that every syllable begins with a consonant and ends with a vowel is so important and so general that it is applied not only to words but also to one word in reference to another. In this way the rule can be followed, even when it seems impossible, with words in which the vowel begins the syllable and the consonant ends it. We resolve, as it were, the difficulty, and succeed in satisfying the French ear, which always wants to hear first the consonant and then the vowel. Here are a few examples:

> 'Il est' is pronounced i-lest
> 'Elle a' : è-la
> 'pauvre enfant' : pau-vren-fant
> 'femme admirable' : fa-ma-dmi-ra-ble.

An obvious conclusion is: *French is a language based completely on vowels*, the opposite of English.

For example: In English one pronounces 'subtle' and only one vowel is heard, the rest being consonants. In French the same word is 'subtil' and one hears mostly the two vowels 'u' and 'i', with distinct, quick consonants. In the word 'opera', in English one hears a strong 'op' and nothing much more. In French one hears: [ɔ]p[e]r[a], three vowels with two swift consonants.

This leads to the observation that the French stresses and rhythms are the antithesis of the English.

In English, in most words, there is *one* syllable which is strongly stressed and the rest is hardly perceptible. (It is obvious in the two words we have just considered.) The place of this stress is irregular (and this is one of the main difficulties for foreigners). The accented syllable can be on the first, the second, the third syllable, etc. (photograph, photographer, photographic).

On the contrary, in French, all syllables are almost equally accented, and the tonic accent, which does exist, is always at the same place: on the last syllable of a word or a group of words (photo, photographe, photographie, ces deux photos là).

There is another difference between the tonic accent in spoken English and spoken French. In English, its nature is primarily of *force*, in French it is of *duration*. But, in singing, obviously, this duration is set down by the composer, and is hoped to be a musical stress! Unfortunately it is not always the case, and sometimes singers must use the accent of force.

This being said, it must be admitted that, in French, *for an expressive reason*, one can occasionally change the normal stress of a word. For example, we say 'une catastrophe' but 'Quelle catastrophe!'

And in singing this means of expression must be used, even when it has not been emphasized by the composer. There will be many examples of this in the following studies of interpretation.

*

All that has been said on *spoken* French is very important, and will be still more important in *sung* French, and must be applied with more care and precision. A fundamental rule can be set down: ' *In French, more so than in any other language, to obtain a proper line, a proper legato, one must fill the entire duration of each note with the vowel sound.*' In other words: in French, one has to carry the vowel sound *unaltered* right through the whole duration of the musical sound, *without anticipating at all the following consonant*. It is the only possible procedure to get both the music of the words and the music itself.

It is perhaps here that we encounter the precise factor which causes non-French people to find the French language less pleasant for singing. It is strictly forbidden in French to sing on the consonants (except, of course, for a very special effect). From this standpoint French is quite different from German, in which one *must* vibrate certain consonants. The same is true of the double consonants in Italian, which should be sounded very clearly.

In French, on the contrary, not only is it forbidden to sing on the consonants, but even the double consonants can only very rarely be emphasized in pronunciation. This has already been said, but it must be insisted on. It will never be a serious error to avoid emphasizing the pronunciation of the double consonants in the small number of words which have been spoken of—words in which emphasis is permissible; but it will always be a serious error to double consonants audibly in words where this is not permitted. Consequently, for singers who are not French born, the safest and most prudent solution is never to double any consonants.

*

Attention has been called to several difficulties that English-speaking singers will encounter in fulfilling successfully the requirements of sung French. A few exercises can be suggested to help them to overcome some of these difficulties.

A good exercise for mastering the vowel sounds is to sing them on one note:

[ɑ] [ɔ] [o] [u]	and then in the opposite direction:
[u] [o] [ɔ] [ɑ]	using the lips and being specially aware of the difference between [ɔ] and [o].
[a] [ɛ] [e] [i]	and
[i] [e] [ɛ] [a]	using the tongue, and being well aware of the difference between [ɛ] and [e].
[a] [œ] [ø] [y]	and
[y] [ø] [œ] [a]	using both the tongue and the lips, and being well aware of the difference between [œ] and [ø].

[y] is specially difficult. A good exercise is to sing (always on one note), starting on the [i] and, keeping the tongue in the same position, to move the lips to the form of [u]: [i] [y] [i] [y] [i] [y]. The same exercise is also the only possible method of working on the difficult compound sound [ɥi] (je suis, la nuit).

To work on the nasal sounds the best possible procedure is to begin singing (on one note), on the pure vowel sound and then to drop the soft palate to make it nasal: [ɑɑ̃]-[oõ]-[ɛɛ̃]-[œœ̃].

Special exercises are very useful to break the habit of anticipating consonants. The best one and the simplest is to sing the French poem one has to perform on one note, before singing it on the musical line, very carefully dividing all the syllables *after the vowels*. (Verlaine: 'Clair de lune'): Vo-tra-m'eʃ-t'un-pai-i-sa-ge-choi-si-. (Verlaine: 'Mandoline'): Leʃ-do-nneu-rde-sé-ré-na-des.

In this exercise one must be very careful not to move the mouth *at all* (lips, tongue) while singing the vowel sounds, in order to avoid completely any diphthong.

The same exercise is still more important in such a phrase (Théophile Gautier: 'Sur la lagune' or 'Lamento'): 'Co-nnai-ssez-vous la-blan-che-tom-be', where sounding the 'n' and the 'm' in the two nasal sounds must be completely avoided; and thus the syllables should be still more carefully divided after the vowels—in this case two nasal vowels.

To break this bad habit of sounding the 'n' or the 'm' in nasal vowels, the method of alternating such words as 'passer' and 'penser' has already been mentioned. There is also the device of singing the words with nasal vowels on one note, starting on the second syllable: 'che-blan-che-blan-che' and 'be-tom-be-tom-be'.

French being completely based on vowel sounds, there is also the good device of singing the musical line of the song only on the vowel sounds, with no consonants at all. It is an excellent way of improving the legato and the phrasing.

Finally, to avoid any 'aspiration' after 't', 'p', and 'k', it is a good test to sing words starting with these consonants, at the same time putting the back of the hand before the mouth; one should not feel any breath escaping.

*

The French language has one more peculiarity which foreigners find very puzzling, it is the question of the '*liaison*'. It is not at all easy to sum this up in a few words. Books on French pronunciation devote many pages to the question, and it is not possible in this book to go into so many details.

First of all, what exactly is a liaison? It is the pronouncing of the last consonant of a word with the vowel beginning the next word, when this consonant would otherwise be silent. Or to put it another way—the last consonant, which is mute in an isolated word, is at times pronounced when followed by a word beginning with a vowel: 'petit' but 'petit_enfant'.

(*Note*: One cannot speak of liaison when the ending consonant of the first word is normally pronounced: 'pour_aller', 'le lac_est grand'; this is only the normal linking up.)

Of course, according to the fundamental rule which has been formulated, when the liaison occurs, the final consonant of the first word begins the first syllable of the next word: 'petit enfant' sounds p[œ]-ti-t[ã]-f[ã].

This being said, it must be added that the liaison should *not always* be made. There are three possibilities:

1. The liaison is forbidden.

Barton College Library
Wilson, N.C. 27893

  2. The liaison is compulsory.
  3. The liaison is optional.

It is only possible here to give a few general rules, admitting that there are a good many exceptions and quite a few special cases.

1. *Forbidden liaison*

(a) The liaison is forbidden, first of all, between two words which are not closely connected by their meaning: 'Ils vont, | ils viennent'. (This can often be detected by the fact that, when speaking the text, in order to make the meaning clearer, there can be a silence between these words.)

(b) After a noun in the singular: 'L'enfant | a peur'.
    (But after a noun in the *plural*, one must make the liaison: 'Les enfants‿ont peur'.)

(c) After a proper name: 'Paris | est beau'.

(d) After the conjunction 'et': 'et | aussi'.

(e) Before the adverb 'oui': 'Je dis | oui'.

(f) Before the nouns of the numbers: un, huit, onze: 'Les | onze hommes'.

(g) Before an aspirate 'h': 'Les | héros'.

2. *Compulsory liaison*

The liaison is compulsory:

  after an article: 'les‿hommes', 'des‿enfants'.
  after an adjective: 'un saint‿homme', 'un grand‿arbre'.
  after a personal pronoun: 'nous‿aimons', 'eux‿aussi'.
  after a verb: 'aimer‿encore', 'il était‿aimé'.
  after an adverb: 'mieux‿encore', 'tellement‿amoureux'.
        (The liaison is made with the p in the two adverbs: 'trop' and 'beaucoup'.)
  after a preposition: 'sous‿un‿arbre', 'depuis‿une‿heure'.
  after a conjunction (except 'et', as we have said): 'mais‿aussi', 'quant‿à moi'.

There is a special rule for the nasals. After a nasal sound when the liaison is not compulsory, it is forbidden. The compulsory liaisons are *after* the words: un, en, on, mon, son, ton, bien, rien, and also the adjectives ending in nasals, but some of them lose their nasalization:

> 'un bon élève': œ̃-bɔ-ne-lɛ-və
> 'au moyen-âge': o-mwa-jɛ-na-ʒə
> 'un vilain enfant': œ̃-vi-lɛ-nã-fã

There is a special rule for the words in the *singular* ending with 'rs', 'rt' and 'rd' (rare). It is the 'r' (which is normally pronounced in the word) which has to be linked: 'Heureux qui meurt ici' (Fauré: 'Au cimetière'), 'me penchant vers elle' (Chausson: 'Poème de l'amour et de la mer').

There are exceptions after the words 'toujours' and 'plusieurs'— the liaison with the 's' is generally accepted. After the adverb 'fort' the liaison with the 't' is also accepted.

Of course, in the ending 'rs', when the 's' is the sign of the plural it is normally linked: 'des vers‿admirables'.

3. *Optional liaison*

There are a great number of cases when the liaison is optional, and left to the taste of the performer.

The liaison occurs much less in informal conversation than when reading aloud or delivering a lecture; it occurs more when reciting poetry than prose, and still more when singing a poem.

But here again it is a matter of taste and of style. For instance, when singing a lyrical poem many liaisons should be made, but when singing a folk-song scarcely any, it would be too refined and out of place.

It should not be forgotten also that the liaison is made for a harmonious purpose, to avoid the ugly hiatus. The liaison should not be used when it would create sounds more disagreeable to the ear than its absence.

Neither should the liaison be used when it would make the poem less understandable, or would produce an ambiguity. Here is a funny example: 'I don't care for the sea; I am too much a man of the land.'

In French: 'Je n'aime pas la mer; je suis trop homme de terre.' It would be a dangerous liaison to say: 'trop‿homme de terre', 'pomme de terre' meaning 'potato'!

For all the mélodies studied in this book the recommended liaisons will be indicated in the text of the poem, with the sign ‿, as in the above examples.

*

A few words should be said concerning the final 'e', the so-called 'e' mute. It must be made clear that when it comes before a vowel sound, it is always completely elided:

Elle‿est, [ɛ]l[ɛ]

Notre‿ami, n[ɔ]tr[a]m[i]

Apart from this, the musical phrase, the position of the 'e' mute in the phrase, and the value of the note attributed to it, decide whether it is sounded strongly, or weakly, or not at all.

The same thing occurs in English with the ending 'ed'.

In these phrases:

the final vowel sound must be sounded but, if possible, diminuendo.

In these phrases:

my be - lo - ved
je vous ai - me

my be - lo - ved
je vous ai - me

in English only the consonants 'v' and 'd' are pronounced, in French only the consonant 'm' is pronounced.

In the case of a final [ə] following a vowel sound, the same thing occurs. In the first three examples above, the [ə] must be sounded but, if possible, diminuendo.

In the following examples the final [ə] is short, almost as short as the ending [ə] after the [i] in the English word 'dear'.

sous la plui - e
bien ai - mé - - e
très jo - li - - e

sous la plui - e
bien ai - mé - - e
très jo - li - - e

A few more examples can be given, taken from mélodies studied in this book:

1. *Well* sung [ə]:
   Fauré: 'Arpège':

L'â - me d'une flû - te sou - pi - re ————

Fauré: 'Mandoline':

Et les bel——les é - cou-teu-ses   E - changent   des pro-pos

fa - des   Sous les ra - mu - res chan - teu———ses

Poulenc: 'Tel jour telle nuit':

Comme u - ne   pier———————re————

2. *Not* sounded:

Debussy: 'Green':

a - vec   vos   deux   mains   blanches

Poulenc: 'Tel jour telle nuit':

pp

Ce mélo - drame   nous arra - che

Ravel: *Shéhérazade* 'La flûte enchantée':

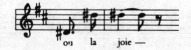

ou   la   joie——

3. *Briefly* sounded:

Debussy: 'Il pleure dans mon cœur':

Pour un cœur qui s'en-nui-e, O le bruit de la pluie!

*

The importance of this chapter cannot be sufficiently emphasized. It will be extremely boring for a superficial reader, but anyone who wishes to interpret the French vocal repertoire should make the effort to study and practise it carefully and patiently.

An effort has been made to expound, as clearly and briefly as possible, the main characteristics of spoken French, and to set down principles and rules which will form a solid basis for the performance of sung French.

If these principles and rules have not been assimilated, if the main technical difficulties have not been overcome, it is to be feared that the English-speaking singers for whom this book is written will not be the 'flawless executants' they will have to be, if they are to aspire to the imposing title of 'interpreters' of the French vocal repertoire.

*

I should like to mention a few books which have been the basis of this chapter, and from which I have borrowed some striking examples. They can be most useful for those interested in French pronunciation:

Pierre Fouché: *Traité de prononciation française* (Klincksieck, Paris)
Ph. Martinon: *Comment on prononce le français* (Larousse, Paris)
The Yersin phono-rhythmic French method (Lippincott, Philadelphia)
Pierre Delattre: *Principles de phonétique française à l'usage des étudiants anglo-américains* (P. Delattre, University of Colorado)
Pierre Delattre: *Advanced training in French pronunciation* (P. Delattre, University of Colorado)

3 | The Interpretation of French Mélodies

It is obvious that there can be no overall, single style of interpretation for French mélodies—how could there be? One does not play or sing Brahms like Schubert, or Wolf like Schumann; and similarly one does not sing Debussy like Duparc, or Poulenc like Fauré. Furthermore, one cannot interpret the early songs of Fauré and Debussy, in which influences prevailing during their youthful years are still evident, in the same style as the songs which they composed in their maturity, when their individuality and personality were strongly marked.

It would be impossibly difficult in a short chapter to demonstrate clearly and usefully such subtle nuances as these; they can be indicated only when dealing with the typical songs of the various composers. In the following studies, such an attempt is made. However, a few general characteristics common to all French mélodies—indeed, to all French music—can be briefly defined, and from these basic principles the discussion of style and interpretation will naturally arise.

A revealing guide to a certain French conception of music is given by an observation made by Debussy: 'Music should humbly seek to give pleasure.' What exactly does this mean? Firstly that the composer must seek for beauty of sonority, rare and subtle harmony, supple modulation, and the resulting interplay of colours, while at the same time seeking the beauty and charm of the melodic line. In short, the aim is to give aesthetic pleasure through pure music, stripped of all philosophical, literary, or humanistic significance, such as that which goes so willingly hand in hand with German music.

Debussy goes on to write that 'clarity of expression, precision and concentration of form are qualities peculiar to the French genius'. These qualities are indeed most noticeable when again compared with the German genius, excelling as it does in long, uninhibited outpourings, directly opposed to the French taste, which abhors overstatement and venerates concision and diversity. The French 'clarity of expression' is also the antithesis of the slow and misty metaphysical Germanic reveries; did not the German Nietzsche say in speaking of Bizet: 'His refinement is that of a race, not of an individual: it presupposes a listener who is not only musical but also intelligent. One leaves behind the North, damp with the mists of the Wagnerian ideal. This music possesses what is common to warm climates: the dryness and limpidity of the air.'

The mixture of harmonic sensuousness and clarity of thought explains why French music so well conveys precise and colourful description, or the suggestion of a poetic climate. The composer Henry Barraud writes: 'A French musician knows that one does not reach poetical achievement, the one aim of all aesthetic creation, merely through verbalism and self-exhibition. Other quicker, surer roads are to be found, and there is nothing like the unexpressed, to make the inexpressible understood.'

It is indeed possible that the art of the greatest French composers is an art of suggestion, more often expressing moods and impressions than precise emotions. This is not to say that lyricism or even passion is absent in French music; but just as severity of spirit controls the sensuousness of sound, so emotions and feelings are refined, purified and controlled by reason. The writer André Gide said: 'The most beautiful things are those which madness inspires and reason writes'; and according to the poet and philosopher Paul Valéry: 'Whoever wants to write his dream must be completely awake.'

These two latter comments apply with equal force to French poetry and French music. A song, being a union of music and a poem, presents a synthesis of these two characteristic elements of the same genius, which emphasizes, to an even greater extent, the particular qualities of this art form. Schumann is as remote from Fauré as Heine is from Verlaine, and Wolf as remote from Poulenc as Mörike from Apollinaire.

A French mélodie is a musico-literary work in which the heart plays its part, but which, in its poem and its music, is an art infinitely more concerned with sensitive perceptions and impressions, more intellectual and more objective, than a German Lied, which is almost always subjective, both musically and poetically. As Heine said:

> 'Aus meinen grossen Schmerzen
> Mach' ich die kleinen Lieder.'
>
> (Out of my deep sorrows
> I make little songs.)

In this, the Lied is essentially a Romantic phenomenon, whereas the French mélodie is post-Romantic and often reacts against sentimental effusion.

Finally another basic difference, as Evelyne Reuter says, is that the French mélodie never shows this close relationship with popular song which characterizes the Lied—an art form springing directly from the folk-song. Echoes of folk music are found even in the most advanced Lieder of Brahms and Mahler.

What conclusions can a performer draw from these short comments? The 'clarity of expression and the precision' of French music have already been stressed; hence the first duty of the performer is to cultivate this precision in performance. It can even imply a certain severity, particularly as regards tempo: as a general rule *rubato* is virtually excluded. Only when this precision has been attained can the performer begin to consider the sensuousness of sound, which has already been mentioned as being one of the characteristics of French music.

I have already insisted, and I would like to emphasize this again, that to consider the vocal line as 'quasi parlando' in style is to show a completely faulty conception of the French mélodie. Nothing could be further from the truth. To obtain the necessary beauty of sound, it is above all essential for the vocal line to be phrased with extreme smoothness—sustained—'sung' in the fullest sense of the word. Naturally the interpretation of the poem is important! But the first consideration should be given to the music, as in any vocal work in any language. The vocal line must not be sacrificed to the declamation of the poem, any more in Fauré than in Schumann, in Wolf than in Poulenc.

I would remark in passing that Italian and German are languages with a very strong tonic accent, and the composer who sets them to music is naturally forced to observe it very strictly. But in French the tonic accent is weaker, which, in the words of Darius Milhaud, 'opens the door to freedom for the composer'. Yes, but it also opens the door to freedom for the singer, and it must be admitted that the rhythmic and expressive declamation of a recitative of Rameau, or a phrase of Debussy, is extremely subtle.

To sum up: in the French mélodie the singer and the pianist must succeed in combining precision with lyricism. But it must be controlled lyricism, for just as the French composer never gives way to sentimentality or emphasis and abominates overstatement, so in the same way his interpreters must have a sense of moderation of expression, a critical capacity, which after all is no more than one of the most vigorous forms of intelligence.

There can be no doubt that it is easier for performers to give themselves up to the sentimental outpourings of German music and poetry than to re-create the subtle poetic climate, the intellectual refinement and the controlled profundity of French music and poetry.

To take a concrete example, it is certainly easier to find the right expression for the 'Moonlight' (Mondnacht) of Eichendorff and Schumann or Brahms, than for the 'Moonlight' (Clair de Lune) of Verlaine and Fauré or Debussy. The sombre, romantic forest haunted by mysterious hunters, elves and fairies, is replaced in French art by great parks with neatly pruned trees, peopled with charming figures, without sentimental or philosophical problems, but whose presence is imbued with an elusive and powerful poetry.

Let it be said that for the listener himself the access to the enchanted world of French music and poetry probably demands a greater collaboration. But this very demand makes its access free to people of the greatest sensibility and taste, of whatever nationality. In music, as in any art, one can only enjoy the pleasure one deserves.

4 | Berlioz, Gounod

HECTOR BERLIOZ

Hector Berlioz (1803–69) wrote about fifty mélodies. In speaking of them himself, he said: 'They have nothing of the form or style of Schubert.' On the contrary they show the conspicuous influence of the 'romance', and also that of the lyric theatre which was flourishing at that time. They often have an emphatic quality of romantic grandiloquence, which is certainly opposed to the essential characteristics and finest merits of the French mélodie. However, some of them are not only typical of the musical taste of the period, but true masterpieces, namely: 'Les Nuits d'Été'.

These six songs, four of which are included here, are settings of poems by Théophile Gautier, first published with piano accompaniment in 1841, and later orchestrated. It is in this orchestral version that they show their genuine worth; the piano accompaniment, badly written for the instrument, at times obscures the true beauty of the music. The character of these songs is often close to that of an operatic aria, and consequently their interpretation is similar in style.

ABSENCE

Reviens, reviens, ma bien-aimée!
Comme une fleur loin du soleil,
La fleur de ma vie est fermée
Loin de ton sourire vermeil!

ABSENCE

Return, return, my beloved!
Like a flower far from the sun,
the flower of my life is closed
far from your rosy smile!

Entre nos cœurs quelle distance!

Tant d'espace entre nos baisers!
O sort amer! ô dure absence!
O grands désirs inapaisés!

Reviens, reviens, ma bien-aimée!
Comme une fleur loin du soleil,
La fleur de ma vie est fermée
Loin de ton sourire vermeil!

D'ici là-bas que de campagnes,
Que de villes et de hameaux,
Que de vallons et de montagnes,
A lasser le pied des chevaux!

Reviens, reviens, ma bien-aimée!
Comme une fleur loin du soleil,
La fleur de ma vie est fermée
Loin de ton sourire vermeil!

Théophile Gautier

Between our hearts, how great a
distance!

So much space between our kisses!
O bitter fate! O harsh absence!
O great unappeased desires!

Return, return, my beloved!
Like a flower far from the sun,
the flower of my life is closed
far from your rosy smile!

From here to there how many plains,
how many towns and villages,
how many valleys and mountains,
to weary the hooves of the horses.

Return, return, my beloved!
Like a flower far from the sun,
the flower of my life is closed
far from your rosy smile!

This is probably the most famous of Berlioz's mélodies. It is best suited to a warm lyric soprano voice. The original key is F sharp, but it is often sung in F, even with orchestra. The indicated tempo ($\quarternote = 44$) is excellent with orchestra, but it may seem a little too slow with piano accompaniment, especially if the singer does not have a big voice.

The musical form is very simple, following closely the form of the poem: three refrains repeated with no modification, separated by two stanzas of eleven bars (the second one a third higher than the first one) and both in tempo *un poco animato*.

The interpretation seems quite obvious; the poem and the music have no subtleties. The *animato* and the crescendo of the two stanzas should be made without fear of exaggeration, but in the second one, a return to the *tempo primo* must be made on 'à lasser le pied des chevaux'. (This important indication is omitted in the Augener edition.) In the third refrain 'ma bien aimée' should be *pp* with no crescendo whatsoever. (English-speaking singers have to be careful not to sing 'ma bien aimé-y-e'. Not [e] [i] [ə] but [e] [ə].)

VILLANELLE

Quand viendra la saison nouvelle,
Quand auront disparu les froids,
Tous les deux nous irons, ma belle,
Pour cueillir le muguet | aux bois.

Sous nos pieds | égrenant les perles
Que l'on voit | au matin trembler,
Nous irons écouter les merles
            Siffler.

Le printemps | est venu, ma belle,
C'est le mois des amants béni;
Et l'oiseau, satinant son aile,
Dit des vers | au rebord du nid.
Oh! viens donc sur ce banc de mousse
Pour parler de nos beaux amours,
Et dis moi de ta voix si douce,
            Toujours!

Loin, bien loin, | égarant nos courses,
Faisons fuir le lapin caché,
Et le daim, | au miroir des sources,

Admirant son grand bois penché;
Puis chez nous, tout heureux,
    tout aises,
En paniers | enlaçant nos doigts,
Revenons rapportant des fraises
            Des bois!

Théophile Gautier

VILLANELLE

When the new season comes,
when the cold has vanished,
we shall go together, my fair one,
to gather the lilies of the valley in the
            woods.
Our feet scattering the pearls of dew
that are seen trembling at morn,
we shall go to hear the blackbirds
            warbling.

The spring has come, my fair one,
it is the month blessed by lovers;
and the bird preening its wing,
sings a refrain on the edge of the nest.
Oh! Come then to this mossy bank
to talk of the delights of our love,
and say to me in your sweet voice,
            for ever!

Far, very far, straying from our paths,
let us put to flight the hidden rabbit,
and the deer, in the mirror of the
            springs,
admiring its great bending antlers;
then towards home, quite happy,
            quite contented,
with interlaced fingers for baskets,
let us return bringing the strawberries
            from the woods.

The original key is A. The indicated tempo seems rather slow, and $\downarrow$ = 120 more advisable.

The three stanzas are differentiated only by subtle modulations. The first stanza ends without a *ritardando*, but at the end of the other two stanzas a *ritardando* is marked, which is more pronounced at the end of the last one; but the last two notes of the voice must always be *a tempo* —on the words 'toujours' and 'des bois'.

The little mélodie should be sung quite blithely and simply, almost in the style of a folk-song.

LE SPECTRE DE LA ROSE	THE SPECTRE OF THE ROSE
Soulève ta paupière close	Raise your closed eyelids
Qu'effleure un songe virginal!	caressed by a virginal dream,
Je suis le spectre d'une rose	I am the spectre of a rose
Que tu portais | hier au bal.	which you wore yesterday at the ball.
Tu me pris | encore emperlée	You took me still bepearled
Des pleurs d'argent de l'arrosoir,	with silver tears from the sprinkler,
Et parmi la fête étoilée,	and amid the starry festival
Tu me promenas tout le soir.	you carried me all the evening.
O toi qui de ma mort fus cause,	O you who were the cause of my death,
Sans que tu puisses le chasser,	you will be powerless to drive away
Toutes les nuits mon spectre rose	my rosy spectre which every night
A ton chevet viendra danser.	will come to dance by your pillow.
Mais ne crains rien, je ne réclame	But have no fear, I ask
Ni messe ni De Profundis.	neither a Mass nor De Profundis.
Ce léger parfum | est mon âme,	This light perfume is my soul
Et j'arrive du paradis.	and I come from paradise.
Mon destin fut digne d'envie,	My destiny was worthy of envy,
Et pour avoir un sort si beau	and to have known so fair a fate
Plus d'un | aurait donné sa vie,	more than one would have given his life,
Car sur ton sein j'ai mon tombeau,	for my tomb is upon your breast.
Et sur l'albâtre où je repose	And on the alabaster where I rest
Un poète | avec un baiser	a poet with a kiss
Écrivit: 'Ci-gît | une rose	has inscribed: 'Here lies a rose
Que tous les rois vont jalouser.'	that all kings will envy.'

Théophile Gautier

This poem by Théophile Gautier is the subject of the wellknown ballet with the same title, staged by Diaghilev in 1911, with which Nijinsky became identified. The music of the ballet was the 'Invitation to the Waltz' by Karl Maria von Weber, orchestrated by Berlioz.

This is probably the most beautiful mélodie of the cycle. The accompaniment is quite orchestral, the style, however, is much less operatic than in 'L'Absence'.

In Augener's edition for voice and piano, the important prelude of eight bars is omitted. In the same edition, eleven bars before the end of the mélodie, the text is erroneous. It should be:

Car sur ton sein   j'ai   mon tom - beau

The indicated tempo ♪ = 96 is excellent. I think it should be observed, even though it may seem a little slow in performance with piano accompaniment. All the beginning of the mélodie is *p*, until the first *mf* on the words: 'Et parmi la fête étoilée'. The *poco ritenuto* and the *rallentando* on 'O toi qui de ma mort fus cause' should be well observed. A breath can be taken after 'O toi'. From there onwards the tempo is very slightly more *animato*, and the dynamics *p*. It is best to pronounce the Latin words 'De Profundis' as in Italian, in spite of the rhyme with 'paradis'. 'Ce léger parfum est mon âme' must be *pp* and mysterious, before beginning a big crescendo of seven bars, which will reach its climax on the *last* 'j'arrive du paradis' in the *allargando* (the first one being only *mf*). One has now returned to the real *tempo primo* and to the dynamics *p* and *pp* up to the end of the mélodie. It is advisable to break between the words 'baiser' and 'Écrivit'; and again between 'Ci-gît' and 'une rose'.

A mysterious and calmly poetic atmosphere should emanate from this beautiful mélodie.

SUR LES LAGUNES

Ma belle amie est morte,
Je pleurerai toujours;
Sous la tombe elle emporte
Mon âme et mes amours.
Dans le ciel sans m'attendre,
Elle s'en retourna;
L'ange qui l'emmena
Ne voulut pas me prendre.

ON THE LAGOONS

My beautiful beloved is dead,
I shall weep for ever;
to the tomb she bears away
my soul and my love.
To Heaven without waiting for me
she has returned;
the angel who led her away
would not take me.

Que mon sort est amer!	How bitter is my fate!
Ah! sans amour s'en aller sur la mer!	Ah! to sail out on the sea without love!
La blanche créature	The white creature
Est couchée au cercueil;	is lying in her coffin;
Comme dans la nature	How in nature
Tout me paraît en deuil!	all seems in mourning!
La colombe oubliée	The unremembered dove
Pleure et songe à l'absent;	weeps and dreams of the absent one;
Mon âme pleure et sent	my soul weeps and feels
Qu'elle est dépareillée.	itself abandoned.
Que mon sort est amer!	How bitter is my fate!
Ah! sans amour s'en aller sur la mer!	Ah! to sail out on the sea without love!
Sur moi la nuit	immense	Over me the immense night
S'étend comme un linceul,	spreads like a shroud,
Je chante ma romance	I sing my song
Que le ciel entend seul.	for the heavens alone to hear.
Ah! comme elle était belle	Ah! how fair she was
Et comme je l'aimais!	and how I loved her!
Je n'aimerai jamais		Never shall I love
Une femme autant qu'elle...	a woman as I loved her....
Que mon sort est amer!	How bitter is my fate!
Ah! sans amour s'en aller sur la mer!	Ah! to sail out on the sea without love!

Théophile Gautier

This poem has also been set by Gounod under the title 'Ma belle amie est morte', and by Fauré under the title 'Chanson du Pêcheur'. There are slight differences in the literary text due to the different editions of the poem used by the composers.

The original key is F minor. The indicated tempo seems a little fast, and ♪ = 120 is more advisable, but in this mélodie the tempo is not rigid, and the most should be made of the indications *appassionato* and *con fuoco*. The music is extremely romantic, and one should not be afraid of being rather bombastic, within the limits of good taste.

The first stanza and the first refrain should be sung in the mood of a sombre lamentation. The second stanza begins with more serenity, but gradually grows more intense and expressive, as also the second refrain.

The third stanza is sombre and tragic at first, but soon breaks out passionately, and the last refrain returns by degrees to calmness and despair, whilst the voice gradually fades away as the singer sails out on the sea.

CHARLES GOUNOD

Charles Gounod (1818–93) is the true originator of the French mélodie. He wrote more than two hundred, certainly of very uneven quality, but some are undoubtedly masterpieces. (A well-chosen group of Gounod mélodies is worth including in a recital programme as being typical of an epoch.)

These mélodies are often still very close to the 'romance' in their strophic form, and even at times in their spirit; but their musical quality ranks much higher, as also the literary quality of the poems which inspired them. Gounod set the verses of the great poets who were his contemporaries: Lamartine, Victor Hugo, Alfred de Musset, etc., and he set them with care and a quite remarkable sense of prosody.

Gounod had an exquisite melodic invention—the contour of his musical phrase is quite personal and soon reveals the name of its composer. Often the piano part is still no more than an 'accompaniment', but the harmonies are refined and sensitive.

Generally speaking, Gounod's mélodies should be sung with great regard for the melodic line, for the vocal curve. One should not be afraid of purely vocal effects, and of a certain *rubato*, within the limits, of course, of what we today consider to be good taste. Certainly we should not go as far as the interpreters of the period, whose style would undoubtedly be unacceptable to us now.

There exist four collections of Gounod's mélodies published by Choudens, in two different keys, and two collections published by Lemoine, also in two different keys.

SÉRÉNADE	SERENADE
Quand tu chantes bercée	When you sing cradled
Le soir entre mes bras,	at evening in my arms,

Entends-tu ma pensée   do you hear my thoughts
Qui te répond tout bas?   which softly respond to you?
Ton doux chant me rappelle   Your sweet song recalls
Les plus beaux de mes jours.   the happiest days of my life.
Chantez, chantez ma belle,   Sing, sing, my fair one,
Chantez, chantez toujours.   sing, sing on!

Quand tu ris, | sur ta bouche   When you laugh, upon your lips
L'amour s'épanouit,   love flowers,
Et soudain le farouche   and suddenly fierce
Soupçon s'évanouit.   suspicion vanishes.
Ah! le rire fidèle   Ah! the faithful laughter
Prouve un cœur sans détours!   shows a guileless heart!
Riez, riez, ma belle,   Laugh, laugh, my fair one,
Riez, riez, toujours!   laugh, laugh always!

Quand tu dors calme et pure   When you sleep calm and pure
Dans l'ombre sous mes yeux,   in the shadows, beneath my gaze,
Ton haleine murmure   your breath murmurs
Des mots harmonieux.   harmonious words.
Ton beau corps se révèle   Your lovely form is revealed
Sans voile et sans atours.   without veil and without attire.
Dormez, dormez, ma belle,   Sleep, sleep, my fair one,
Dormez, dormez toujours!   sleep, sleep on!

Victor Hugo

This well-known mélodie, published by Leduc in three keys and also in Choudens' first collection, is essentially a *bel canto* piece. The suppleness of the melodic contour and the coloratura at the end of each stanza can admirably exhibit the vocal qualities of the performer. The three stanzas of the poem are set to the same music ($\downarrow$. = 58). The dynamics, which should be varied according to the meaning of the words, are clearly suggested by Hugo's poem.

The first stanza can be *mf*, and the long note 'Ah!' gives an opportunity to display a beautiful crescendo and decrescendo. The second stanza is *f*, and on the long 'ah!' there is a crescendo but no diminuendo, leading to full *f* attack on 'riez', and this *f* is kept up to the end of the stanza.

The last stanza should be *pp* and a shade slower in tempo, with a little crescendo–diminuendo again on 'Ah!' and a *portamento* link to 'dormez' without a breath. *pp* to the end.

CHANSON DE PRINTEMPS

Viens, | enfant, la terre s'éveille
Le soleil rit au gazon vert!
La fleur au calice entr'ouvert
Reçoit les baisers de l'abeille.
Respirons cet air pur!
Enivrons-nous d'azur!
Là-haut sur la colline
Viens cueillir l'aubépine!
La neige des pommiers
Parfume les sentiers.

Viens, | enfant, voici l'hirondelle
Qui passe en chantant dans les airs,
Ouvre ton âme aux frais concerts
Éclos sous la feuille nouvelle.
Un vent joyeux, là-bas,
Frémit dans les lilas,
C'est la saison bénie,
C'est l'amour, c'est la vie!
Qu'un fleuve de bonheur
Inonde notre cœur.

Viens, | enfant, c'est l'heure charmante
Où l'on voudrait rêver à deux,
Mêlons nos rêves et nos vœux

Sous cette verdure naissante.
Salut règne des fleurs
Des parfums, des couleurs,
Les suaves haleines
Voltigent sur les plaines,
Le cœur épanoui
Se perd dans l'infini.

SONG OF SPRINGTIME

Come, child, the earth is awakening
the sun smiles on the green grass!
The flower in its half-opened cup
receives the kisses of the bee.
Let us breathe this pure air!
Let us revel in the blueness of the sky!
Above on the hill
come let us gather the hawthorn!
The snow of the apple trees
perfumes the paths.

Come, child, here is the swallow
that passes singing through the air,
open your soul to the fresh chorus
dawning under the new leaves.
A joyous wind, yonder,
rustles in the lilac,
it is the blest season,
it is love, it is life!
Let a flood of happiness
fill our heart.

Come, child, it is the charming hour
when we would dream together,
let us mingle our dreams and our
 vows
beneath this newly-springing foliage.
Hail kingdom of flowers
of perfumes, of colours!
The gentle zephyrs
hover over the plains,
the heart full of joy
loses itself in infinity.

Eugène Tourneux

The same contrasted dynamics will fit this mélodie (published by Choudens in four keys) admirably. A great freshness, a springlike enthusiasm must emanate from the interpretation. ($\downarrow$ = 72).

The first stanza *mf*, with the indicated dynamics. The second stanza *f*, and the piano part must make no diminuendo at the end of the *ritornello*. In the fifth bar there is a variation in the turn of the phrase, which can be *rubato*. The same effect can be made in the same bar of the third stanza, which begins *pp* with tenderness; but from ' Salut règne des fleurs' it should be *mf* with a big crescendo up to the end.

AU ROSSIGNOL

Quand ta voix céleste prélude
Au silence des belles nuits,
Barde ailé de ma solitude
Tu ne sais pas que je te suis.
Tu ne sais pas que mon oreille
Suspendue à ta douce voix
De l'harmonieuse merveille
S'enivre longtemps sous les bois!
Tu ne sais pas que mon haleine
Sur mes lèvres n'ose passer!
Que mon pied muet foule à peine
La feuille qu'il craint de froisser!

Ah! ces douces scènes nocturnes,
Ces pieux mystères du soir
Et ces fleurs qui penchent leurs urnes

Comme l'urne d'un encensoir,
Et cette voix mystérieuse
Qu'écoutent les anges et moi,
Ce soupir de la nuit pieuse,
Oiseau mélodieux, √ c'est toi!
Oh! mêle ta voix à la mienne,
La même oreille nous entend,
Mais ta prière aérienne
Monte mieux au ciel qui l'attend!

A. de Lamartine

TO THE NIGHTINGALE

When your celestial voice begins
in the silence of the lovely nights,
winged poet of my solitude
you do not know that I follow you.
You do not know that my ear
spellbound by your sweet voice
with its miracle of melody
is long enraptured under the trees!
You do not know that my breath
does not dare to pass my lips!
That my silent foot barely treads
on the leaves that it fears to rustle!

Ah! these sweet nocturnal scenes,
these devotional mysteries of evening
and these flowers that incline their
      chalices
like the chalice of a censer,
and this mysterious voice
heard by the angels and by me,
this sigh of the devout night,
melodious bird, it is you!
Oh! mingle your voice with mine,
the same ear listens to us,
but your ethereal prayer
rises better to the heaven which
      awaits it!

Only two stanzas of the poem written by the great romantic poet, Lamartine, are given here, as it is advisable when performing this mélodie (published by Choudens in three keys) to sing only the first and last stanzas.

The tempo must be slow, about ♩ = 66. All the same the first two lines should be sung in one breath, in spite of the short rest indicated by the very kind Gounod—it is much more beautiful so. The quiet, even pace must be maintained throughout this lovely mélodie, which is quite impressive when sung with a perfect legato and great tranquillity. The end of the second stanza can be very much *allargando*, especially on 'monte mieux au ciel', and a breath may be taken before 'qui l'attend'.

MIGNON

Connais–tu le pays, | où dans
    l'immense plaine
Brille comme de l'or̲ le fruit des̲
    orangers,
Où sous des cieux bénis | une
    amoureuse haleine ✓
Recueille et porte au loin le parfum
    des vergers?

Ce pays | où le jour plus radieux se
    lève
Le connais–tu, dis–moi, le connais–tu?

C'est là, mon bien aimé̲ que
    m'emporte mon rêve!
C'est là̲ que je voudrais m'en aller̲
    avec toi!

Connais–tu la maison toute blanche ✓
    et posée͡
Dans les bosquets de myrte | aimés
    des papillons,
Et les champs lumineux | où la fraîche
    rosée
Sème ses diamants dans l'herbe des
    sillons?

Ce pays | où le jour...
Louis Gallet

MIGNON

Do you know the country, where on
    the immense plain
the fruit of the orange-tree shines like
    gold,
where under blest skies a tender
    breeze
gathers and carries far the fragrance
    of the orchards?

That country where dawns a more
    radiant day
do you know it, tell me, do you
    know it?
It is there, my beloved, that my
    dream takes me!
It is there that I would go with you!

Do you know the white house lying

among thickets of myrtle beloved of
    butterflies,
and the luminous fields where the
    fresh dew
sows its diamonds in the grassy
    furrows?

That country where dawns...

To this poem, very freely inspired by Goethe's 'Kennst du das Land', Gounod wrote another of his strophic mélodies (published by Choudens in three keys), but with a coda. The tempo ($\downarrow$ = 69) seems excellent, as also the indicated dynamics. They should be observed without fear of excess. Thus the beginning of the two refrains 'Ce pays où le jour…' must be truly *p*, with a very fast crescendo on the first four bars, be-becoming a real *f* on 'le connais-tu?'. Then *subito p* to build up another crescendo. In spite of the indicated rests, it is far more effective to sing: 'Ah! c'est là, √ c'est là que je voudrais m'en aller avec toi' with only this one breath. There are too many rests—I have indicated in the text a few links. The same dynamics can be used for the two stanzas. The end of the coda gives an opportunity for a beautiful vocal effect, the last 'c'est là' being *f* fading away in a lovely diminuendo.

This mélodie should be sung with great sincerity and lyricism. If a man sings it, 'Mon bien aimé' can be changed to 'Ma bien aimée'.

VIENS, LES GAZONS SONT VERTS

Si tu dors, jeune fille,
Debout, debout! voici le soleil!
Chasse de tes‿yeux l'indolent
   sommeil
C'est l'heure du réveil!

Suis-moi, vive‿et gentille,
Pieds nus‿, viens, √ les gazons sont
   verts!
Les ruisseaux jaseurs par les bois
   déserts
Promènent leurs flots clairs!

Jules Barbier

COME, THE LAWNS ARE GREEN

If you are sleeping, maiden,
arise, arise! Here is the sun!
Chase lazy sleep from your eyes

it is time to wake up!

Follow me, quickly and sweetly,
barefoot, come, the lawns are green!

The babbling brooks in the lonely
   woods
are flowing with clear water!

This short text is by Jules Barbier, who was one of the librettists of Gounod's *Faust*. The mélodie (published by Lemoine in two keys) is charming. Sung lightly with freshness and wit, it is always very success-ful, and can be an excellent encore, short and fast ($\downarrow$ = 120).

The dynamics of the two stanzas may be varied, but the most impor-tant point is to observe these dynamics in the coda.

In the last bar it is far better to sing, as indicated above, two quavers (as in the piano part), instead of two crotchets.

L'ABSENT	THE ABSENT ONE

O silence des nuits dont la voix
    seule est douce
        Quand je n'ai plus sa voix,
Mystérieux rayons qui glissez sur la
    mousse
        Dans l'ombre de ces bois.
	O silence of the nights whose voice
	    alone is sweet
	        when I hear her voice no more,
	mysterious rays that glide across the
	    moss
	        in the shadow of these woods.

Dites-moi si ses yeux, à l'heure où
    tout sommeille
        Se rouvrent doucement,
Et si ma bien-aimée, alors que moi je
    veille,
        Se souvient de l'absent.
	Tell me if her eyes, at the hour when
	    all is sleeping,
	        gently open,
	and if my beloved, at the time when
	    I am waking,
	        remembers the absent one.

Quand la lune est aux cieux,
    baignant de sa lumière
        Les grands bois et l'azur,
	When the moon is in the sky,
	    bathing with its light
	        the great forests and the blue
	        heavens,

Quand des cloches du soir qui
    tintent la prière
        Vibre l'écho si pur;
	when the bells of evening tolling for
	    prayer
	        awaken so pure an echo;

Dites-moi si son âme un instant
    recueillie
        S'élève avec leur chant,
Et si de leurs accords la paisible
    harmonie
        Lui rappelle l'absent.
	tell me if her soul, for a moment
	    contemplative,
	        arises with their song,
	and if the peaceful harmony of their
	    strains
	        reminds her of the absent one.

Charles Gounod

This poem is by Gounod himself (he wrote it when he was in London, caught in the net of the terrible Mrs. Weldon) and the mélodie (published by Lemoine in two keys) is very beautiful. It is not in strophic form, but rather in that of the Lied: A.B.A. There is a certain Schumannesque spirit in this mélodie. It should be sung with great tranquillity ($\downarrow = 58$), and with a perfect legato. The refined modulations suggest sensitive inflexions and varied shadings. The second stanza: (Dites-moi...) is a gradually increasing crescendo up to 'Se souvient de l'absent', with a *subito p* on the repeat of these words. This effect can be repeated in the last stanza. Two bars may be cut in the overlong piano conclusion.

5 | Franck, Lalo, St-Saëns, Delibes, Bizet, Massenet

Among Gounod's contemporaries, there are at least five composers whose mélodies, although not accounted among their finest work, should nevertheless be included in this book, and should find a place in recital programmes.

CÉSAR FRANCK

César Franck (1822–90) wrote about fifteen mélodies, but only four or five of them are really worthy of a musician who was the founder of a school among his contemporaries, and had such a great influence on several French composers, among them Duparc and Chausson, who were his pupils.

NOCTURNE

O fraîche nuit, nuit transparente,
Mystère sans obscurité,
La vie est noire et dévorante,
O fraîche nuit, nuit transparente,
Donne-moi ta placidité.

O belle nuit, nuit | étoilée,
Vers moi tes regards sont baissés,
Éclaire mon âme troublée,

NOCTURNE

O fresh night, transparent night,
mystery without obscurity,
life is black and devouring,
O fresh night, transparent night,
give me your serenity.

O lovely night, starry night,
you are looking down on me,
bring light to my troubled soul,

O belle nuit, nuit | étoilée,
Mets ton sourire en mes pensers.

O sainte nuit, nuit taciturne,
Pleine de paix | et de douceur,
Mon cœur bouillonne comme une
    urne,
O sainte nuit, nuit taciturne,
Fais le silence dans mon cœur.

O grande nuit, nuit solennelle,
En qui tout est délicieux,
Prends mon être entier sous ton aile,

O grande nuit, nuit solennelle,
Verse le sommeil en mes yeux.

O lovely night, starry night,
let your smile pervade my thoughts.

O saintly night, taciturn night,
full of peace and gentleness,
my heart is seething like a cauldron,

O saintly night, taciturn night,
bring silence to my heart.

O grand night, solemn night,
in which all is delicious,
take my whole being under your
    wing,
O grand night, solemn night,
pour sleep into my eyes.

L. de Fourcaud

This very beautiful mélodie, published by Enoch in two keys, should be sung more often; it is quite typical of the style of Franck, with its harmonic texture full of chromaticism.

The three first stanzas of the poem are set to the same music ($\rabbr = 58$), with only a few changes in the voice part to suit the prosody, and also a different rhythm in the piano part for each stanza. These stanzas can be varied in mood and expression according to the feelings expressed in the poem. In the first one, the poet asks the 'fresh' and 'transparent' night to give him its 'serenity'. These three words are enough to suggest the shading of the voice and its calmness in the *p*. In the second stanza the night is 'beautiful' and 'starry' and the poet asks for its 'smile in his thoughts'. It suggests a *mf* with a crescendo. In the third stanza, the night is 'holy' and 'taciturn', and he asks for its 'silence in his heart'. The *pp* is imperative. But the final stanza changes to the major and a rather slower tempo, with a harp-like piano part. Although *p* is indicated at the beginning, the voice should be full and the declamation broad, in order to suggest that the night is now 'great' and 'solemn'; and there should be a big crescendo, leading to a quick diminuendo on the last two bars, with a definitely *p* attack on the last note. This is not easy.

LA PROCESSION	THE PROCESSION
Dieu s'avance à travers les champs!	The Host moves across the fields!
Par les landes, les prés, les verts taillis de hêtres.	By the heath, the meadows, the green beech coppices.
Il vient, suivi du peuple et porté par les prêtres.	It comes followed by the people and borne by the priests.
Aux cantiques de l'homme, oiseaux mêlez vos chants!	With the hymns of man, birds mingle your songs!
On s'arrête. La foule autour d'un chêne antique	They halt. The crowd round an ancient oak tree
S'incline en adorant sous l'ostensoir mystique.	kneels in adoration beneath the mystical monstrance.
Soleil! darde sur lui tes longs rayons couchants!	Sun! cast upon it your long sunset beams!
Aux cantiques de l'homme, oiseaux mêlez vos chants!	With the hymns of man, birds mingle your songs!
Vous, fleurs, avec l'encens	exhalez votre arôme!	You, flowers, with the incense exhale your fragrance!
O fête! tout reluit, tout prie et tout embaume!	O festival! All is shining, all is prayer, all is fragrance!
Dieu s'avance à travers les champs.	The Host moves across the fields.

Ch. Brizeux

In this mélodie, published by Leduc in two keys, there are two contrasted expressions to be emphasized: that of an objective description, and that of the enthusiasm it arouses in the poet's mind.

The long piano (or orchestral) prelude ($\downarrow$ = 63) based on the plainsong 'Lauda Sion', suggests the march of the procession through the fields, and helps the singer to create the right atmosphere from the beginning, describing with simplicity and nobility the religious retinue. Then, for four bars only, comes an emotional call to the birds to join the songs of men, after which the quiet description is resumed. A quick crescendo in the piano part brings the great call, with full voice, to the sun to beam on the monstrance. Four bars of piano, exalting the musical theme, end with a modulation introducing a new episode *p*, in which the piano *wie Harfenton* supports a long lyrical crescendo, the poet and the musician (therefore the interpreter) pouring forth their religious fervour. The opening theme and the descriptive mood return to end the mélodie in quiet serenity.

ÉDOUARD LALO

Édouard Lalo (1823–92), composer of the opera *Le Roi d'Ys*, of the well-known 'Symphonie Espagnole' for violin and orchestra, and of the ballet *Namouna* much admired by Debussy, wrote about thirty mélodies, settings of the great romantic poets. The best (published by Hamelle in two keys) are probably: 'Marine', 'L'esclave', 'Guitare'; but there is not space here to study them in detail.

CAMILLE ST-SAËNS

Camille St-Saëns (1835–1921), composer of the opera *Samson and Delilah*, was a very prolific composer in all forms of music, but he wrote only about fifty mélodies. Two of these, settings of poems by Victor Hugo, are studied here. St-Saëns had a great admiration for this poet, and in an article devoted to him he gave expression to his conception of the art of the mélodie: 'Could singing not emerge from poetry as a kind of blossoming? The rhythms, the sonorities of the verses, do they not ask for singing to emphasize them, singing being only a superior form of declamation?' The two following mélodies (published by Durand in two keys) seem to realize this intention quite successfully.

LA CLOCHE

Seule en ta sombre tour aux faîtes
    dentelés,
D'où ton souffle descend sur les
    toits ébranlés,
O cloche suspendue au milieu des
    nuées,
Par ton vaste roulis si souvent
    remuées,

THE BELL

Alone in your dark tower with its
    serrated pinnacles,
from where your breath descends
    upon the shaken roofs,
O bell hanging amid clouds

so often disturbed by your mighty
    swinging,

Tu dors en ce moment dans l'ombre,
✓et rien ne luit
Sous ta voûte profonde ✓ où sommeille
le bruit!
Oh! tandis qu'un esprit qui jusqu'à
toi s'élance,
Silencieux aussi, contemple ton
silence,
Sens-tu par cet instinct vague et
plein de douceur
Qui révèle toujours une sœur à la
sœur,
Qu'à cette heure où s'endort la
soirée expirante,
Une âme est près de toi, non moins
que toi vibrante,
Qui bien souvent aussi jette un bruit
solennel,
Et se plaint dans l'amour comme toi
dans le ciel!

you are sleeping now in the shadows,
and there is no gleam of light
under your deep vault where the
sound sleeps!
Oh! while a spirit which leaps
towards you
silent also, contemplates your silence,
do you feel with that vague instinct,
full of sweetness,
which always reveals one sister to
another,
that at this hour when the dying
evening falls asleep,
a soul is close to you, no less vibrant
than your own,
who also speaks at times in solemn
tones,
and mourns in love as you do in the
sky!

Victor Hugo

L'ATTENTE

THE WAITING ONE

Monte, écureuil, monte au grand
chêne,
Sur la branche des cieux prochaine,
Qui plie et tremble comme un jonc.

Climb, squirrel, climb into the tall
oak tree,
on to the branch near to the skies,
that bends and trembles like a reed.

Cigogne aux vieilles tours fidèle,
Oh! vole et monte à tire d'aile
De l'église à la citadelle,
Du haut clocher | au grand donjon.

Stork, faithful to ancient towers,
Oh! fly and soar swiftly
from the church to the citadel,
from the high belfry to the tall turret.

Vieil aigle, monte de ton aire,
A la montagne centenaire
Que blanchit l'hiver éternel.

Old eagle, rise from your eyrie,
to the age-old mountain
whitened by eternal winter.

Et toi qu'en ta couche inquiète

And you, who from your restless
sleeping place
Jamais l'aube ne vit muette,
never in silence see the dawn,
Monte, monte vive alouette,
ascend, ascend, lively lark,
Vive alouette monte au ciel!
lively lark ascend to the sky!

Et maintenant du haut de l'arbre,	And now from the top of the tree,
Des flèches de la tour de marbre,	from the spires of the marble tower,
Du grand mont, du ciel enflammé,	from the great mountain, from the blazing sky,
A l'horizon parmi la brume,	on the horizon in the mist,
Voyez-vous flotter une plume,	do you see a feather swaying,
Et courir un cheval qui fume,	and a steaming horse galloping,
Et revenir mon bien aimé?	and my beloved returning?

Victor Hugo

These mélodies should be sung in a broad and dramatic style; they do not ask for much subtlety in their interpretation. The dynamics are very well indicated. They are admirably suited to a big voice, and will show its beauty to advantage.

The beginning of 'La Cloche' with its low and heavy octaves (♩ = 76) suggests the tolling of a great bell, and the piano part accelerates its rhythm, while the words and the vocal line become more and more exalted.

'L'attente', with its agitated and rhythmic piano part (♩ = 144), suggests the burning impatience of a medieval lady for her lover's return. Crisp and clear articulation is required to give an adequate performance of this beautiful mélodie.

LÉO DELIBES

Léo Delibes (1836–91), who composed the opera *Lakmé*, and the ballets *Coppélia* and *Sylvia*, wrote only a few mélodies, and these are of uneven quality. One of the best known, published by Gallet, is a setting of verses by Alfred de Musset:

LES FILLES DE CADIX	THE DAUGHTERS OF CADIZ
Nous venions de voir le taureau,	We had just seen the bullfight,
Trois garçons, trois fillettes,	three lads, three young girls,
Sur la pelouse il faisait beau	on the green it was fine
Et nous dansions un boléro	and we danced a bolero

Au son des castagnettes:

to the sound of the castanets:

Dites-moi, voisin,

tell me, neighbour,

Si j'ai bonne mine,

if my looks please you,

Et si ma basquine

and if my skirt

Va bien, ce matin.

is becoming this morning.

Vous me trouvez la taille fine?

Do you think my waist is slender?

Les filles de Cadix aiment assez cela!

The daughters of Cadiz have a liking for that!

Et nous dansions un boléro

And we danced a bolero

Un soir c'était dimanche,

on a Sunday evening,

Vers nous s'en vint un hidalgo,

a Hidalgo approached us,

Cousu d'or, la plume au chapeau,

raiment stitched with gold, a feather in his hat,

Et le poing sur la hanche:

and his fist on his hip:

Si tu veux de moi,

if you fancy me,

Brune au doux sourire,

brunette with the sweet smile,

Tu n'as qu'à le dire,

you need only say so,

Cet or est à toi.

this gold is yours.

Passez votre chemin, beau sire...

Go on your way, handsome Sir...

Les filles de Cadix n'entendent pas cela!

the daughters of Cadiz do not listen to that!

Et nous dansions un boléro

And we danced a bolero

Au pied de la colline,

at the foot of the hill,

Sur le chemin passait Diégo

on the road Diégo passed

Qui pour tout bien n'a qu'un manteau

whose only belongings were a cloak

Et qu'une mandoline.

and a mandolin.

La belle aux doux yeux,

Fair one with the sweet eyes,

Veux-tu qu'à l'église

would you like it if to church

Demain te conduise

tomorrow you should be escorted

Un amant jaloux?

by a jealous lover?

Jaloux! Jaloux! quelle sottise!

Jealous! Jealous! What stupidity!

Les filles de Cadix craignent ce défaut là!

The daughters of Cadiz fear that fault!

Alfred de Musset

This mélodie is suited to a light, brilliant soprano voice, and when performed with wit and skill is quite successful.

The tempo is about ♩ = 144, but very *rubato* and supple. For instance the bars set in the first stanza to 'Et nous dansions un boléro', should always be very freely phrased, the *rallentandi* on the following bars well observed, but all the coloratura phrases on 'Ah!' must be in tempo. The last line of each stanza, repeated three times, should be crescendo and slightly *accelerando*. It is easy to vary the three stanzas; the first one sung with much coquetry; the second ironical and mocking, the coloratura on 'Ah!' being like peals of laughter; and the final stanza easy, sprightly and gay.

GEORGES BIZET

Georges Bizet (1838–75), the composer of *Carmen*, seems to have lost much of his strong personality when writing mélodies. At least two of them, both published by Choudens, must, however, be mentioned:

CHANSON D'AVRIL	SONG OF APRIL
Lève-toi! lève-toi! le printemps vient de naître!	Arise! Arise! Spring is just born!
Là-bas sur les vallons flotte un réseau vermeil!	Yonder over the valleys rosy gossamer floats!
Tout frissonne au jardin, tout chante et ta fenêtre	Everything thrills in the garden, everything sings, and your window
Comme un regard joyeux, | est pleine de soleil!	like a joyous glance, is full of sun!
Du côté des lilas | aux touffes violettes,	Beside the lilac with its purple clusters,
Mouches et papillons bruissent à la fois,	flies and butterflies hum together,
Et le muguet sauvage, | ébranlant ses clochettes,	and the wild lily-of-the-valley, ringing its tiny bells,
A réveillé l'amour endormi dans les bois!	has awakened love asleep in the woods!
Puisqu'Avril a semé ses marguerites blanches,	Since April has sown its white daisies,
Laisse ta mante lourde et ton manchon frileux,	put off your heavy cloak and your cosy muff,

Déjà l'oiseau t'appelle et tes sœurs les pervenches	already the bird calls you and your sisters the periwinkles
Te souriront dans l'herbe en voyant tes yeux bleus!	will smile in the grass on seeing your blue eyes!
Viens partons! | au matin la source est plus limpide!	Come let us go! At morn the springs are more limpid!
N'attendons pas du jour les brûlantes chaleurs,	Let us not wait for the burning heat of the day,
Je veux mouiller mes pieds dans la rosée humide,	I would moisten my feet in the damp dew,
Et te parler d'amour sous les poiriers en fleurs.	and tell you of my love beneath the flowering pear trees.

Louis Bouilhet

This charming mélodie could very well have been written by Gounod, for it has a similar grace of musical phrase. The two stanzas should be sung with freshness and simplicity ($\quarternote$ = 92).

LES ADIEUX DE L'HÔTESSE ARABE	THE FAREWELL OF THE ARABIAN HOSTESS
Puisque rien ne t'arrête en cet heureux pays,	Since nothing will keep you in this happy land,
Ni l'ombre du palmier, ni le jaune maïs	neither the shade of the palm trees, nor the yellow corn,
Ni le repos, ni l'abondance,	not the restfulness, nor the abundance,
Ni de voir à ta voix battre le jeune sein,	nor to see palpitating at the sound of your voice, the young breasts
De nos sœurs dont, les soirs, le tournoyant essaim	of our sisters, who in a whirling bevy at evening
Couronne un coteau de sa danse,	encircle the hillside with their dancing,
Adieu, beau voyageur! Oh! que n'es-tu de ceux	farewell, handsome traveller! Oh! you are not of those
Qui donnent pour limite à leur pieds paresseux	whose lazy feet are bounded
Leur toit de branches ou de toiles!	by their roof of branches or of tiles!
Qui rêveurs, sans en faire, écoutent les récits,	Who, dreamers, listen in silence to narratives,

Et souhaitent, le soir, devant leur
    porte assis,
      De s'en aller dans les étoiles!
Si tu l'avais voulu, peut-être une de
    nous,
O jeune homme, eut aimé te servir à
    genoux
      Dans nos | huttes toujours
      ouvertes.
Elle eut fait, | en berçant ton
    sommeil de ses chants,
Pour chasser de ton front les
    moucherons méchants,
      Un éventail de feuilles vertes.
Si tu ne reviens pas, songe un peu
    quelquefois
Aux filles du désert, sœurs à la
    douce voix,
      Qui dansent pieds nus sur la
      dune.
O beau jeune homme blanc, bel
    oiseau passager,
Souviens-toi, car peut-être, | ô rapide
    étranger,
      Ton souvenir reste à plus d'une!

Hélas! adieu! bel étranger!
    Souviens-toi!

Victor Hugo

and wish at evening, sitting outside
    their door,
      to be off to the stars!
Had you wished it, perhaps one of us,

O young man, would have liked to
    serve you kneeling
      in our ever open huts.

She would have made, while rocking
    you asleep with her songs,
to drive the troublesome midges
    from your brow
      a fan of green leaves.
If you do not return, dream a little
    sometimes
of the daughters of the desert, sisters
    of the sweet voice,
      who dance barefoot on the
      sandhills.
O handsome, white young man,
    beautiful bird of passage,
remember, for perhaps, o swiftly
    passing stranger,
      your memory remains with
      more than one!

Alas! farewell! handsome stranger!
    Remember!

This mélodie is a good example of a certain inclination towards orientalism which flourished in France during the romantic period: among the poets Victor Hugo ('Les Orientales'), among the painters Delacroix and among the musicians Berlioz ('La captive'); Lalo ('L'esclave'); St-Saëns ('Mélodies persannes').

The piano part suggests the incessant beating of a tabor ($\quarternote = 72$). This makes it obvious that the mélodie must be performed with absolutely firm rhythm, in accordance with its character. It also requires a deep and nostalgic romanticism, which must, however, remain within the limits of what we at present consider to be good taste, even when faced with such indications by the composer as 'd'une voix entrecoupée par les sanglots' (with a voice broken by sobs).

JULES MASSENET

This short chapter cannot end without mentioning the name of Jules Massenet (1842–1912), so well known for his operas. Debussy wrote: 'Massenet was the most really loved of the musicians of his time. He has been much imitated . . ., . . . by Debussy himself in the mélodies of his youth! Massenet wrote about two hundred mélodies. Unfortunately he did not observe the precept set forth by Debussy in the same article: 'In art, one has more often to fight only against one-self, and the victories one wins are perhaps the most beautiful.' Massenet abandoned himself to his unique gift and fluency which, in his mélodies, led to a sugary sentimentalism. They cannot be recommended.

6 | Henri Duparc
(1848–1933)

It is certainly unique in musical history for a composer to win international fame with an output of fourteen songs only—yet such is the case of Henri Duparc, who was born in Paris in 1848, three years after Fauré. Duparc wrote these fourteen songs in sixteen years, between the ages of twenty and thirty-seven; he died in 1933, having lived for another forty-eight years without producing a single note of music. Unfortunately he suffered from a nervous disease which unduly intensified and exaggerated his critical sense. Duparc was a pupil of César Franck. The songs are published by Salabert in one volume in high (original) and medium keys. A lower key is published by The International Music Co., New York.

CHANSON TRISTE

Dans ton cœur dort un clair de lune,
Un doux clair de lune d'été,
Et pour fuir la vie importune
Je me noierai dans ta clarté.

J'oublierai les douleurs passées,
Mon amour, quand tu berceras
Mon triste cœur et mes pensées,
Dans le calme aimant de tes bras.

SORROWFUL SONG

In your heart moonlight sleeps,
gentle summer moonlight,
and to escape from the stress of life
I will drown myself in your radiance.

I will forget past sorrows,
my love, when you cradle
my sad heart and my thoughts
in the loving peacefulness of your
arms.

Tu prendras ma tête malade
Oh! quelquefois sur tes genoux,
Et lui diras_une ballade
Qui semblera parler de nous.

You will take my aching head
Oh! sometimes upon your knee,
and will relate a ballad
that seems to speak of ourselves.

Et dans tes yeux pleins de tristesses,
Dans tes yeux | alors_je boirai
Tant de baisers | et de tendresses
Que, peut-être, | je guérirai...

And in your eyes full of sorrows,
in your eyes then I will drink
so deeply of kisses and of tenderness
that, perhaps, I shall be healed....

Jean Lahor

Hope is the theme of this poem by Jean Lahor; a rather over-sweet lyric that inspired the young composer—this was his first mélodie— to write tender, melancholy music, the sentimentality of which must not be emphasized in performance. The prefatory indication: 'with tender and intimate feeling' is most important, and should dominate the interpretation. The marks of expression are certainly excellent, but as *f* and *p* can never be taken in an absolute sense, but only in relationship to the work in question, *f* in this melodie should rather be *mf*. The feelings of intimacy which must prevail throughout, the lovers being so close to one another, should prevent the formidable outbursts of some singers, anxious to achieve a good top A—outbursts entirely out of place in this quiet mélodie. Care must be taken to give all the quavers their full value, to sing them well. The general tempo, about ♩. = 56, should be supple and *senza rigore*. A *rubato*, for instance, is permissible on the words 'mon amour', which should be *pp*, as in tender parenthesis, the tempo picking up again on 'quand tu berceras Mon triste cœur et mes pensées' which is *mf* and in crescendo. Then attack *subito p* on 'Dans le calme aimant de tes bras'. The marks of expression should be well observed in the last stanza, especially the crescendo on the words 'Dans tes yeux alors je boirai'. It is preferable not to make too much of a diminuendo on the last line of the poem. The main thing is to suggest all the hope expressed by the words and the music; to achieve this, the singer must give the impression that his last phrase does not conclude the song, the conclusion is in the piano part.

I have suggested above, in the poem, liaisons and breaks for the last stanza, which are not compulsory. To make no liaison before 'alors' gives more stress to this word. The liaison 'baisers-z-et' is, in my opinion, not very pretty; and it is more expressive to have a 'Luftpause' between 'que, peut-être' and 'je guérirai'.

*

Duparc has set two other poems by Jean Lahor—'Extase' and 'Sérénade Florentine'. These pale verses evoke for me Pre-Raphaelite paintings.

EXTASE	ECSTASY
Sur un lys pâle mon cœur dort	On a pale lily my heart sleeps
D'un sommeil doux comme la mort...	a sleep sweet as death...
Mort exquise, mort parfumée	Exquisite death, death perfumed
Du souffle de la bien-aimée...	by the breath of the beloved...
Sur ton sein pâle mon cœur dort	On your pale breast my heart sleeps
D'un sommeil doux comme la mort...	a sleep sweet as death...

Jean Lahor

This is a beautiful, Wagnerian nocturne for the piano (♩ = 56), over which the vocal line floats in a dreamlike manner. The first stanza should be *p*, keeping the effect of *pp* for the last stanza. It is better to give up the idea of singing this mélodie, if the phrasing on the words 'Du souffle de la bien-aimée'—*poco crescendo* and *diminuendo molto*—cannot be perfectly achieved with a beautiful *pianissimo* on the top note.

SÉRÉNADE FLORENTINE	FLORENTINE SERENADE
Étoile dont la beauté luit	Star whose beauty shines
Comme un diamant dans la nuit,	like a diamond in the night,
Regarde vers ma bien-aimée	look down upon my beloved
Dont la paupière s'est fermée,	whose eyelids are closed,
Et fais descendre sur ses yeux	and let fall upon her eyes
La bénédiction des cieux.	the blessing of heaven.

Elle s'endort... Par la fenêtre |	She falls asleep. . . . Through the window
En sa chambre heureuse | pénètre:	of her happy room, enter,
Sur sa blancheur, comme un baiser,	upon her whiteness, like a kiss,
Viens jusqu'à l'aube te poser,	come and rest until the dawn,
Et que sa pensée, alors, rêve	and let her thought, then, dream
D'un astre d'amour qui se lève!	of a star of love which is rising!

Jean Lahor

The singer should choose a clear, floating tone. The legato must be perfect, as also the rhythm, ($\rfloor$. = 54), which at times is a little awkward with the offbeats of the piano part. The only *ritardando* is on 'Elle s'endort', the effect being of a slight hesitation before the first beat of the *a tempo* bar. The prosody of the line 'Par la fenêtre En sa chambre heureuse pénètre' does not make the bad poetic inversion clear; a slight re-attack between 'fenêtre' and 'en', and another one between 'heureuse' and 'pénètre' may help. Observe the little crescendo on 'Et que sa pensée alors' leading to a *pp* on 'rêve'. The whole mélodie should be sung *p* and *pp*, in serene and blissful tranquillity.

*

Let us now consider three mélodies best suited to men's voices:

LE MANOIR DE ROSEMONDE   THE MANOR OF ROSAMUND

De sa dent soudaine et vorace,	With its sudden and voracious fang,
Comme un chien, l'amour m'a mordu.	like a dog, love has bitten me.
En suivant mon sang répandu,	By following the blood I have shed,
Va, tu pourras suivre ma trace.	go! You will be able to follow my trail.
Prends un cheval de bonne race,	Take a thoroughbred horse,
Pars, | et suis mon chemin ardu,	set out, and follow my arduous way,
Fondrière ou sentier perdu,	bog or hidden path,
Si la course ne te harasse!	if the ride does not exhaust you!
En passant par où j'ai passé,	In passing where I have passed,
Tu verras que seul et blessé,	you will see that alone and wounded,
J'ai parcouru ce triste monde,	I have ranged this sad world,
Et qu'ainsi je m'en fus mourir	and that thus I went to die

Bien loin, bien loin, sans découvrir √	far away, far away, without discovering
Le bleu manoir de Rosemonde.	the blue manor of Rosamund.
R. de Bonnières	

There are two sharply contrasted parts in this poem. In the first part the poet gives, with bitterness, an image of his arduous life, and in the second, with lassitude, he tells how he went to die far away, without discovering the inaccessible domain of the beloved of his dreams. The composer has succeeded wonderfully in expressing these feelings in music.

In the first part the rhythm is of prime importance, both for the singer and the pianist—it must be perfectly precise and firm (♩. = 88). The singer must also have a strong and biting declamation. In the text I have indicated expressive stresses in the difficult first two lines. The dynamic markings are constantly *f* and *ff*.

The second part of the mélodie—the last two stanzas of the sonnet—is in slower tempo (♩ = 60), and above all in a completely different mood—*p*, legato, but always precise in rhythm. There must be a big crescendo on the line 'J'ai parcouru ce triste monde', and a real *f* on 'Et qu'ainsi je m'en fus mourir'. The first 'bien loin' will still be *f*; the second one being *p*, an echo; and by his way of pronouncing the words, by the shading of his voice, the singer must give the impression of distance. He must think: 'bien loin ah! bien loin', the 'ah!' being a silent expressive breath. At the end of this *rallentando* the pianist must carefully observe the silence, and attack the following chord *p*, but with a stress, imitating horns. The *a tempo* is, of course, the *tempo più lento*. The *rallentando* on the last phrase of the song will depend upon the breath of the singer. (The more closed the vowel [ø] in 'bleu', the bluer will be the manor . . .) On the last note of the voice: *a tempo lento* for the piano; and suddenly *a tempo primo* but *p*, for the last measure.

LA VAGUE ET LA CLOCHE	THE WAVE AND THE BELL
Une fois, terrassé par un puissant breuvage	Once, laid low by a potent drink
J'ai rêvé que parmi les vagues | et le bruit⌐	I dreamed that amid the waves and the roar

De la mer, je voguais sans fanal √ dans la nuit,
Morne rameur, √ n'ayant plus l'espoir du rivage.

L'océan me crachait ses baves sur le front,
Et le vent me glaçait d'horreur jusqu'aux_entrailles.
Les vagues s'écroulaient | ainsi que des murailles
Avec ce rythme lent qu'un silence͜ interrompt.

Puis tout changea. La mer et sa noire mêlée
Sombrèrent. Sous mes pieds s'effrondra le plancher͡
De la barque. Et j'étais seul dans_un vieux clocher,
Chevauchant_avec rage une cloche ́ ébranlée.

J'étreignais la criarde | opiniâtrement,

Convulsif | et fermant dans l'effort mes paupières.
Le grondement faisait trembler les vieilles pierres,
Tant j'activais sans fin le lourd balancement.

Pourquoi n'as–tu pas dit, o rêve √ où Dieu nous mène?
Pourquoi n'as–tu pas dit s'ils ne finiraient pas
L'inutile travail et l'éternel fracas

Dont_est faite la vie, hélas, la vie humaine!

François Coppée

of the sea, I rowed without a ship's lantern in the night,
mournful oarsman, with no more hope of reaching the shore.

The ocean spat its foam on my brow,

and the wind froze me to the entrails with horror.
The waves crashed down like walls

with that slow rhythm punctuated with silence.

Then all changed. The sea and its dark conflict
sank down. Under my feet the bottom
of the boat gave way.
       And I was alone in an old belfry,
riding furiously on a ringing bell.

I stubbornly gripped the clangorous thing,
violently and closing my eyes with the effort,
the booming made the old stones tremble,
so unceasingly did I activate the heavy swinging.

Why did you not say, O dream, where God is leading us?
Why did you not say if there is to be no end
to the useless toil and the eternal strife
of which, alas, human life is made!

This mélodie, with its tumultuous romanticism, requires a rich baritone voice. The poet, François Coppée, tells of two successive nightmares he had, the meaning of which remains for him an enigma, giving no answer to his distressed interrogation. Both nightmares—the stormy night and the ringing bell—are admirably suggested by the music, due mainly to the very important piano part, which is quite orchestral. The pianist must have a good technique, a warm temperament and . . . a singer with a powerful voice.

The two-bar theme of the tempest is repeated by the piano seven times (the expression mark in the second bar of the phrase is important), while the singer, broadly but rather *mf* and simply, sings the first two lines (♩ = 92/96). Then comes a $\frac{9}{8}$ in broader tempo (♩. = 63). After the return, twice, of the tempest theme, the piano remains in $\frac{3}{4}$ for the introduction of a new rhythmic theme, but the voice remains in $\frac{9}{8}$ and the singer has the first *ff*. On the last line of the stanza there is a *diminuendo*, but small and without losing the timbre of the voice. All the duplets in the voice part are rather *marcato*. After the broad and rather free 'Puis, tout changea', it is important to be *a tempo*, even on the words 'le plancher De la barque', whose rhythm ♩♪ ♪♪♪ is excellent.

Then comes the second nightmare. The toll of the bell should be about ♩ = 69, and should be kept steady for the whole stanza. The singer should follow only slightly the expression marks $>$ over the two last lines of this section.

Now comes the great peroration, the pathetic interrogation of the last stanza. It is in broader tempo, and the voice should sing only *mf*, this giving, curiously enough, more expression and intensity.

TESTAMENT	TESTAMENT
Pour que le vent te les apporte	So that the wind may carry them to you
Sur l'aile noire d'un remord,	on the black wing of remorse,
J'écrirai sur la feuille morte	I will write upon a dead leaf
Les tortures de mon cœur mort!	the torments of my dead heart!
Toute ma sève s'est tarie	All my sap is dried up
Aux clairs midis de ta beauté,	in the clear midday sun of your beauty,

Et, comme à la feuille flétrie,	and, like a withered leaf,
Rien de vivant ne m'est resté.	nothing living remains to me.
Tes yeux m'ont brûlé jusqu'à l'âme	Your eyes have burned me to the soul
Comme des soleils sans merci!	like merciless suns!
Feuille que le gouffre réclame,	Leaf that the abyss claims,
L'autan va m'emporter aussi...	the south wind will bear me away too. . . .
Mais avant, pour qu'il te les porte	But first, so that they are borne to you
Sur l'aile noire d'un remord,	on the black wing of remorse,
J'écrirai sur la feuille morte	I will write upon a dead leaf
Les tortures de mon cœur mort!	the torments of my dead heart!
Armand Silvestre	

This mélodie, which is not without grandiloquence, is certainly not the best of Duparc. It requires a generous voice and a firm articulation. The tempo, approximately ♩ = ♩. = 88, should be *senza rigore*. The very romantic and passionate feeling is obvious in the vocal line, and still more so in the orchestral piano part.

SOUPIR	SIGH
Ne jamais la voir ni l'entendre,	Never to see or hear her,
Ne jamais tout haut la nommer,	never to speak her name aloud,
Mais, fidèle, toujours l'attendre,	but, faithful, ever to wait for her,
Toujours l'aimer.	ever to love her.
Ouvrir les bras, | et, las d'attendre,	To open my arms, and weary of waiting,
Sur le néant les refermer!	to close them on a void!
Mais encor, ✓ toujours les lui tendre,	Yet still, always to stretch them towards her,
Toujours l'aimer.	ever to love her.
Ah! ne pouvoir que les lui tendre	Ah! to be able only to stretch them towards her
Et dans les pleurs se consumer,	and to be consumed in tears,
Mais ces pleurs toujours les répandre,	yet ever to shed these tears,
Toujours l'aimer.	ever to love her.

Ne jamais la voir ni l'entendre,
Ne jamais tout haut la nommer,
Mais d'un amour toujours plus tendre,
  Toujours l'aimer.

Never to see or hear her,
never to speak her name aloud,
but with a love always more tender,
  ever to love her.

Sully Prud'homme

This is a very touching and moving mélodie when it is performed with simplicity and sincerity. The pianist should use a beautiful quality of tone and expressive phrasing ($\quad$ = 56). The voice should barely attain the *mf* marked on the two climaxes: 'Toujours' and 'Ah! ne pouvoir' (no break between 'Ah' and 'ne'). It is essential to sing the last stanza *pp*, even on the top notes. To make sure of this effect it is advisable to sing the first stanza only *p*.

It is important in this mélodie to vary the expression of the refrain: 'Toujours l'aimer', which should continue the feeling of the preceding lines in each verse. The first stanza should be sung simply and sadly. The second should be more intense, suggesting the arms stretched out to the beloved; a long expressive breath will join 'Toujours l'aimer', sung with the same intensity. The third stanza should begin by maintaining this same intensity, but after the first two lines, the long silence for the voice is filled with the help of the pianist, who must not drag, but rather play his chromatic descent a shade faster. The recitative on one note should be sung with great emotion, and again a long expressive breath will link 'Toujours l'aimer' in the same emotion as the preceding line.

ÉLÉGIE

Oh! ne murmurez pas son nom! qu'il
  dorme dans l'ombre,
Où froide et sans honneur repose sa
  dépouille.
Muettes, tristes, glacées, tombent nos
  larmes,
Comme la rosée de la nuit qui sur sa
  tête | humecte le gazon.

Mais la rosée de la nuit, bien qu'elle
  pleure en silence,

ELEGY ON THE DEATH OF ROBERT EMMET

Oh! breathe not his name, let it sleep
  in the shade,
Where cold and unhonour'd his
  relics are laid.
Sad, silent, and dark, be the tears
  that we shed,
As the night-dew that falls on the
  grass o'er his head.

But the night-dew that falls, though
  in silence it weeps,

Fera briller la verdure sur sa couche,	Shall brighten with verdure the grave where he sleeps,
Et nos larmes, | en secret répandues,	And the tear that we shed, though in secret it rolls,
Conserveront sa mémoire fraîche et verte ✓ dans nos cœurs.	Shall long keep his memory green in our souls.

Thomas Moore

The original poem of Thomas Moore is given here; the French text was a prose translation, made probably by Duparc himself (he had married an Irish wife). The two stanzas of the poem express two different feelings, given beautiful expression in music by the composer. First the poet deplores in calm despair the death of the Irish patriot, but afterwards, he convinces himself that this very despair will immortalize the memory of the departed.

The first part—which, of course, recalls Wagner's Wesendonck Lied: 'Träume'—should be played at a really slow tempo ($\quarternote$. = 50). I suggest that the first two lines be sung *pp*, with no crescendo whatsoever, even when the vocal line rises. Then a crescendo begins and continues to 'tombent nos larmes', and the last line of the stanza is *p*, but not *pp*. The second stanza should be only very little faster, the impression of movement being given mostly by the flowing accompaniment. The long crescendo of the first line should be very gradual, and the second line sung, if possible, in one breath. The third line should begin *mf* before a new crescendo. A little stress should be made on the second beats of 'fraîche' and 'dans', and only a little *diminuendo* and *ritardando* to the end, to express the faith of the poet in this unforgettable memory.

*

Let us consider now two settings of poems by Théophile Gautier. For his 'Lamento', Duparc chose only three stanzas of a long poem already set in its entirety by Berlioz, under the title 'Au Cimetière'.

LAMENTO	LAMENT
Connaissez-vous la blanche tombe	Do you know the white tomb
Où flotte avec un son plaintif	where sways with a plaintive sound
L'ombre d'un if?	the shadow of a yew tree?

ose, ô Phidylé! Midi sur les
iillages
Rayonne ✓ et t'invite au sommeil!
e trèfle et le thym, seules, | en
in soleil
Chantent les abeilles volages;

haud parfum circule au détour
s sentiers,
La rouge fleur des blés s'incline,
oiseaux, rasant de l'aile la
line,
Cherchent l'ombre des églantiers.

quand l'Astre incliné ✓ sur sa
urbe éclatante,
Verra ses ardeurs s'apaiser,
ton plus beau sourire ✓ et ton
illeur baiser
Me récompensent ✓ de l'attente!

Leconte de Lisle

Rest, O Phidylé! the midday sun on
the leaves
is shining and invites you to sleep!
In the clover and the thyme, alone,
in full sunlight
the hovering bees are humming;

a warm fragrance haunts the winding
paths,
the red poppy of the cornfield droops,
and the birds, skimming the hill on
the wing,
seek the shade of the sweet briar.

But when the sun, sinking lower on
its resplendent orbit,
finds its fire abated,
let your loveliest smile and your most
ardent kiss
reward me for my waiting!

his beautiful and long mélodie is a setting of the poem by Leconte
isle, the 'Parnassian poet' often inspired by Greek antiquity, as we
observe in other poems of his, set by Chausson and Fauré.
ere, the poet is embodied in a young man who, lying down beside
beloved, rests in an idyllic landscape, at noon, under a warm,
literranean sun. He describes the beauty of his surroundings, the
ds, the fragrance; and addressing the sleeping girl he says: 'Rest,
hidylé, but when the sun is setting you will awake, and then I
have my reward!' Any sadness or sentimentality would thus be
pletely out of place in the interpretation of this mélodie.

he song can be divided into five parts: (1) the first quatrain; (2)
irst two lines of the second quatrain; (3) the last two lines of this
 quatrain; (4) a musical episode based on the repetition of the
ds 'Repose, O Phidylé' (which are not in the poem at this point);
he last quatrain.

) This first page, absolutely static in a rather slow tempo (♩ = 48),
ng with perfect legato and evenness, with no nuance at all. The

Sur l'if | une pâle colombe,
Triste et seule au soleil couchant,
Chante son chant.

On dirait que l'âme éveillée

Pleure sous terre ✓ à l'unisson
De la chanson,
Et du malheur d'être oubliée
Se plaint dans un roucoulement
Bien doucement.

Ah! jamais plus près de la tombe
Je n'irai, ✓ quand descend le soir
Au manteau noir,
Écouter la pâle colombe
Chanter sur la branche de l'if
Son chant plaintif!

Théophile Gautier

On the yew a pale dove,
sad and alone in the setting sun,
sings its song.

One would say that the awakened
soul
weeps under the earth in unison
with the song,
and the distress of being forgotten
laments in a cooing
very softly.

Ah! nevermore near to the tomb
shall I go, when evening descends
in its dark cloak,
to listen to the pale dove
singing on the branch of the yew tree
its plaintive song!

The first two stanzas are set to exactly the same music, with only a
few changes of rhythm in the vocal line to suit the prosody, which is
extremely good. In the very slow tempo (♩ = 50), the singer must
achieve a perfect legato, stretching his vowel sounds as much as
possible. (The first line seems to be particularly difficult for English-
speaking singers:—there should be no double or anticipated consonants.) There should be very few nuances in these two stanzas—the
poco *f* is really *pochissimo*—the *pp* has to be maintained without involuntary crescendi, and without trying to make any difference
between the first and the second stanza, continuing a depressed, hopeless mood. The third stanza, with more animation (♩ = 80), should,
however, never become dramatic, even on the attack of 'Ah! jamais
plus', which is only relatively *f*, and always with the feeling of a
'lamento'.

AU PAYS OÙ SE FAIT LA GUERRE

TO THE COUNTRY WHERE THEY ARE AT WAR

Au pays | où se fait la guerre
Mon bel ami s'en est allé,

To the country where they are at war
my dear love has departed,

Il semble à mon cœur désolé	it seems to my desolate heart
Qu'il ne reste que moi sur terre.	that no one is left on earth but myself
En partant, | au baiser d'adieu,	On leaving, with a farewell kiss,
Il m'a pris mon âme à ma bouche...	he took my soul from my lips. . . .
Qui le tient si longtemps, mon Dieu?	Who keeps him so long, dear God?
Voici le soleil qui se couche,	Now the sun is setting,
Et moi toute seule en ma tour,	and I, all alone in my tower,
J'attends encore son retour.	I still await his return.
Les pigeons sur le toit roucoulent,	The doves on the roof are cooing,
Roucoulent | amoureusement,	cooing amorously,
Avec un son triste et charmant;	with a sad and charming sound;
Les eaux sous les grands saules coulent.	the waters under the big willows are flowing.
Je me sens tout près de pleurer,	I feel near to tears,
Mon cœur comme un lys plein s'épanche,	my heart unfolds like a full-blown lily,
Et je n'ose plus espérer,	and I dare hope no longer,
Voici briller la lune blanche.	now the pale moon is shining.
Et moi toute seule en ma tour,	And I, all alone in my tower,
J'attends encore son retour.	I still await his return.
Quelqu'un monte à grands pas la rampe...	Someone is climbing the stairs with big strides . . .
Serait-ce lui, mon doux amant?	could it be he, my sweet love?
Ce n'est pas lui, mais seulement	It is not he, but only
Mon petit page avec ma lampe...	my little page with my lamp. . . .
Vents du soir, volez, dites-lui	Winds of evening, fly, tell him
Qu'il est ma pensée et mon rêve	that he is my thought and my dream
Toute ma joie et mon ennui.	all my joy and my anxiety.
Voici que l'aurore se lève.	Now the dawn is rising.
Et moi toute seule en ma tour,	And I, all alone in my tower,
J'attends encore son retour.	I still await his return.
Théophile Gautier	

This resembles a medieval ballad; it is written for a mezzo-soprano voice. The composer has followed the pattern of the poet: three

---

stanzas, ending with a refrain which is the leitmotiv of the

The repetition and the monotony of this refrain should be e to suggest the long, long waiting of the 'chatelaine in her ca indicated by the last line of each stanza: the sun setting, shining, dawn rising.

The first stanza should start *mp*, with a naturally sad but cali The indicated metronomic tempo is on the fast side and $\boldsymbol{\downarrow} =$ advisable. Gradually despair should increase in the voice u climax: 'Qui le tient si longtemps, mon Dieu?' The last lin refrain should be only *mf*.

The second stanza is a little faster, but in a way this more tempo will help to keep it less intense. It should be sung entir *pp*, and very simply.

Thus the intensely dramatic beginning of the third stanza w its full effect, with the faster tempo, the orchestral piano p breathlessness of 'quelqu'un...', and the hopeful question: 'S lui, mon doux amant?' One should not be misled by the *dim* indicated on these last three words; in spite of it, the interrogatio maintain its intensity and its hope up to the end. It is only dur following measures for the piano, that the singer gradually real deception, and the leitmotiv must be played in a really slow te allow the singer to say, with infinite weariness: 'Ce n'est pa Then an *accelerando* of five bars will begin, and on 'vents du soir one should have returned to the fast tempo of the beginnin third stanza. The *tempo primo* returns only for the refrain. Th the mélodie should be intensely dramatic.

PHIDYLÉ

L'herbe est molle au sommeil sous les frais peupliers,	The grass is soft for sleeping the fresh poplars,
Aux pentes des sources moussues,	on the slopes by the mossy
Qui dans les prés en fleurs germant par mille issues,	which in the flowery mead in a thousand rills,
Se perdent sous les noirs | halliers.	to be lost under dark thick

young man, half asleep himself, lazily describes the beauty of nature around him. (There can be no liaison between 'noirs' and 'halliers', but a re-attack, as in German.)

(2) The young man tenderly addresses the girl in her sleep: 'Repose, O Phidylé' (with only one 'l', please!). The tempo can be a little faster, ($\quarternote$ = 66) tempo II, and *poco rubato*. The piano has the important part, and must state the theme with lyricism, but also simplicity (only one 'm' in 'sommeil', please!).

(3) The young man describes the splendours of the noontide around him, thus the voice sings with warmth, but with no real *f*, and no sentimentality, quite objectively. The tempo is still faster, about $\quarternote$ = 72, and can be always more *animato*, reaching $\halfnote$ = 50, as it is better to count in two from: 'Un chaud parfum...'. No *ritardando* on the very melodic phrase: 'Et les oiseaux rasant de l'aile la colline', which can suggest the meaning of the words, when sung with beautiful phrasing and legato. The *rallentando* is only on the bar: 'l'ombre des églantiers' and brings back the second tempo: $\quarternote$ = 66.

(4) This is the counterpart of (2), in tempo and mood. The piano again has the important part, but the singer, in spite of his long silences, and his text repeated three times, must succeed in maintaining the intensity by his 'presence', and the subtle and tender variation of his inflexions.

(5) It is the second tempo which must be taken for this last part, to allow the 'ampleur' (breadth) for which the composer asks. The piano part is quite orchestral, and the voice in its fullness and warmth will express the joy of the young man in receiving his long-awaited reward. The *diminuendo* indicated on 'meilleur baiser' is rather a 'no crescendo', to bring out the attack *più f* on the first 'me récompensent', the second one being softer (but not *p*) and very intense and *marcato* —a little line over each note. This will also allow the singer to make as effective a crescendo as possible on 'de l'attente'—not easy in the tessitura!

The important conclusion of the song is given to the piano, which must maintain its orchestral lyricism. The *poco a poco diminuendo* is indicated much too soon.

*

We shall now study two mélodies which, in my opinion, are the most beautiful in the collection. It may be because they are settings of two superb poems by the great poet Charles Baudelaire: 'L'Invitation au Voyage' and 'La Vie antérieure'. In the first one, the poet depicts his visions of a future life in 'order, beauty, luxuriousness, calm, and sensuous delight' of an 'Orient of the Occident', as he says in a prose poem on this same subject; and in the second one his visions of a 'vie antérieure', a former life, in the 'splendour' and the 'calm, sensuous delight' of an Orient of dreams. The density, the richness of these poems have inspired the composer to write music of sumptuous lyricism, where the synthesis of the poetic and the musical beauty is exceptionally well realized.

L'INVITATION AU VOYAGE

Mon enfant, ma sœur,
Songe à la douceur
D'aller là-bas vivre‿ensemble!
Aimer‿à loisir,
Aimer‿et mourir
Au pays qui te ressemble!
Les soleils mouillés
De ces ciels brouillés
Pour mon‿esprit √ ont les charmes⌐
Si mystérieux
De tes traitres‿yeux
Brillant‿à travers leurs larmes.

Là, tout n'est qu'ordre‿et beauté,
Luxe, calme | et volupté.

Vois sur ces canaux⌐
Dormir ces vaisseaux
Dont l'humeur est vagabonde;
C'est pour assouvir
Ton moindre désir
Qu'ils viennent √ du bout du monde.

Les soleils couchants
Revêtent les champs,

INVITATION TO A JOURNEY

My child, my sister,
dream of the sweetness
of going yonder to live together!
To love at leisure,
to love and to die
in a country that resembles you!
The humid suns
of these hazy skies
have for my spirit the charm
so mysterious
of your betraying eyes
shining through their tears.

There, all is order and beauty,
luxuriousness, calm and sensuous
delight.

See on these canals
these sleeping ships
whose nature is to roam;
it is to fulfil
your least desire
that they come from the ends of the
earth.

The setting suns
invest the fields,

Les canaux, la ville entière,	the canals, the whole town,
D'hyacinthe et d'or ;	with hyacinth and gold ;
Le monde s'endort	the world falls asleep
Dans une chaude lumière !	in a warm light !
Là, tout n'est qu'ordre et beauté,	There, all is order and beauty,
Luxe, calme | et volupté.	luxuriousness, calm and sensuous
Charles Baudelaire	delight.

The original poem has three stanzas, but Duparc has set only these two. The poet expresses a longing to live in the country of his dreams, and the country here evoked is Holland, as confirmed in Baudelaire's prose poem. One must take care not to sing this mélodie with sadness, as singers too often do, but on the contrary, with an ecstatic sense of joy in the imagined realization of the vision.

The prefatory marking *presque lent* (almost slow), according to the form of the piano part and the curves of the vocal line, should be about ♩. = 52. The singer must take care to give full value to the quavers. The whole of the first stanza is sung 'softly and tenderly' as specified by the composer, in the atmosphere of the 'humid suns of the hazy skies' and barely reaching *mf.* After the *poco ritenuto* on 'pour mon esprit', a breath should be taken in order to be able to sing in one breath 'ont les charmes Si mystérieux'. On the line: 'Brillant à travers leurs larmes', a beautiful vocal effect can be achieved, with a big *diminuendo* and a real *pp* on the top note.

Now comes the first refrain, which is marked 'a little faster', but which most singers take 'a little slower'. Yet it is easy to find this tempo, as the second refrain, at the end of the mélodie, should be in the same tempo; and this tempo starts where 'a little faster' is again indicated, where the $\frac{9}{8}$ and the arpeggios of the piano begin. It seems to be about ♩. = 69. It is the singer who must establish this tempo in the first refrain, and he must respect the rhythm with exactness. (Roll both the 'r's in the word 'ordre'; and in the word 'beauté' the first syllable must be a rich, long [o]; the final [ə] in 'luxe' and 'calme' must be extremely light.) The *rallentando* on the measure 'et volupté' should be well established—the last quaver on the syllable 'lu' must be long enough (remain on the vowel [y] without anticipating the consonant 'p') to give plenty of time for the pianist to play without haste the bass of his following chord. (No double 'l' on the word 'volupté', please!) The whole of this refrain should be sung *p*, but with intensity, in the ecstasy of a wonderful vision.

To link the second stanza, it is better if there is no breath between the major and the minor chord in the piano part. I have been told that for the second stanza Duparc liked a tempo just a shade faster than the *tempo primo*. The crescendo should be established gradually, and the first big climax of the mélodie is on the words 'qu'ils viennent', and the whole of this line of this stanza, in the medium of the voice, should be *f* with no *diminuendo* on 'monde'.

The last part of the mélodie (in the tempo ♩. = 69) should be sung broadly. Even the *più p* marked on 'd'hyacinthe et d'or' should be less *f* but not *p*, and very intense. The duplets on 'la ville entière' *poco marcato*. By the richness of his voice and the breadth of his declamation, the singer must suggest the sumptuousness of a sunset whose colours are all warm, rich and brilliant.

The last refrain is *p* but full and intense, and exactly in tempo. Only a slight *ritardando* should be made on the word 'volupté'. The expression should be that of the first refrain, but with more exaltation. The ending for the piano should be very flexible; it is a long *rallentando*, written rhythmically, which should be played *senza rigore*.

LA VIE ANTÉRIEURE	THE FORMER LIFE
J'ai longtemps‿habité sous de vastes portiques	For a long time I dwelt beneath vast porticoes
Que les soleils marins teignaient de mille feux,	coloured by the marine suns with a thousand fires,
Et que leurs grands piliers, droits‿et majestueux,	whose great columns, straight and majestic,
Rendaient pareils, le soir, ✓ aux grottes basaltiques.	resembled, at evening, basaltic grottoes.
Les houles, | en roulant les‿images des cieux,	The surging waves, rolling the mirrored skies,
Mêlaient d'une façon solennelle‿et mystique	mingled in a solemn and mystical way

Les tout-puissants_accords de leur riche musique √	the mighty harmonies of their sonorous music
Aux couleurs du couchant √ reflété par mes_yeux.	with the colours of the sunset reflected in my eyes.
C'est là que j'ai vécu dans les voluptés calmes,	It is there that I lived in the calm delight of the senses,
Au milieu de l'azur, des vagues, des splendeurs	surrounded by the azure skies, the waves, the splendours,
Et des esclaves nus, tout_imprégnés d'odeurs,	and the naked slaves, imbued with fragrant essences,
Qui me rafraîchissaient le front | avec des palmes,	who cooled my brow with waving palms,
Et dont l'unique soin | était √ d'approfondir	and whose sole care was to deepen
Le secret douloureux qui me faisait languir.	the sorrowful secret that made me languish.

Charles Baudelaire

This magnificent sonnet inspired Duparc to write his last mélodie, and the composer's evolution since the charming and sweet 'Chanson Triste' is noticeable.

The first part of the mélodie—the setting of the first quatrain—is built on two measures for the piano repeated seven times, in a tempo 'slow and solemn', about ♩ = 56. Their harmonic immobility, their firm rhythm, and the nobility of the vocal line, form the grand introduction, or, to use the words of the poem, the majestic portico of the mélodie. It is sung, of course, *mf* with rich quality in the voice and broad declamation. No nuance, perfect legato. The poet's vision is best suggested by complete evenness and stability.

Thus the striking contrast with the second part of the mélodie (the second quatrain) is established. The agitated piano part, suggesting the vast motion of the surging waves, and thereby giving the expression of more movement, is sufficient to fulfil the composer's indication *un peu plus vite, mais très peu* for the first six bars of this second part. Then begins a very big crescendo and *accelerando* of twelve bars, which must be enormously and gradually increased in strength and in tempo, up to the last flashing of foam of the great piano arpeggio.

After a long silence, the voice attacks with all its fullness and power the last part of the mélodie: the climax of the poet's vision. It is important here to take exactly the tempo of the introduction ($\quarternote = 56$), and it is the singer, with his upbeat on 'C'est', who must set this tempo. At the measure in $\frac{2}{4}$ the indication of the composer is quite precise and applies to the whole of the rest of the mélodie: 'almost half voice, with no nuance, like a vision'. The extraordinary poetic atmosphere which should be created by this page could not be better suggested to the interpreters: the splendid vision, voluptuously calm, and secretly painful, of the poet and of the musician. The prosody is excellent; the evenness of the triplets must be observed; an expressive stress should be made on the first syllable of the word 'splendeur'. It will be noticed that while the voice sings almost on the same note 'qui me rafraîchissaient le front avec des palmes', the piano plays in canon the expressive theme 'dans les voluptés calmes'. (According to the rule there can be no liaison between 'front' and 'avec'.) A breath should be taken between 'était' and 'd'approfondir'. For the poem it would be better to breathe before 'était', for the music it is better to breathe before 'd'approfondir'. As always, we must serve the music first. There should be a *rallentando* on the three crotchets of 'd'approfondir', the last one prolonged to emphasize the modulation and the return, *p subito*, to the first tempo and to the key of the introduction, but now in the minor. The long conclusion for the piano must succeed in prolonging, up to its end, the depth, the intensity, the magic of this glorious mélodie.

7 | Emmanuel Chabrier
(1841–94)

Emmanuel Chabrier is a musician too often disregarded and mis-judged by the international public. Though a certain gift for humour in music is granted to him, he is often reproached with vulgarity. This opinion is violently combated by all the French musicians from Debussy to the contemporary composers, who declare that without Chabrier they would not have been what they are. Ravel never tired of repeating: 'How can one accuse a musician of vulgarity, when it is impossible to hear two of his chords without attributing them at once to him, and to him alone.' And Henri Barraud writes: 'Chabrie· is absolutely, typically French. He is the most gifted inventor o. unimagined harmonies, of rare combinations of timbres, the most vigorous colourist and the most straightforward melodist,' Un-doubtedly he gave back to French music its humour and joy, as well as the most delicate traits and finest shades of tenderness.

Chabrier, unfortunately, composed only a small number of mélodies (published by Enoch, in two keys). All are strophic songs, but the rhythm is very cleverly modified in each stanza to suit the prosody of the literary text. They require, together with perfect precision, a supple, elegant style of interpretation, slightly whimsical; a 'laissé-aller contrôlé', as Poulenc said. The best example of this style is given by the mélodie:

L'ÎLE HEUREUSE	THE HAPPY ISLE
Dans le golfe aux jardins ombreux	In the gulf by the shady gardens
Des couples blonds d'amants heureux	blond pairs of happy lovers
Ont fleuri les mâts langoureux	have decked with flowers the
	languorous masts
De ta galère.	of your galley,
Et caressé de doux été,	and caressed by gentle summer
Notre beau navire enchanté	our beautiful enchanted ship
Vers des pays de volupté	bound for the country of delight
Fend l'onde claire.	cleaves the clear water.
Vois, | nous sommes les souverains	See, we are the monarchs
Des lumineux déserts marins,	of luminous marine deserts,
Sur les flots ravis et sereins	on the waves, delightful and serene,
Berçons nos rêves!	let us rock our dreams!
Tes pâles mains ont le pouvoir	Your pale hands have the power
D'embaumer au loin l'air du soir,	to perfume from afar the evening air,
Et dans tes yeux je crois revoir	and in your eyes I think to see again
Le ciel des grèves!	the sky of the shores!
Mais là-bas, là-bas | au soleil,	But yonder, yonder in the sun,
Surgit le cher pays vermeil	appears the dear brightly coloured
	land,
D'où s'élève un chant de réveil	from whence arises a song of
	awakening
Et d'allégresse.	and of joy.
C'est l'île heureuse | aux cieux légers	It is the happy isle of clear skies
Où parmi les lys étrangers	where among exotic lilies
Je dormirai dans les vergers,	I will sleep in the orchards
Sous ta caresse!	beneath your caress!

Ephraïm Mikhaël

This *mélodie*, the poem of which is mediocre and rather unimportant, requires a lyricism approaching caricature, and must be interpreted as indicated *molto rubato ed appassionato*, with all the prettiest effects possible in the voice and in the piano: *portamenti, rubati*, etc. This must, of course, remain within the limits of good taste. All the dynamics, the nuances, the *rubati*, are precisely indicated, and should be made without fear of exaggeration, but without breaking the general *con slancio* gaiety and enthusiasm of the whole *mélodie*. This is most important.

The general tempo is about ♩ = 112. The *ritornelli* of the piano are difficult to play with their precision and their freedom. In the second stanza the *poco meno mosso* and *pp* from 'Tes pâles mains' should be well observed. In the third stanza: 'C'est l'île heureuse aux cieux légers' should start *after* the arpeggio of the piano, and be very *ritenuto*. Then *a tempo* and gradually *ritardando* up to the end. The phrase: 'Où parmi les lys étrangers Je dormirai dans les vergers' should be sung in one breath. (Or a little catch breath can be taken before 'dans les vergers'.)

CHANSON POUR JEANNE

Puisque les roses sont jolies,
Et puisque Jeanne l'est aussi,
Tout fleurit dans ce monde-ci,
Et c'est la pire des folies
Que de mettre ailleurs son souci,
Puisque les roses sont jolies,
Et puisque Jeanne l'est aussi!

Puisque vous gazouillez, mésanges,
Et puisque Jeanne gazouille aussi,
Tout chante dans ce monde-ci,
Et les | harpes saintes des anges
Ne feront jamais mon souci,
Puisque vous gazouillez, mésanges,
Et puisque Jeanne gazouille aussi!

Puisque la belle fleur est morte,
Morte l'oiselle, et Jeanne aussi...
Rien ne vit dans ce monde-ci!
Et j'attends qu'un souffle m'emporte

Dans la tombe, mon seul souci...
Puisque la belle fleur est morte,
Morte l'oiselle, et Jeanne aussi.

Catulle Mendès

SONG FOR JEANNE

Since roses are pretty,
and so is Jeanne,
everything flowers in this world,
and it is the worst of follies
to care about anything else,
since roses are pretty,
and so is Jeanne!

Since you warble, tomtits,
and so does Jeanne,
everything in the world sings,
and the sainted harps of the angels
will be no concern of mine,
since you warble, tomtits,
and so does Jeanne!

Since the lovely flower is dead,
dead the tiny bird, and Jeanne too...
nothing in the world is living!
And I wait for a breath of air to bear
me away
to the tomb, my sole concern...
since the lovely flower is dead,
dead the tiny bird, and Jeanne too.

This is another *mélodie* extremely *rubato*. The numerous changes in tempo, the dynamics and nuances are carefully indicated and should be observed. The initial tempo is about ♩ = 88. It should be sung with tenderness; the first two stanzas being very gay and happy, to make marked contrast with the third stanza, in the minor, which is *più lento* with a desolate but simple expression.

LIED	SONG
Nez | au vent, cœur plein d'aise	Facing the wind, contented of heart
Berthe emplit, fraise à fraise,	Berthe fills, strawberry by strawberry,
Dans le bois printanier,	in the springtime wood,
Son frais panier.	her fresh basket.
Les déesses de marbre	The marble goddesses
La regardent sous l'arbre	watch her under the trees
D'un air plein de douceur,	with an air full of sweetness,
Comme une sœur,	like a sister,
Et dans de folles rixes	and in crazy combat
Passe l'essaim des Nixes |	the swarms of nixies pass,
Et des Elfes badins, ✓	of playful elves,
Et des Ondins.	and of water genies.
Un Elfe dit à Berthe:	An elf says to Berthe:
'Là-bas sous l'ombre verte,	'Yonder in the green shade,
Il est dans les sentiers	on the paths there are
De beaux fraisiers.'	some beautiful strawberry plants.'
Un Elfe a la moustache	An elf has a moustache
Très fine | et l'air bravache	very natty, and the swaggering air
D'un reître ou d'un varlet	of a cavalry officer or of a page
Quand il lui plaît...	when it pleases him. . . .
'Conduisez-moi,' dit Berthe,	'Direct me,' says Berthe,
'Là-bas, sous l'ombre verte,	'yonder, in the green shade,
Où sont dans les sentiers	to where on the paths are
Les beaux fraisiers!'	the beautiful strawberry plants!'
Leste comme une chèvre,	Nimble as a goat,
Berthe courait: 'Ta lèvre	Berthe ran: 'Your lips
Est un fraisier charmant,'	are a charming strawberry plant',
Reprit l'amant.	replied the lover.
'Le baiser, fraise rose,	'The kiss, rosy strawberry,
Donne à la bouche éclose	gives to the open mouth
Qui le laisse saisir,	which is allowed to cull it,
Un doux plaisir!'	a sweet pleasure!'
'S'il est ainsi,' dit Berthe,	'If this is so,' says Berthe,
'Laissons sous l'ombre verte	'let us leave in the green shade
En paix, dans les sentiers,	in peace, on the paths,
Les beaux fraisiers!'	the beautiful strawberry plants!'

Catulle Mendès

This charming and fresh mélodie, in contrast to the two preceding ones, should be performed in an immutable tempo ($\bullet$. = 104), and with no *rubato*. The singer, however, must endeavour, with the precision of his diction, and a great variety of colours and expression, to enhance the gay, naughty, (and very 1890) little poem, so wonderfully expressed musically. I recommend exactness of rhythm and well-sung vocal line.

*

Chabrier composed a series of mélodies on animal subjects. The poems are by Edmond Rostand or his wife Rosemonde Gérard. This merry music must be interpreted with much wit and good taste, in order to realize all the possible 'effects', without ever falling into exaggeration or caricature for, beyond the obvious humour of the poets and of the musician, it is a poetic atmosphere which should prevail.

BALLADE DES GROS DINDONS	BALLAD OF THE BIG FAT TURKEYS
Les gros dindons, à travers champs,	The big fat turkeys, across the fields,
D'un pas solennel et <u>tran</u>quille,	with solemn, placid steps,
Par les matins, par les couchants,	every morning, every evening,
Bêtement marchent‿à la file,	stupidly march in a row,
Devant la pastoure qui file,	in front of the shepherdess who spins
En fredonnant de vieux fredons,	as she hums old tunes,
Vont‿en procession docile	they form a docile procession,
Les gros dindons.	the big fat turkeys.
Ils vous‿ont l'air de gros marchands	They look like wealthy merchants
Remplis d'une morgue‿<u>im</u>bécile,	full of absurd pride,
De baillis rogues‿et méchants	or haughty, spiteful magistrates
Vous regardant d'un œil hostile :	regarding one with a hostile eye :
Leur rouge pendeloque | <u>os</u>cille ;	their red pendants oscillate ;
Ils semblent parmi les chardons	among the thistles they seem
Gravement tenir un concile,	to be gravely holding council,
Les gros dindons.	the big fat turkeys.
N'ayant jamais trouvé touchants	Having never been moved
Les sons que le rossignol file,	by the notes of the nightingale,

Ils suivent, lourds | et trébuchants,
L'un d'eux, | digne comme un édile;

Et lorsqu'au lointain campanile
L'angélus fait ses lents: | din! | dons!

Ils regagnent leur domicile,
    Les gros dindons!

Prud'hommes gras, leurs seuls
    penchants
Sont vers le pratique | et l'utile,
Pour eux, l'amour et ses doux chants
Sont un passe-temps trop futile;
Bourgeois de la gent volatile,
Arrondissant de noirs bedons,
Ils se fichent de toute idylle,
    Les gros dindons!

they follow, heavy and stumbling,
one of their number, dignified as a
    town councillor,

and when from the distant belfry
the angelus chimes its slow
    ding! dong!

they return to their habitat,
    the big fat turkeys!

Pompous and portly, their only
    leaning
is towards the practical and the useful,
for them, love and its sweet songs
are too futile a pastime;
philistines of the bird world,
with plump, black bellies,
they care nothing for romance,
    the big fat turkeys!

Edmond Rostand

The first four bars of this mélodie, with their heavily struck chords, about ♩ = 60, and the indication 'bêtement' (stupidly), are enough to suggest to the singer the spirit and the colour he has to employ—that of a grotesque pomposity. All the *sf* and stresses must be observed. Suddenly for four bars: 'Devant la pastoure qui file, En fredonnant de vieux fredons', comes a touch of poetry, with more legato. I suggest a crescendo when the voice goes down on: 'Vont en procession do...' and *pp* on '...ciles' with a slight *portamento* going up, and no *sf* in the piano part on this *pp*. The same effect should be made in each stanza (in the ⁶₈ the ♩. is equal to the preceding ♩). The *ritornello* imitating comically the mandoline accompaniment of the 'Serenade' of Mozart's *Don Giovanni* should be played with no *rubato* at all, no hurry, flatly and fatuously.

The second stanza is in the same spirit (do not miss the *sf* on 'im*bé*cile'). I suggest that the third stanza be only *mf* and less heavy, with a real *p* and a poetic effect on: 'Et lorsqu'au lointain campanile L'angélus fait ses lents: din! dons!', these last three notes being *rallentando* to imitate the tolling of the bells. Then *subito f* and *a tempo* on: 'Ils regagnent leur domicile'.

The last stanza is again heavily grotesque (the 'r's exaggeratedly rolled), and more *p* only on: 'Pour eux l'amour et ses doux chants sont un passe-temps trop futile'. The last *ritornello* without any hurry, ending *f*, with a stupid crescendo and little *ritardando* on the very last bar.

VILLANELLE DES PETITS CANARDS	VILLANELLE OF THE LITTLE DUCKS
Ils vont, les petits canards, Tout au bord de la rivière, Comme de bons campagnards!	They go, the little ducks, all along the bank of the river, like good countrymen!
Barboteurs | et frétillards, Heureux de troubler l'eau claire,	Dabblers and waddlers, happily making the clear water muddy,
Ils vont, les petits canards, Ils semblent un peu jobards, Mais ils sont à leur affaire, Comme de bons campagnards!	they go, the little ducks, they seem silly mugs, but they are about their business, like good countrymen!
Dans l'eau pleine de têtards, Où tremble une herbe légère, Ils vont, les petits canards, Marchants par groupes épars, D'une allure régulière, Comme de bons campagnards!	In the water full of tadpoles, where a delicate weed trembles, they go, the little ducks, walking in scattered groups, with a regular gait, like good countrymen!
Dans le beau vert d'épinards De l'humide cressonnière, Ils vont, les petits canards, Et quoiqu'un peu goguenards, Ils sont d'humeur débonnaire Comme de bons campagnards!	In the beautiful spinach green of the moist watercress, they go, the little ducks, and though rather roguish, they have easy-going natures like good countrymen!
Faisant, en cercles bavards, Un vrai bruit de pétaudière, Ils vont, les petits canards, Dodus, lustrés et gaillards, Ils sont gais à leur manière, Comme de bons campagnards!	Making in chattering circles, a veritable bedlam of noise, they go, the little ducks, plump, glossy and lively, they have a gaiety all their own, like good countrymen!

Amoureux | et nasillards,
Chacun | avec sa commère,
Ils vont, les petits canards,
Comme de bons campagnards!

Rosemonde Gérard

Amorous and nasal,
each one with her crony,
they go, the little ducks,
like good countrymen!

This charmïng and cheerful mélodie will only be successfully performed if its rhythm and tempo are precise and immutable. The
different stanzas should be linked with no stop at all. The only *allargando*
comes on the last four bars. The general tempo is about ♩ = 88/92. The
detached notes must not be played or sung too dryly or too lightly. One
has to suggest the clumsy and loutish pace of the ducks. All the dynamics
are indicated and can be well asserted. In the 'coda' the word
'amoureux' should be exaggeratedly legato, 'et nasillard' with a bit
too much nasal quality. All the 'ils vont' always *diminuendo*, the last
'les petits canards' whispered, and the final bars subito *f* and *molto
allargando*.

LES CIGALES

Le soleil est droit sur la sente,
L'ombre bleuit sous les figuiers,

Ces cris au loin multipliés,
C'est Midi, c'est Midi qui chante!
Sous l'astre qui conduit le chœur,

Les chanteuses dissimulées
Jettent leurs rauques ululées,
De quel infatigable cœur!

Les cigales, ces bestioles,
Ont plus d'âme que les violes,
Les cigales, les cigalons,
Chantent mieux que les violons!

S'en donnent elles, les cigales,
Sur les tas de poussière gris,
Sous les oliviers rabougris,
Etoilés de fleurettes pâles.

THE CICADAS

The sun is directly above the path,
the shadow turns blue under the fig-
    trees,
these distant cries multiply,
it is noon, it is noon that sings!
Beneath the sun which conducts the
    choir,
the hidden singers
utter their raucous cries,
from how tireless a heart!

The cicadas, these tiny beasts,
have more soul than the viols,
the cicadas, the little cicadas,
sing better than the violins!

They revel in it, the cicadas,
on the heaps of grey dust,
under the stunted olive-trees,
starred with pale flowerets.

Et grises de chanter_ainsi,	And delirious with their singing,
Elles font leur musique folle;	they make their mad music;
Et toujours leur chanson s'envole	and their song rises unceasingly
Des touffes du gazon roussi!⌐	from the tufts of russet grass!
Les cigales, ces bestioles,	The cicadas, these tiny beasts,
Ont plus d'âme que les violes,	have more soul than the viols,
Les cigales, les cigalons,	the cicadas, the little cicadas,
Chantent mieux que les violons!	sing better than the violins!
Aux rustres_épars dans le chaume,	Upon the rustics dispersed in the stubble,
Le grand_astre torrentiel,	the great torrential sun,
A larges flots, du haut du ciel,	flooding down from on high,
Verse le sommeil et son baume.	pours sleep and its balm.
Tout_est mort, rien ne bruit plus⌐	All is dead, nothing makes a sound
Qu'elles, toujours, les forcenées,	except these crazy creatures, always heard
Entre les notes_égrénées	between the scattered notes
De quelque lointain_angélus!	of some far distant angelus!
Les cigales, ces bestioles,	The cicadas, these tiny beasts,
Ont plus d'âme que les violes,	have more soul than the viols,
Les cigales, les cigalons,	the cicadas, the little cicadas,
Chantent mieux que les violons!	sing better than the violins!

Rosemonde Gérard

A sparkling but very difficult mélodie, and unlike the preceding ones, the author's indications are not precise enough.

The tempo 'très animé' is about ♩ = 168. The piano part suggests the grating of the cicadas in the warm atmosphere of the south of France at noon. Thus *pp*, the arpeggios very even and quickly but clearly played. The voice starts mezzavoce, as if drowned by the heat and the intensity of the light. But on 'Ces cris au loin multipliés' there is a big and very fast crescendo. 'C'est Midi, c'est Midi qui chante' is really *ff* and with a stress on the syllable 'Mi'. The following phrases are very lyrical. A good breath should be taken before 'De quel infatigable cœur—Les cigales, ces bestioles' for these two lines have to be sung in one breath, with a slight *portamento* between 'cœur' and 'les cigales'. On this very bar there is a little *ritardando* and the refrain is again in tempo. At the end of the refrain: 'Chantent mieux que les violons' with no *ritardando* at all, and the three syllables: 'vi-o-lons' must be well detached. The *ritornello* of the piano is *a tempo* and very brilliant.

The first eight bars of the second stanza are *p* for the voice and *pp* for the piano. Then crescendo and with lyricism. The same effect as in the first stanza must be made to link the refrain.

The third stanza starts also *p*, with *a tempo*, but already on 'A larges flots, du haut du ciel' with the crescendo, a little *allargando* should begin. The line 'Verse le sommeil et son baume' must be *much* slower, to give the impression of the burning sun sending men and nature to sleep. The *a tempo* is indicated one bar too soon; it is only on in the piano part. The voice whispers: 'Tout est mort' and remains *pp* on the following lines. There is a *ritardando* on 'lointain angélus', and again the indication *a tempo* comes one bar too soon. The same effect should be made of linking the refrain with a *portamento*, but this time the piano brings back the tempo with one bar of *accelerando*.

The end of the last refrain is different from the others: 'Chantent mieux' is sustained on long notes and can be freely slower, as well as the four following chords. Then after a silence and an expressive breath, 'que les violons' is *a tempo*, but this last word is now legato. The 'coda' for the piano is extremely brilliant, with the contrasts of dynamics and no *ritenuto* at all to the end.

8 | Ernest Chausson
(1855–99)

Ernest Chausson composed about forty mélodies; most of them are published in two collections, one edited by Hamelle, the other by Salabert (Rouart–Lerolle).

These mélodies are still quite romantic in style, and the best of them are often in a sad and elegiac mood. They require a warm and expressive interpretation, quite different from the discreet restraint required in the interpretation of Fauré, or Debussy.

The following mélodies are from the first (Hamelle) collection.

NANNY

Bois chers aux ramiers, pleurez, doux feuillages,
Et toi, source vive, et vous frais sentiers,
    Pleurez, | o bruyères sauvages,
    Buissons de houx | et d'églantiers.

Printemps, roi fleuri de la verte année,

O jeune dieu, pleure! Été mûrissant,

    Coupe ta tresse couronnée,
    Et pleure, automne rougissant.

NANNY

Woods dear to the doves, weep, gentle leaves,
and you flowing spring, and you cool footpaths,
    weep, O wild heather,
    holly bushes and sweet briars.

Springtime, king of the green year adorned with flowers,

O young god, weep! Ripening summer,

    cut your crowned tresses,
    and weep, reddening autumn.

L'angoisse d'aimer brise un cœur
fidèle,
Terre et ciel, pleurez! Oh! que je
l'aimais!
    Cher pays, ne parle plus d'elle;
    Nanny ne reviendra jamais!
	The anguish of loving breaks a
	faithful heart,
	earth and sky, weep! Oh! how I
	loved her!
	    Dear land, speak of her no more;
	    Nanny will never return!

Leconte de Lisle

These verses, in which the poet invites all nature to join him in the despair of his love, inspired Chausson to write his first and one of his best mélodies. It should be sung with a subdued lyricism and great sincerity of expression. This is made easy by the perfection of the prosody and the charm of the vocal line. The tempo is about ♩ = 60, but the second page is *più animato* with great warmth, before coming back to the *tempo primo* for the return of the theme. The last eight bars of the mélodie become progressively slower.

LE CHARME	THE CHARM
Quand ton sourire me surprit,	When your smile caught me unawares,
Je sentis frémir tout mon être,	I felt a trembling throughout my being,
Mais ce qui domptais mon esprit	but the reason for the subjection of my spirit
Je ne pus d'abord le connaître.	I did not at first know.
Quand ton regard tomba sur moi, Je sentis mon âme se fondre, Mais ce que serait cet émoi, Je ne pus d'abord en répondre.	When your glance fell on me, I felt my soul melt, but what this emotion was, I could not at first tell.
Ce qui me vainquit à jamais, Ce fut un plus douloureux charme, Et je n'ai su que je t'aimais, Qu'en voyant ta première larme.	That which vanquished me for ever, was a more sorrowful charm, and I knew that I loved you only when I saw your first tears.

Armand Silvestre

The musical setting of this poem is constructed on a very simple plan: each quatrain has eight bars, starting in a rather fast tempo: ♩ = 84 (the first two lines being spirited), and slowing down regularly (the last two lines being more grave). The final quatrain, however, has twelve bars, because the *rallentando* is formed by the lengthening of the musical values. For this last quatrain, the dynamics should be from *mf* to *f* (in place of *p* to *mf* for the two earlier ones), to give great expressive intensity, especially in such a low tessitura.

LES PAPILLONS	THE BUTTERFLIES
Les papillons couleur de neige	The snow-coloured butterflies
Volent par essaim sur la mer;	fly in swarms over the sea;
Beaux papillons blancs, quand pourrai-je	Beautiful white butterflies, when can I
Prendre le bleu chemin de l'air?	take the blue path of the air?
Savez-vous, | o belle des belles,	Do you know, O fairest of the fair,
Ma bayadère aux yeux de jais,	my dancing girl with the jet black eyes,
S'ils me voulaient prêter leurs ailes,	if they would lend me their wings,
Dites, savez-vous, | où j'irais?	tell me, do you know where I would go?
Sans prendre un seul baiser | aux roses,	Without taking a single kiss from the roses,
A travers vallons et forêts,	across valleys and forests,
J'irais à vos lèvres mi-closes,	I would go to your half-closed lips,
Fleur de mon âme, et j'y mourrais.	flower of my soul, and there I would die.
Théophile Gautier	

This short and sprightly mélodie can be useful as a contrast in a group of Chausson. The piano part, light and sparkling, suggests the wavering flight of the butterflies, and when brilliantly performed makes the success of this little mélodie. The tempo is about ♩ = 126. The voice part should be sung legato and with young and enthusiastic feeling. All the indicated *ritardandi* should be carefully adjusted; at the seventeenth bar, scarcely made, but nineteen and twenty bars further on, on the contrary, strongly marked. Before the last four bars of the voice, the piano must slow down very much and very regularly. 'Fleur de mon âme' is quite free. (The ⌒ is definitely on 'â', not the weak syllable 'me'.) 'Et j'y mourrais', according to the taste of the performer, can either be more *ritenuto*, or, on the contrary, gradually picking up the tempo to launch the piano coda, which must fly away *pp* and with no *rallentando*.

SÉRÉNADE ITALIENNE	ITALIAN SERENADE
Partons en barque sur la mer	Let us sail in a boat over the sea
Pour passer la nuit | aux étoiles.	to pass the night under the stars,
Vois, il souffle juste assez d'air	See, there is just enough breeze
Pour enfler la toile des voiles.	to inflate the canvas of the sails.
Le vieux pêcheur italien	The old Italian fisherman
Et ses deux fils, qui nous conduisent,	and his two sons, who steer us,
Écoutent mais n'entendent rien	listen but understand nothing
Aux mots que nos bouches se disent.	of the words which we speak.
Sur la mer calme et sombre, vois,	On the sea, calm and dark, see,
Nous pouvons échanger nos âmes,	our souls may commune,
Et nul ne comprendra nos voix,	and none will understand our voices
Que la nuit, le ciel ✓ et les lames.	but the night, the sky and the waves.

Paul Bourget

In spite of its title this beautiful mélodie is not a serenade, and in spite of its poem, is not a barcarolle. It should be sung *con slancio* ($\downarrow = 63$), with pretty vocal effects. 'Vois, il souffle juste assez d'air' is sung in one breath (but no liaison between 'vois' and 'il'). Same effect for: 'Vois, nous pouvons échanger nos âmes', and the two long notes on the word 'Vois' can be crescendo–decrescendo. To perform the end of the mélodie successfully, a very big *rallentando* should be made. The piano begins this *molto ritenuto* on the bar before 'que la nuit', starting to count in 6, instead of 3, and the *ritenuto* should continue becoming slower and slower, up to the *a tempo* of the piano coda, which has just a little *rallentando* on its last ascending line.

HÉBÉ	HEBE
Les yeux baissés, rougissante et candide,	With downcast eyes, blushing and ingenuous,
Vers leur banquet quand Hébé s'avançait,	when Hebe approached their banquet,
Les Dieux charmés tendaient leur coupe vide,	the delighted Gods held out their empty cup,
Et de nectar l'enfant la remplissait.	and the child refilled it with nectar.

Nous tou<u>s</u> | aussi, quand passe la jeunesse,	We all likewise, when youth passes,
Nous lui tendons notre coupe à l'envie,	hold out our cup to her in longing,
Quel est le vin qu'y verse la ⌒ Déesse ?	what is the wine that the Goddess pours therein ?
Nous l'ignorons; il eniv<u>re</u> et ravit.	We do not know; it elates and enraptures.
Ayant souri dans sa grâce im̲mortelle	Having smiled with her immortal grace
Hébé s'éloigne; ✓ on la rappell<u>e</u> en vain.	Hebe goes away; one calls her back in vain.
Longtemp<u>s</u>_encor, sur la rout<u>e</u> éternelle,	On the eternal path, for a long time still
Not<u>re</u> œil en pleurs suit l'échanson divin.	our eyes in tears follow the divine cup-bearer.

L. Ackermann

The subtitle of this mélodie is revealing: 'Greek song in the Phrygian mode'. With the bareness of a few thirds (about ♩ = 92) and their modal ambiguity, the composer creates an atmosphere which the singer must match with the linear purity of his singing, and the clarity of a timbre with no *vibrato*, to suggest the ingenuous Hébé, servant of the Olympian gods. (The two *poco ritenuto* should be well observed.) But Hébé, for the poet, is the image of youth, which 'elates and enraptures'. Thus the composer has set the second quatrain of the poem in complete contrast, and it should be sung quite lyrically with a warm voice, in a very supple and slightly faster tempo (two beats in the bar). For the final quatrain, the initial theme and tempo returns to describe the young Hébé withdrawing (in this bar *a ritenuto*), and the whole end of the mélodie, *a tempo*, should have the nostalgia of youth 'recalled in vain'.

LE COLIBRI   THE HUMMING-BIRD

Le vert colibri, le roi des collines,	The green humming-bird, the king of the hills,
Voyant la rosée et le soleil clair	seeing the dew and the bright sun
Luire dans son nid tissé d'herbes fines,	shining into his nest, woven of fine grasses,
Comm<u>e</u> un frais rayon s'é<u>ch</u>appe dans l'air.	darts into the air like a ray of light.

Il se hâte | et vole aux sources voisines,	He hurries and flies to the nearby springs,
Où les bambous font le bruit de la mer,	where bamboos make a sound like the sea,
Où l'açoka rouge aux odeurs divines	where the red hibiscus with its divine fragrance
S'ouvre et porte au cœur un humide éclair.	unfolds the dewy brilliance at its heart.
Vers la fleur dorée il descend, se pose,	He descends to the golden flower, alights,
Et boit tant d'amour ✓ dans la coupe rose,	and drinks so much love from the rosy cup,
Qu'il meurt ✓ ne sachant s'il l'a pu tarir!	that he dies, not knowing if he had exhausted its nectar!
Sur ta lèvre pure, | ô ma bien-aimée,	On your pure lips, O my beloved,
Telle aussi mon âme eut voulu mourir,	likewise my soul wished to die,
Du premier baiser ✓ qui l'a parfumée.	of the first kiss which perfumed it.

Leconte de Lisle

This little love poem does not ask for many subtleties of interpretation; it is quite descriptive, and only the last tercet of the poem is subjective and expressive. But it inspired the composer to write a beautiful piece of vocal music, and it is the beauty of the phrasing, the quality of the sonorities, the suppleness of the rhythm in 5 ($\quarternote = 80$), the charm of the vocal curves, that give this mélodie all its value. It is a true piece of 'bel canto', and it is not easy to fulfil successfully all its vocal requirements. Such a phrase as:

le   roi   des   collines
ô   ma   bien - aimé - e

must have great charm. Thus the E and the F should be more *p* than the D, and a slight *portamento* made between the F and the C. This same effect, but with much more tenderness, should be made again in the same bar of the last stanza: 'ô ma bien-aimée'. The long crescendo and *poco accelerando* of the second stanza should lead to the *f* and *a tempo* of 'Vers la fleur dorée', all the third stanza, to the contrary, being gradually *diminuendo* and *rallentando*. The end of the mélodie affords an opportunity for a beautiful vocal effect.

LA CIGALE	THE CICADA
O cigale, née avec les beaux jours,	O cicada, born with the fine weather,
Sur les verts rameaux, dès l'aube posée,	perched at early dawn on the green branches,
Contente de boire un peu de rosée,	content to drink a little dew,
Et telle qu'un roi, tu chantes toujours.	and like a king, you always sing.
Innocente à tous, paisible et sans ruses,	Completely innocent, peaceful and guileless,
Le gai laboureur, du chêne abrité,	the gay labourer, under the shady oak tree,
T'écoute de loin √ annoncer l'Été.	hears you from afar announcing the arrival of summer.
Apollon t'honore autant que les Muses,	Apollo honours you as greatly as the Muses,
Et Zeus t'a donné l'Immortalité!	and Zeus has rendered you immortal!
Salut, sage enfant de la terre antique,	Hail, wise child of the ancient world,
Dont le chant	invite à clore les yeux,	whose song invites the eyes to close,
Et qui, sous l'ardeur du soleil attique,	and who, beneath the heat of the Attic sun,
N'ayant chair ni sang, √ vis semblable aux Dieux!	having neither flesh nor blood, lives like the gods!

Leconte de Lisle

The light, high soprano voices do not have a very rich concert repertoire, and this mélodie suits them perfectly. It must be performed in a fast tempo, one in a bar ($\downarrow$. = 120), to sing the glory of the cicada. The voice should be brilliant and the expression unrestrained.

*

The mélodies of the second collection, published by Salabert (Rouart–Lerolle), are for the most part very elegiac and marked with a soft and hopeless sadness.

NOCTURNE   NOCTURNE

La nuit | était pensive et ténébreuse;   The night was pensive and sombre;
   à peine⁀   faintly
Quelques‿épingles d'or scintillaient   some pins of gold sparkled in the
   dans l'ébène   ebony
     De ses grands cheveux déroulés,   of its long uncoiled hair,
Qui, sur nous, ✓ sur la mer lointaine,   which over us, over the distant sea,
   et sur la terre‿   and over the earth
Ensevelie en‿un sommeil plein de   enshrouded in sleep full of mystery,
   mystère,
     Secouaient des parfums‿ailés.   scattered winged perfumes.

Et notre jeune‿amour, naissant de nos   And our young love, dawning in our
   pensées,   thoughts,
S'éveillait sur le lit de cent roses   awakened on a bed of a hundred
   glacées   frozen roses
     Qui n'avaient respiré qu'un jour;   which had lived but a day;
Et moi, je lui disais, pâle‿et tremblant   and I, I said to her, pale and
   de fièvre,   trembling with fever,
Que nous mourrions tous deux, le   that we should die together, a smile
   sourire‿à la lèvre,   on our lips,
     En même temps que notre‿amour.   at the same time as our love.

               Maurice Bouchor

    This is a beautiful mélodie in spite of its very bad poem. It has an
ambiguous rhythm: it is in $\frac{4}{4}$ (♩ = 96) but the piano part gives the
impression of being in $\frac{9}{8}$. Thus one should take care to perform it
with perfect rhythmic precision and evenness. The dynamic must be
uniformly *p*, avoiding any involuntary nuance. Only the final stanza
can be more intense, but certainly not dramatic. One must try to
create the atmosphere of the 'pensive and gloomy' night, and to
maintain it undisturbed during the entire mélodie.

LE TEMPS DES LILAS   THE TIME OF LILAC

Le temps des lilas | et le temps des   The time of lilac and the time of
   roses   roses
Ne reviendra plus | à ce printemps-ci,   will not return this spring,
Le temps des lilas | et le temps des   the time of lilac and the time of roses
   roses |
Est passé, le temps des‿œillets‿aussi.   has passed, the time of carnations too.

Le vent | a changé, les cieux sont
  moroses,
Et nous n'irons plus courir, √ et
  cueillir⌢
Les lilas‿en fleur | et les belles roses;

Le printemps | est triste et ne peut
  fleurir.

O joyeux‿et doux printemps de
  l'année,
Qui vins, l'an passé, nous‿ensoleiller,

Notre fleur d'amour est si bien fanée,
Las! que ton baiser √ ne peut
  l'éveiller!

Et toi, que fais-tu? pas de fleurs‿
  écloses,
Point de gai soleil, ni d'ombrages
  frais;
Le temps des lilas | et le temps des
  roses,
Avec notre amour est mort, √ à
  jamais.

The wind has changed, the skies are
  sullen,
and we will go no more to roam, and
  to gather
the lilac in flower and the lovely
  roses;
the spring is sad and cannot bloom.

O joyous, sweet springtime of the
  year,
that came, in the past year, to shine
  upon us,
our flower of love is so faded,
alas! that your kiss cannot revive it!

And you, what are you doing? No
  blossoming flowers,
never any gay sun, nor cool shade;

the time of lilac and the time of roses,

with our love is dead for ever.

Maurice Bouchor

   This mélodie is really the last part of a long piece for voice and orchestra, called 'Le poème de l'Amour et de la Mer', a work of great lyricism and typical of its composer's genius. After expressing varying states of mind: hope, happiness, enthusiasm, then heart-break, sorrow and grief, the composer ends his work with this elegy of sombre sadness. It should be sung with perfect legato, and a feeling of the deepest despair.
   The initial tempo is ♩ = 66, and there is an *accelerando* for two bars leading to the *tempo più animato* of the third quatrain, which is about ♩ = 92. (On the big climax, the 's' of the word 'Las!' should be pronounced: it is a shortened form of 'hélas!') This fast tempo should be maintained through 'Et toi, que fais-tu, pas de fleurs écloses', and a gradual *rallentando* on 'Point de gai soleil, ni d'ombrages frais' brings

back the *tempo primo* on this last word. After three bars, the tempo *lent* is definitely slower than the *tempo primo*, up to the end of the mélodie, with still another little *rallentando* on 'à jamais' (a long 'ja' and half an 'm'.) All this last part of the mélodie is of course *p*, but very intense and expressive.

LES HEURES	THE HOURS
Les pâles heures, sous la lune,	The pale hours under the moon,
En chantant jusqu'à mourir,	singing until death,
Avec un triste sourire,	with a sorrowful smile,
Vont | une à une,	go one by one,
Sur un lac baigné de lune,	upon a lake bathed in moonlight,
Où, avec un sombre sourire,	where, with a sombre smile,
Elles tendent, | une à une,	they stretch out, one by one,
Les mains qui mènent à mourir ;	hands which lead to death;
Et certains, | blêmes sous la lune,	and some, deathly pale under the moon,
Aux yeux d'iris sans sourire,	with dark, unsmiling eyes,
Sachant que l'heure est de mourir,	knowing that the hour of death is come,
Donnent leurs mains | une à une ;	give their hands one by one;
Et tous s'en vont dans l'ombre et dans la lune,	and all depart in the shadow and the moonlight,
Pour s'alanguir et puis mourir,	to languish and then to die,
Avec les heures | une à une,	with the hours one by one,
Les heures au pâle sourire.	the hours with the pallid smile.

Camille Mauclair

With its relentless pedal of A, with the range of the voice never exceeding an octave, with the repetition of the same words in the poem and the use of only two rhymes, this mélodie attempts to give the impression of the monotony and the fatality of the passing hours. The prefatory indications 'Slow and resigned' is excellent ($\quartern = 50$). Scarcely any nuances should be made.

CANTIQUE A L'ÉPOUSE	SONG OF PRAISE TO A WIFE
Épouse au front lumineux,	Consort with the luminous brow,
Voici que le soir descend,	now evening descends,
Et qu'il jette dans tes yeux	and sends into your eyes
Des rayons couleur de sang.	blood-red rays of light.

Le crépuscule féerique
T'environne d'un feu rose,
Viens me chanter un cantique √
Beau comme une sombre rose.

Ou plutôt ne chante pas,
Viens te coucher sur mon cœur,
Laisse-moi baiser tes bras √
Pâles comme l'aube en fleur.

La nuit de tes yeux m'attire,
Nuit frémissante, mystique,
Douce comme ton sourire
Heureux | et mélancolique.

Et soudain √ la profondeur
Du passé religieux,
Le mystère et la grandeur,
De notre amour sérieux,

S'ouvre au fond de nos pensées,
Comme une vallée immense
Où des forêts délaissées
Rêvent dans un grand silence.

Albert Jounet

The fairylike dusk
encircles you with a rosy fire,
come sing to me a song
beautiful as a dark rose.

Or rather do not sing,
come lie on my heart,
let me kiss your arms
pale as the dawn in flower.

The night of your eyes attracts me,
tremulous, mystical night,
sweet as your smile
happy and melancholy.

And suddenly the profundity
of the devout past,
the mystery and the grandeur
of our true love,

is revealed in our inmost thoughts,
like an immense valley
where deserted forests
dream in a great silence.

This poem of conjugal love inspired Chausson to write a beautiful mélodie which, by its musical texture and the nobility of its character, recalls his master César Franck. The interpreters, singer and pianist, must give the impression of serene calm and profound happiness, using broad and peaceful phrasing. The tempo is about ♩ = 66, except for the brief and warmer episode: 'La nuit de tes yeux', etc. after which one returns to the broad *tempo primo*, which continues up to the end, in spite of the long breath required for the final phrase: 'Rêvent dans un grand silence'.

CHANSON PERPÉTUELLE

Bois frissonants, ciel étoilé,
Mon bien-aimé s'en est allé,
Emportant mon cœur désolé.

SONG WITHOUT END

Quivering woods, starry sky,
my beloved has gone,
bearing away my despairing heart.

Vents, que vos plaintives rumeurs,
Que vos chants, rossignols charmeurs,

Aillent lui dire que je meurs.

Winds, let your plaintive sounds,
let your songs, enchanting nightin-
      gales,
tell him that I am dying.

Le premier soir qu'il vint̲ ici,
Mon âme fût̲ à sa merci,
De fierté je n'eus plus souci.

Since the first evening of his coming
my heart was at his mercy,
I cared no more for pride.

Mes regards̲ étaient pleins d'aveux,
Il me prit dans ses bras nerveux,
Et me baisa près des cheveux.

My gaze confessed my love,
he took me in his strong arms
and kissed my brow.

J'en̲ eus̲ un grand frémissement.
Et puis, je ne sais plus comment,
Il est devenu mon̲ amant.

I was seized by a great trembling
and then, I know no longer how,
he became my lover.

Je lui disais: 'Tu m'aimeras
Aussi longtemps que tu pourras'.
Je ne dormais bien qu'en ses bras.

I said to him: 'You will love me
as long as you can.'
My only restful sleep was in his arms.

Mais lui, sentant son cœur éteint,
S'en̲ est̲ allé, l'autre matin,
Sans moi, dans̲ un pays lointain.

But he, feeling his heart grown cold,
went away one morning,
without me, into a distant land.

Puisque je n'ai plus mon̲ ami,
Je mourrai dans l'étang parmi
Les fleurs, sous le flot | endormi;

Since I no longer have my lover,
I will die in the pool among
the flowers, beneath the sleeping
      waters.

Sur le bord̲ arrivée, ✓ au vent,⌒
Je dirai son nom ✓ en rêvant⌒

When I reach the bank, to the winds
I will speak his name, in a reverie of
      remembrance

Que là je l'attendis souvent.

that there I often awaited him.

Et comme̲ en̲ un linceul doré,
Dans mes cheveux défaits, au gré

Du vent je m'abandonnerai.

And as if in a golden shroud,
my flowing hair around me, to the
      will
of the wind I will abandon myself.

Les bonheurs passés verseront
Leur douce lumière sur mon front,
Et les joncs verts m'enlaceront,

Past joys will shed
their gentle light upon my brow,
and the green rushes will entwine me,

Et mon sein croira, √ frémissant
Sous l'enlacement caressant,
Subir l'étreinte √ de l'absent!

Charles Cros

and my breast will believe, trembling
beneath the caressing entanglement,
that I submit to the embrace of the
absent one!

The accompaniment to this mélodie, in its original form, is written for string quartet. The performance does not require a strict tempo, and, in fact, the indications of the composer must be modified in several places.

In the first two tercets of the poem, the forsaken young woman confides her despair to nature, but according to the composer's conception, her accent is more of profound desolation. The indicated initial tempo ($\quarternote = 40$) is excellent and should be maintained, also for the following five bars of instrumental interlude.

In the five following tercets, the young woman recalls the whole of her love story, from the first meeting to the relinquishment of her lover. After the indication *très peu retenu* on 'Mon âme fût à sa merci', *tempo primo* is found again, but one should not fear to make an *accelerando poco a poco* of seven bars, followed by a *rallentando poco a poco* on the three bars of 'Et puis, je ne sais plus comment, Il est devenu mon amant'. Thus the increasing emotion of the young woman can be more easily suggested in the quivering of the quartet, and her simple and grave avowal.

One is now back to the *tempo primo* for the exposition of a new musical theme, which is important to the whole end of the mélodie. This theme becomes more animated six bars further on, and soon returns to the initial theme and tempo. However, this tempo should certainly be taken a little faster, and from the end of the phrase 'Dans un pays lointain' the quartet should definitely animate the tempo. Now, with the last five tercets of the poem comes the tragic conclusion. It is already with exaltation, an exaltation which, however, must be able to increase up to the end, that the young woman cries out: 'Puisque je n'ai plus mon ami', etc. All this part of the mélodie should be in a more and more agitated tempo. The *retenu* on 'je m'abandonnerai' should not bring back the *tempo primo*, that is impossible; it should be to the *tempo agitato* ('Puisque je n'ai plus mon ami'), and gradually an *animato poco a poco* is made to the end. The singer must be able to show the greatest exaltation and the greatest lyricism. Of course an *allargando* must be made on 'de l'absent'.

This long mélodie, quite Wagnerian, is suitable for a generous mezzo-soprano voice.

9 | Gabriel Fauré
(1845–1924)

It has often been said that Fauré is the French Schumann. This assertion is acceptable only in so far as it is taken to mean that each of these two musicians is typical of his own country in the particular art of song writing. In actual fact, their songs exemplify the antithesis existing between the Lied and the mélodie. A certain Schumannesque romanticism may at times be noticed in some (and not the best) of Fauré's very early mélodies; but generally speaking, these early mélodies, with their strophic form, graceful melodic line and simple accompaniments, show a far greater affinity with Gounod's songs, from which they are directly descended.

In complete contrast with Duparc, born three years later, who wrote only fourteen mélodies in sixteen years, Fauré produced more than one hundred over a period of sixty years. During all this time he was never at all influenced by the other composers who were his contemporaries, for instance, Debussy, Ravel, Stravinsky, etc. A striking and steady evolution can be observed in Fauré's art. Between the romances written before 1870 and his last work, *L'Horizon Chimérique*, written in 1922, Fauré's mélodies follow a direct line along which his music becomes always more subtle in form and harmony, and likewise, purer and more restrained in expression.

There are approximately three periods in Fauré's song writing: the first one, from 1863 to 1887, includes almost all the mélodies of the first and second collections in the Hamelle edition, up to the famous 'Clair de lune' which opens the second period, that of Fauré's marvellous encounter with the poetry of Verlaine. This second period, from 1887 to 1906, is one of magnificent fecundity; it comprises the admirable *Bonne Chanson*, and the mélodies of the third Hamelle collection. The third period begins in 1906, and is that of four cycles less well known but genuinely beautiful.

*

Among the early mélodies contained in the first book, only four can be included here.

CHANSON DU PÊCHEUR	SONG OF THE FISHERMAN
Ma belle amie est morte,	My beautiful beloved is dead,
Je pleurerai toujours!	I shall weep for ever;
Sous la tombe elle emporte	to the tomb she bears away
Mon âme et mes amours.	my soul and my love.
Dans le ciel sans m'attendre,	To heaven without waiting for me,
Elle s'en retourna,	she has returned;
L'ange qui l'emmena	the angel who led her away
Ne voulut pas me prendre.	would not take me.
Que mon sort est amer!	How bitter is my fate!
Ah! sans amour s'en aller sur la mer!	Ah! to sail out on the sea without love!
La blanche créature	The white creature
Est couchée au cercueil,	is lying in her coffin:
Comme dans la nature	how in nature
Tout me paraît en deuil!	all seems in mourning!
La colombe oubliée	The unremembered dove
Pleure et songe à l'absent,	weeps and dreams of the absent one;
Mon âme pleure et sent	my soul weeps and feels
Qu'elle est dépareillée!	itself abandoned.
Que mon sort est amer!	How bitter is my fate!
Ah! sans amour s'en aller sur la mer!	Ah! to sail out on the sea without love!

Sur moi la nuit | immense	Over me the immense night
Plane comme un linceul,	spreads like a shroud,
Je chante ma romance	I sing my song
Que le ciel entend seul!	for the heavens alone to hear.
Ah! comme elle était belle |	Ah! how fair she was
Et combien je l'aimais!	and how I loved her!
Je n'aimerai jamais |	Never shall I love
Une femme autant qu'elle!	a woman as I loved her ...
Que mon sort est amer!	How bitter is my fate!
Ah! sans amour s'en aller sur la	Ah! to sail out on the sea without
mer!	love!

Théophile Gautier

This poem has also been set by Berlioz and Gounod. However different Fauré's setting may be, it is nevertheless his most romantic *mélodie*. A baritone (or possibly a mezzo-soprano) is the most suitable voice to render the sombre 'lamento' of the poor fisherman. The original key is F minor, the tempo ♩ = 69. The first two stanzas are set to the same music; in the singing, the marked dynamics should be carefully observed; but even in the *p* the voice should be full and dark, and the declamation broad.

Fauré escapes from the rigid strophic form for the third stanza, in which he attains a dramatic climax. A pathetic *p* is marked on the line: 'Ah! comme elle était belle, Et combien je l'aimais!'; it precedes and prepares the outburst: 'Je n'aimerai jamais Une femme autant qu'elle', and on the very last line there is no *diminuendo*.

LYDIA

Lydia, sur tes roses joues	Lydia, on your rosy cheeks
Et sur ton col frais et si blanc	and on your neck so fresh and white
Roule étincelant	rolls shining down
L'or fluide que tu dénoues;	the flowing gold that you unbind;
Le jour qui luit | est le meilleur;	the day that is dawning is the best;
Oublions l'éternelle tombe,	let us forget the eternal tomb,
Laisse tes baisers de colombe	let your dove-like kisses
Chanter sur ta lèvre en fleur.	sing on your blossoming lips.

Un lys caché répand sans cesse	A hidden lily exhales unceasingly
Une odeur divine en ton sein;	a divine fragrance in your breast;
Les délices comme un essaim	joys in abundance
Sortent de toi, jeune déesse.	emanate from you, young goddess.
Je t'aime et meurs, | ô mes amours,	I love you and I am dying, O my love,
Mon âme en baisers m'est ravie!	your kisses ravish my soul!
O Lydia, rends-moi la vie,	O Lydia, give me back my life,
Que je puisse mourir toujours!	that I may die again and again!
Leconte de Lisle	

This is the first time that Fauré was inspired to set one of the exotic and epicurean poems of Leconte de Lisle. The others are 'Nell', 'Les Roses d'Ispahan', 'La Rose' and 'Le Parfum Impérissable'. It can be said that these are among his best songs. 'Lydia' is in his opus 4, and how surprising it is to find that it is the same opus as 'Chanson du Pêcheur'! There is such a contrast between the Italian expressiveness of the latter song, and the hellenic nudity of 'Lydia', which already foreshadows the ascetic purity of the last cycles. It demands from the singer a much brighter and more transparent colour in the voice. The original key is F, with a B natural—the 'Lydian' mode—and the tempo is ♩ = 76. It must be perfectly steady, the line pure, the dynamics *p*, with very little variation (no involuntary crescendi when the voice goes up). There is only one small climax *mf* in the second stanza on the line: 'Mon âme en baisers m'est ravie'; then immediately back to the most tender *p*. The triplets should be very even on 'tes baisers de colombe', and can suggest the cooing of the dove. In the first stanza, there is no *ritardando* on the bar 'Chanter sur ta lèvre en fleur', but there is one on the same bar of the second stanza, 'Que je puisse mourir'. This death of love is certainly not dramatic! On the contrary . . . as proved by the enchanting piano coda and its aerial thirds.

APRÈS UN RÊVE	AFTER A DREAM
Dans un sommeil que charmait ton image	In a sleep made sweet by a vision of you
Je rêvais le bonheur, | ardent mirage;	I dreamed of happiness, passionate illusion;

Tes yeux_étaient plus doux, ta voix pure et sonore,	your eyes were more tender, your voice pure and ringing,
Tu rayonnais comme un ciel éclairé par l'aurore.	you shone like a sky lighted by the dawn.
Tu m'appelais │ et je quittais la terre	You called me and I left the earth
Pour m'enfuir avec toi vers la lumière;	to fly with you towards the light,
Les cieux pour nous, │ entr'ouvraient leurs nues,	the skies drew apart their clouds for us,
Splendeurs_inconnues, lueurs divines_entrevues...	unknown splendours, glimpses of divine fires . . .
Hélas! ✓ Hélas, ✓ triste réveil des songes!	Alas, alas, sad awakening from dreams!
Je t'appelle, ✓ ô nuit, rends-moi tes mensonges;	I invoke you, O night, give me back your illusions;
Reviens, ✓ reviens radieuse,	return, return, in radiance,
Reviens, ✓ ô nuit mystérieuse!	return, O mysterious night!

Romain Bussine

The purists may think that the accompaniment of this mélodie is too simple, with its repeated chords; but the harmonies are refined and support the most exquisite melodic line which, with its apparent Italian facility, never loses its serene loftiness. This is enough to indicate to the singer that, although he has to sing this mélodie with a true and beautiful *bel canto* line, his style must be always perfectly controlled.

The tempo is about ♩ = 60, and the evenness of all the triplets must be carefully observed.

In the first stanza the poet tells of a blissful dream beguiled by the image of his beloved. It should be kept rather *p* in its happy remembrance. The second stanza will start more *f* and with more exaltation, when the beloved calls him into the splendours of the heavens. After an expressive *p* on: 'Les cieux pour nous, entr'ouvraient leurs nues', the following lines 'Splendeurs inconnues', etc. may be taken more *f* and with rich tone in the low register.

Then, suddenly, a complete change of colour and expression for the third stanza. In the sad awakening from his dream, the poet calls the night to return with its marvellous deception. On the two 'hélas', only a very small, but rather inevitable *rubato*. Observe the breathing as indicated above, and watch the major third in the ascending scale: 'Triste *ré*veil des' and then on two notes on the [ɛ] of 'veil'. *Sempre f* until the *subito p* on the last line: 'Reviens, ô nuit mystérieuse', if possible the breathing as indicated; there is no *ritardando* (pianists please note) at the end of the mélodie.

AU BORD DE L'EAU	ON THE BANK OF THE RIVER
S'asseoir tous deux au bord du flot qui passe,	To sit together on the bank of the flowing stream,
Le voir passer;	watching it flow;
Tous deux, s'il glisse un nuage en l'espace,	together, if a cloud floats by in space,
Le voir glisser;	to watch it floating by;
A l'horizon s'il fume un toit de chaume,	on the horizon, if a thatched roof is smoking,
Le voir fumer;	to watch the smoke;
Aux alentours, si quelque fleur embaume,	around us, if some flower is fragrant,
S'en embaumer;	to bathe in its fragrance;
Entendre au pied du saule où l'eau murmure,	to listen, at the foot of the willow where the water murmurs,
L'eau murmurer;	to the murmuring of the water;
Ne pas sentir tant que ce rêve dure,	while this dream lasts, not to feel
Le temps durer;	the passing of time;
Mais n'apportant de passion profonde,	not feeling deep passion,
Qu'à s'adorer;	only adoring each other;
Sans nul souci des querelles du monde,	without concern for the disputes of the world,
Les ignorer;	to know nothing of them;
Et seuls tous deux devant tout ce qui lasse,	and alone together seeing all that grows weary
Sans se lasser;	without wearying of each other;
Sentir l'amour devant tout ce qui passe,	to feel that love in face of all that passes,
Ne point passer!	will never pass!

Sully Prudhomme

'Everything passes, but not our love,' says the poet (unfortunately in not very inspired words), but the musician succeeds in transfiguring these poor lines with flowing music evoking the streaming water, the gliding clouds, the passing life, etc. The melodic line, which must flow regularly (with perfect evenness of the quavers), is shared between the voice part and the piano part. In his broken line the singer must succeed in 'making the bridge', while the piano completes the phrase. This can be achieved with his 'presence' and an expressive breath.

In this flowing $^6_8$ ($\downarrow$. = 58) there are, curiously enough, only a few bars where the prosody of the text is rather bad. Note the bar: 'pied du saule où l'eau murmure'. In $^6_8$ the stresses are all wrong, one must feel this bar in $^3_4$ 'pied du saule où l'eau murmure'. When the modulation to major comes: 'Et seuls tous deux', etc. and the affirmation of the immutability of the lovers, one must try to give the impression of more solidity, more gravity, but without varying the tempo up to the end.

*

Let us consider now a few songs from the second book of the Hamelle collection. From now on, Fauré has indicated metronomic tempi. They seem, of course, generally right, but I know by personal experience how much composers can alter their conception of the tempo of their own works. This may excuse my suggesting a tempo just a little different from Fauré's indication for a few of these mélodies.

NELL

Ta rose de pourpre à ton clair soleil,
   O Juin, | étincelle enivrée,
Penche aussi vers moi ta coupe dorée:
   Mon cœur à ta rose est pareil.

Sous le mol abri de la feuille
   ombreuse
   Monte un soupir de volupté:
Plus d'un ramier chante au bois
   écarté, √
   O mon cœur, | sa plainte
   amoureuse.

NELL

Your crimson rose in your clear sun,
   O June, glitters in exultation,
incline towards me your golden cup:
   my heart and your rose are alike.

From beneath the soft shelter of the
   shady leaves
   rises a sigh of sensuous delight,
more than one dove sings in the
   lonely wood,
   O my heart, its amorous plaint.

Que ta perle est douce au ciel
    enflammé,
        Étoile de la nuit pensive!
Mais combien plus douce est la
    clarté vive
        Qui rayonne en mon cœur
            charmé!

La chantante mer, le long du rivage,
    Taira son murmure éternel,
Avant qu'en mon cœur, chère amour,
    | O Nell,
        Ne fleurisse plus ton image!

                    Leconte de Lisle

How sweet is your pearl to the
    flaming sky,
        star of the pensive night!
But how much sweeter is the vivid
    light
        that shines in my enraptured
            heart!

The singing sea, along the shore,
    will cease its eternal murmuring,
before, dear love, O Nell, in my heart

    your image no longer flowers!

This charming mélodie must be primarily a delightful display of vocal qualities. The pretty love poem merely provides an occasion for ravishing curves and nuances. The original key is G flat, and it is best suited to a soprano voice—the colour of the voice should be fresh and young. The piano part may suggest a rather fast tempo, but it is not fast, even if Fauré's marking ($\quarternote = 66$) seems a little slow. $\quarternote = 76$ may be preferred and, as usual in Fauré's music, there is no *rubato* at all.

There is a very quick crescendo in the first two bars to express the glory of June. In the ninth bar on the second syllable of the word 'pareil' one has to sustain the voice on the sound [ɛ]. 'Sous le mol abri', etc. should be *pp* with no crescendo on 'Monte', the crescendo begins only on 'Plus d'un ramier', etc. The liaison between 'bois' and 'écarté', which according to the rule should not be made, is here acceptable, as it is much prettier. The breath indicated by Fauré after these words is not very agreeable. I suggest a breath and a break as indicated above. The following stanza is rather *mf*, ending *f* with a *diminuendo* on the last note. The last stanza begins *pp* and there must be no crescendo on 'taira', the crescendo begins only on 'avant qu'en mon cœur'. There is an expressive break between 'Chère amour' and 'O Nell'. The climax on 'fleurisse' should not be too loud, and then comes the difficult vocal effect of a *subito pp* for the last phrase. It is better to give a little more tone than to take too much risk.

AUTOMNE

Automne au ciel brumeux, | aux
   horizons navrants,
Aux rapides couchants, | aux
   aurores pâlies,
Je regarde couler comme l'eau du
   torrent,
    Tes jours faits de mélancolie.

Sur l'aile des regrets mes esprits
   emportés,
Comme s'il se pouvait que notre âge
   renaisse!
Parcourent en rêvant les coteaux
   enchantés √
    Où, jadis, sourit ma jeunesse!

Je sens | au clair soleil du souvenir
   vainqueur,
Refleurir en bouquets les roses
   déliées,
Et monter à mes yeux des larmes,
   qu'en mon cœur √
    Mes vingt ans √ avaient oubliées!
       Armand Silvestre

AUTUMN

Autumn of the misty skies, the heartrending horizons,
the rapid sunsets, the pale dawns,
I watch flowing on like the waters of
the torrent,
your days imbued with melancholy.

My thoughts, borne away on the
wing of regret,
as though it were possible for our
time to come again!
are wandering in dreams on the
enchanted hillsides
where the days of my youth once
smiled.

In the clear sun of victorious memory,
the scent comes to me
of fallen roses flowering once more
in clusters,
and tears come to my eyes, that
in my heart
at twenty had been forgotten!

The original key of this mélodie is B minor and it is best suited to a baritone voice. Fauré's marking is ♩. = 66; 60 may be better. The three stanzas express different feelings and are well differentiated in their setting. The first one describes the sad days of autumn and should be sung with a firm rhythm and a broad declamation, maintaining the *f*, up to the *diminuendo* on 'mélancolie'. Then in the second stanza, the piano part *pp* brings in a new colour and a new feeling, as the poet speaks of the autumn of his life. Thus it is much more subjective, and expressive. Starting *p* the voice makes a crescendo which reaches its dramatic climax on 'jadis' (yore) expressing all the regret of youth. The third stanza begins *p*, in the atmosphere of recollection, remains *p* on the second line, and builds up the big final crescendo. The *f* must be maintained to the end of the last long note of the voice. The piano ending is *sempre f* and *marcato*, with just a small *diminuendo* on the last bar.

POÈME D'UN JOUR (POEM OF A DAY)

This is a little triptych. In the first mélodie the poet meets a woman and, falling in love with her, wonders whether she is going to be his ideal dream always pursued in vain. In the second mélodie, he cries out in despair when she speaks of leaving him. But in the third mélodie (can one imagine a more insulting poem?), he says: even the longest loves are short, so: Farewell . . . These three well-contrasted songs form a nice group. The original key is for medium voice (with, however, good top notes for the second mélodie). The indicated tempi seem excellent.

RENCONTRE	MEETING
J'étais triste et pensif quand je t'ai rencontrée;	I was sad and thoughtful when I met you;
Je sens moins aujourd'hui mon obstiné tourment.	today I feel my persistent anguish lessened.
Ô dis-moi, serais-tu la femme inespérée,	O tell me, could it be that you are the unhoped-for woman,
Et le rêve idéal poursuivi vainement?	and the ideal dream pursued in vain?
Ô passante aux doux yeux, serais-tu donc l'amie	O passer-by with the gentle eyes, could it be that you are the friend
Qui rendrait le bonheur au poète isolé?	who would bring happiness to the lonely poet?
Et vas-tu rayonner sur mon âme affermie,	And will you shine on my strengthened soul
Comme le ciel natal sur un cœur d'exilé?	like the native sky upon a heart in exile?
Ta tristesse sauvage, à la mienne pareille,	Your aloof sadness, like my own,
Aime à voir le soleil décliner sur la mer.	loves to see the sun setting over the sea.
Devant l'immensité ton extase s'éveille,	Your ecstasy awakens before the vastness of space,
Et le charme des soirs,	à ta belle âme est cher.	and the charm of the evenings is dear to your lovely soul.

Une mystérieuse et douce sympathie
Déjà m'enchaîne à toi comme un
vivant lien,
Et mon âme frémit, par l'amour
envahie,
Et mon cœur te chérit, sans te
connaître bien!

Charles Grandmougin

A mysterious and sweet sympathy
already attaches me to you like a
living bond,
and my soul trembles, invaded by
love,
and my heart cherishes you, without
knowing you well!

To be sung at an easy pace, with good legato and phrasing. A little crescendo with the piano on 'tourment'. Stress on 'dis' (O *tell* me). There should be nice supple phrasing on the word 'idéal' and a real *p* on 'passante aux doux yeux', to allow a very gradual crescendo. The second stanza, less *p*, should have supple phrasing again on 'charme des soirs'. The words 'Une mystérieuse et douce sympathie' should be *pp* and mysterious. The crescendo leads to a stronger climax than in the first stanza. As there is no *ritardando* whatsoever towards the end of the mélodie, the long last phrase is quite possible in one breath.

TOUJOURS

Vous me demandez de me taire,
De fuir loin de vous pour jamais,
Et de m'en aller solitaire,
Sans me rappeler qui j'aimais!

Demandez plutôt | aux étoiles
De tomber dans l'immensité,
A la nuit de perdre ses voiles,
Au jour de perdre sa clarté!

Demandez à la mer immense
De dessécher ses vastes flots,
Et, quand les vents sont en démence,
D'apaiser ses sombres sanglots!

Mais n'espérez pas que mon âme
S'arrache à ses âpres douleurs,

Et se dépouille de sa flamme
Comme le printemps de ses fleurs.

Charles Grandmougin

FOR EVER

You ask me to be silent,
to fly far from you for ever,
and to go away alone
without remembering the one I
loved!

Sooner ask the stars
to fall into infinity,
the night to lose its veils,
the day to lose its light!

Ask the immense ocean
to dry up its vast waves,
and, when the winds are wild,
to calm its dismal sobbing!

But do not hope that my soul
will tear itself away from its bitter
sorrow,
and shed its passion
like the springtime sheds its flowers.

The tempo of this violent mélodie is marked ♩ = 152. It helps both the pianist and the singer to count in two instead of four. It is strong declamation rather than volume of voice that will give this mélodie its intensity. However, the first stanza of the poem must be *sempre f*; but in the whole second stanza, one can sing much more *p*, and then begin the third stanza again *f* and very broadly, with a *diminuendo* only on the long note of 'sanglots'. The beginning of the last stanza is *p*, but a *p* with intensity, and crescendo to the end. Again no *ritardando* whatsoever, which makes it possible to sing the last phrase in one breath.

ADIEU

Comme tout meurt vite, la rose
    Déclose,
Et les frais manteaux diaprés
    Des prés;
Les longs soupirs, les bien-aimées,
    Fumées!

On voit dans ce monde léger, ✓
    Changer
Plus vite que les flots des grèves,

    Nos rêves!
Plus vite que le givre en fleurs,

    Nos cœurs!

A vous l'on se croyait fidèle,

    Cruelle,
Mais hélas! les plus longs amours
    Sont courts!
Et je dis en quittant vos charmes
    Sans larmes,
Presqu'au moment de mon aveu,
    Adieu!

        Charles Grandmougin

FAREWELL

How quickly everything dies, the rose
    in bloom,
and the fresh dappled mantle
    of the meadows;
the long sighs, the well-beloveds,
    are but smoke!

One sees in this fickle world,
    change
more quickly than the waves on the
    shore,
    our dreams!
More quickly than the hoar-frost
    flowers,
    our hearts!

To you one believed one would be
    faithful,
    cruel one,
but alas! the longest loves
    are short!
And I say, on leaving your charms
    without tears,
almost at the moment of my avowal,
    farewell!

Very simple and with perfect rhythm and legato. One has to be meticulous about the evenness of the quavers: the second quaver of the beat is too often not sung enough. An expressive stress on the first syllable of the word 'Fumées' can suggest its meaning; just vanishing smoke. . . . Keep the same tempo for the second stanza, a little more lyrical, and for the third back to the music of the first stanza, always very even *p* with no *rallentando* on 'Presqu'au moment de mon aveu'. The last 'adieu' should be *pp* without sadness, meaning only: 'It may be a pity, but it is so . . .'.

*

LES BERCEAUX	THE CRADLES
Le long du quai, les grands vaisseaux,	Along the quay, the great ships,
Que la houle incline en silence,	silently listing to the swell,
Ne prennent pas garde aux berceaux,	are unmindful of the cradles
Que la main des femmes balance.	rocked by the women's hands.
Mais viendra le jour des adieux,	But the day of parting will come,
Car il faut que les femmes pleurent,	for it must be that women weep,
Et que les hommes curieux,	and men with inquiring minds,
Tentent les horizons qui leurrent!	attempt alluring horizons!
Et ce jour-là les grands vaisseaux,	And on that day the great ships,
Fuyant le port qui diminue,	leaving the port growing smaller in the distance,
Sentent leur masse retenue	feel their hulls held back
Par l'âme des lointains berceaux.	by the soul of the distant cradles.
Sully Prudhomme	

The original key is B flat minor. The rhythm ($\bullet$. = 58) suggests both the rocking of the big ships in the port, and that of the small cradles. The first stanza, quite descriptive, is *mp* with no nuances and a good legato, the quavers well sustained. If possible, the lower alternative should be used for the phrase 'Que la main des femmes balance'.

The beginning of the second stanza must be *p*, for an expressive reason: after the immobility and the objectivity of the first stanza, there now comes a feeling of premonition, of warning; it must also be *p* because it is the start of a big and long crescendo of eight bars, which should be gradually established.

Then the last stanza starts *pp*. It is the expressive climax, the result of the prediction. 'Ce jour-là' (on that day) should be emphasized. The last line of the poem, repeated twice, is *f* the first time, with very little *diminuendo*, and *p*, echo, the second time, and more expressive. A little stress on the first syllable of 'lointains' will help to give the impression of the distance.

NOTRE AMOUR	OUR LOVE
Notre amour est chose légère	Our love is a light thing
Comme les parfums que le vent	like the fragrance that the breeze
Prend aux cimes de la fougère,	takes from the tips of the ferns,
Pour qu'on les respire en rêvant.	for us to breathe in dreaming.
Notre amour est chose charmante,	Our love is a charming thing,
Comme les chansons du matin,	like morning songs,
Où nul regret ne se lamente,	when there are no sorrows to lament,
Où vibre un espoir incertain.	where there is the thrill of an
	uncertain hope.
Notre amour est chose sacrée,	Our love is a sacred thing,
Comme les mystères des bois,	like the mysteries of the woods,
Où tressaille une âme ignorée,	where an unknown soul quivers,
Où les silences ont des voix.	where the silences are eloquent.
Notre amour est chose infinie,	Our love is an infinite thing,
Comme les chemins des couchants,	like the paths of the sunsets,
Où la mer, aux cieux réunie,	where the sea, united to the sky,
S'endort sous les soleils penchants.	falls asleep beneath the inclining sun.
Notre amour est chose éternelle,	Our love is an eternal thing,
Comme tout ce qu'un dieu vainqueur	as all that a victorious god
A touché du feu de son aile,	has touched with the fire of his wing,
Comme tout ce qui vient du cœur.	as all that comes from the heart.

Armand Silvestre

This fresh and charming little *mélodie* is best in the original key, E major, and sung by a soprano voice. The indicated tempo is very good: ♪ = 126, *sempre leggiero and legato*, writes Fauré. The five stanzas by themselves, and as they are set, do not permit a great variety of expression and mood. However, after the first stanza, which should be sung quite straightforwardly, a little stress emphasis in the second stanza can be given to the word 'charmante' and to the following bar and its unexpected modulation. The third stanza can be *pp*, 'the mystery of the woods'. The 'infinite' in the fourth stanza asks for a broader expression, and, of course, the last stanza speaking of 'eternal love' is quite lyrical. The upper version is preferable, for the 'ad libitum' of the last top note. No *ritardando* to the end.

LE SECRET	THE SECRET
Je veux que le matin l'ignore	I wish that the morning may know nothing
Le nom que j'ai dit à la nuit,	of the name that I spoke to the night,
Et qu'au vent de l'aube, sans bruit,	and that in the dawn breeze, silently,
Comme une larme il s'évapore.	it may vanish like a tear that dries.
Je veux que le jour le proclame	I wish that the day may proclaim
L'amour qu'au matin j'ai caché,	the love that I have hidden from the morning,
Et sur mon cœur ouvert penché ✓	and leaning over my open heart
Comme un grain d'encens, ✓ il l'enflamme.	may kindle it like a grain of incense.
Je veux que le couchant l'oublie	I wish that the evening may forget
Le secret que j'ai dit au jour,	the secret I have told to the day,
Et l'emporte avec mon amour,	and carry it and my love away,
Aux plis de sa robe pâlie!	in the folds of its pallid robe!

Armand Silvestre

This short poem is in itself a little triptych. Dawn of a love with its secrecy, noon of this love with its climax, and the evening of it as it disappears with the setting sun. Fauré's beautiful music magnifies these rather poor verses.

The original key, by far the best, is for medium voice: D flat major. The indicated tempo is ♪ = 69 and seems good.

To suggest the mystery of the first stanza it should of course be *p* from beginning to end. The little crescendo and *diminuendo* indicated on: 'Comme une larme', etc. should be hardly perceptible, and still more important, there must not be the slightest crescendo in the phrase going up an octave, on the line 'Et qu'au vent de l'aube, sans bruit'.

The secret is to be not too *p* at the start and to make a *diminuendo* as the voice rises. 'Il s'évapore' is *pp*, and by its pronunciation can suggest the meaning of the word.

The second stanza is more *f* throughout, but slightly less so on 'L'amour qu'au matin j'ai caché', and the climax of the following *f* is on the syllable '<u>fla</u>' of the line 'Comme un grain d'encens, il l'en<u>fla</u>mme'. (Note: the final 's' in 'encens' is not sounded.)

The third stanza starts *pp* but with an early crescendo and a contrast for the last line, which should be *pp*, with nice phrasing, and no *rallentando at all*, which gives the impression of a fugitive regret for this love fading away.

LES ROSES D'ISPAHAN	THE ROSES OF ISPAHAN
Les roses d'Ispahan dans leur gaine de mousse,	The roses of Ispahan in their sheath of moss,
Les jasmins de Mossoul, les fleurs de l'oranger,	the jasmines of Mosul, the flowers of the orange-tree,
Ont‿un parfum moins frais, | ont‿ une odeur moins douce,	have a fragrance less fresh, a scent less sweet,
Ô blanche Leïlah! que ton souffle léger.	O pale Leilah! than your light breath.
Ta lèvre‿est de corail et ton rire léger	Your lips are coral and your lilting laugh
Sonne mieux que l'eau vive | et d'une voix plus douce.	has a better sound than running water, and a sweeter voice.
Mieux que le vent joyeux qui berce l'oranger,	Better than the joyous breeze that rocks the orange-tree,
Mieux que l'oiseau qui chante‿au bord d'un nid de mousse.	better than the bird that sings on the edge of its mossy nest.
Ô Leïlah! depuis que de leur vol léger	O Leilah! since on light wing
Tous les baisers‿ont fui de ta lèvre si douce,	all the kisses are flown from your sweet lips,
Il n'est plus de parfum dans le pâle‿ oranger,	there is no longer any fragrance in the pale orange-tree,
Ni de céleste‿arôme‿aux roses dans leur mousse.	no divine aroma from the roses in their moss.

Oh! que ton jeune amour, ce papillon léger,	Oh! that your young love, this airy butterfly,
Revienne vers mon cœur d'une aile prompte et douce,	may return to my heart on quick, sweet wing,
Et qu'il parfume encor la fleur de l'oranger,	and once again give fragrance to the flower of the orange-tree,
Les roses d'Ispahan dans leur gaine de mousse.	to the roses of Ispahan in their sheath of moss.

Leconte de Lisle

('Ispahan' should be pronounced [i|sp[a] [ɑ̃].) This pseudo-oriental love poem has inspired Fauré to write a naïve and sweet mélodie. The interpreters should be careful not to make it *too* sweet. The charm of the vocal line will give it enough 'charm'. There must be no dubious *portamenti*, and a perfectly steady tempo should be maintained (♩ = 60). (There should be no rest on 'Ô blanche Leïlah!') There can be a little change of colour, with a slight touch of sadness, for the minor of the second stanza, but soon the light and tender mood returns for the last stanza. All the dynamics are well indicated.

*

Seven mélodies that Fauré composed on poems by Paul Verlaine will now be studied. Six of these poems have also been set by Debussy. The approach of the two composers is totally different. Fauré seems to capture the whole poetic mood of each poem, and to create an aura around it with his music; whereas Debussy follows much more closely the meaning of each phrase, almost of each word, and magically expresses it musically. The mélodie 'En sourdine' by both composers is a striking example of their different conceptions.

The first encounter of Fauré with Verlaine's poetry ('Clair de lune') opens a new era in his style of song writing. It begins the second of the three periods already mentioned. Although 'Clair de lune' is at the end of the second volume of his songs, it really belongs to the style of his third volume. The great cycle 'La Bonne Chanson', also written to Verlaine's poems, belongs to the same period, and will be studied immediately after the following seven mélodies. The first three are settings from a series of Verlaine's poems called 'Fêtes galantes'. The singular and typically French atmosphere of the 'Fêtes galantes' is that of the eighteenth-century French paintings, particularly the paintings of Watteau. In these pictures, charming figures of both sexes are seen in the delightful costumes of the period, extremely elegant, handsome, refined and sophisticated, trivial and poetic, even sometimes melancholy. They are pictured in great shady parks, with many statues and fountains, sitting or wandering about two by two, or playing the mandoline or the lute, and . . . speaking of love; a kind of love which may be as sincere as romantic love, but which is completely opposite in its expression. The names of these charming figures are: Tircis, Aminte, Clitandre, Damis, etc. But they can also be the fanciful characters of the old Italian Comedy: Scaramouche, Pulcinella, Mezzetino. . . . They have all been evoked at the end of the nineteenth century by Verlaine, in this series of poems called 'Fêtes galantes', and he succeeded in creating with them an extraordinary poetic atmosphere, full of elegance and of mystery, of wit and of melancholy, which inspired both Fauré and Debussy.

CLAIR DE LUNE	MOONLIGHT
Votre âme est un paysage choisi	Your soul is a chosen landscape
Que vont charmant masques et bergamasques,	to which maskers and bergamasks bring delight,
Jouant du luth, | et dansant, ✓ et quasi⁀	playing the lute and dancing, and almost
Tristes sous leurs déguisements fantasques.	sad beneath their fanciful disguises.
Tout en chantant sur le mode mineur	While singing in the minor key
L'amour vainqueur et la vie opportune,	of victorious love and the propitious life,
Ils n'ont pas l'air de croire à leur bonheur	they do not seem to believe in their happiness
Et leur chanson se mêle au clair de lune,	and their song mingles with the moonlight,
Au calme clair de lune triste et beau,	with the calm moonlight, sad and beautiful,
Qui fait rêver les oiseaux dans les arbres	which brings dreams to the birds in the trees

Et sangloter d'extase les jets d'eau,	and makes the fountains sob with ecstasy,
Les grands jets d'eau sveltes √ parmi les marbres.	the tall, slender fountains among the marble statues.
Paul Verlaine	

What did Fauré do to turn this beautiful poem into music? He wrote an elegant and graceful minuet (the original key, by far the best, is B flat minor; ♩ = 78 is a little too fast, 72 seems preferable) which goes on its way through the mélodie, with just a short change and modulation for the 'moonlight'; the voice sings its melodic line and its charming words without disturbing the minuet at all. After the long piano prelude, the voice should give the impression of entering quite unexpectedly; this means that the singer must be completely in the mood during the prelude, must take his breath at least one bar before beginning to sing, and then enter quite easily and naturally, *p*, legato, with clear diction, and almost no nuances, singing with elegance and charm. (There should not be any sadness.) 'Bergamasque' is a poetic word made with 'masque' and 'Bergamo', the Italian town. In the Fauré setting, because of the long note on 'luth', it is better to break before 'et dansant', and then breathe as indicated above. A little stress on '<u>dan</u>sant'. Pronounce 'quasi': k[a]z[i]. The beginning of the second stanza must be as *p* as possible. When the modulation comes and the arpeggios of 'Au calme clair de lune', there must not be the slightest change in tempo, but a wonderful impression of nocturnal 'calm'. No emphasis on the word 'sangloter'; it is merely the sound of the fountains. There is no word in English for a 'jet d'eau' which goes up and then down, as suggested by the last curve of the voice beautifully phrased in tempo.

EN SOURDINE	MUTED
Calmes dans le demi-jour	Calm in the half light
Que les branches hautes font,	made by the tall branches,
Pénétrons bien notre amour	let our love be imbued
De ce silence profond.	with this deep silence.

Mêlons nos_âmes, nos cœurs
Et nos sens_extasiés,
Parmi les vagues langueurs⁀
Des pins √ et des_arbousiers.

Ferme tes_yeux_à demi,
Croise tes bras sur ton sein,
Et de ton cœur endormi
Chasse à jamais tout dessein.

Laissons-nous persuader
Au souffle berceur et doux
Qui vient | à tes pieds √ rider
Les_ondes des gazons roux.

Et quand, solennel, | le soir √
Des chênes noirs tombera,
Voix de notre désespoir,
Le rossignol chantera.

Let us merge our souls, our hearts
and our ecstatic senses
with the vague languors
of the pines and the arbutus.

Half close your eyes,
fold your arms across your breast,
and from your sleeping heart
for ever drive away all purpose.

Let us surrender
to the soothing, gentle zephyr
that comes to ruffle at your feet
the waves of russet grass.

And when, solemnly, evening
falls from the dark oak trees,
voice of our despair,
the nightingale will sing.

Paul Verlaine

A mist of arpeggios shrouds this mélodie (♩ = 63), while sometimes a theme taken from the vocal line hovers over them, like a dialogue with the voice. As always, the dynamics should not be taken in an absolute sense, and the *f* indicated in this mélodie should rather be a *mf*, compared with the climaxes of the songs 'Automne' and 'Toujours', of which we have just been speaking. This mélodie must remain quite subdued, in accordance with the 'silence profond' and the poetic melancholy of the love poem. The original key is E flat and it loses much of its atmosphere when performed in F sharp. The indicated tempo seems just right.

The voice must sing with a perfect line and phrasing, giving a total impression of calm and amorous languor. The first two lines of the third stanza are *pp*, and the triplets precise. The solemnity of the evening allows the last stanza to begin broadly, and the dynamics to be maintained rather *f* on 'Voix de notre désespoir'; this will help to bridge over the long silence of the voice before 'Le rossignol', which should not be too *p*, in order to get the wonderful *subito pp* on the word 'chantera' which vanishes in the silence of the evening.

MANDOLINE	MANDOLIN
Les donneurs de sérénades	The serenaders
Et les belles_écouteuses	and the lovely listeners
Échangent des propos fades	exchange sweet nothings
Sous les ramures chanteuses.	beneath the singing branches.
C'est Tirci̱s et c'est_Aminte,	It is Tircis and Aminte,
Et c'est l'éternel Clitandre,	and the eternal Clitandre,
Et c'est Dami̱s qui pour mainte⌒	and Damis, who for many
Cruelle ✓ fit maint vers tendre.	a cruel fair one has written many a
	tender verse.
Leurs courtes vestes de soie,	Their short silken doublets,
Leurs longues robes_à queues,	their long trailing dresses,
Leur élégance, leur joie	their elegance, their joy,
Et leurs molles_ombres bleues	and their soft blue shadows
Tourbillonnent dans l'extase	whirl in the ecstasy
D'une lune rose̱ et grise,	of a pink and grey moon,
Et la mandoline jase	and the mandolin chatters
Parmi les frissons de brise.	amid the quivering of the breeze.

Paul Verlaine

This perfect Watteau painting has been set by Fauré as a very delicate sérénade, the *pizzicati* of the piano evolving in subtle modulations, and the voice line, ornamented with triplets and coloratura, suggesting the poetic elegance of the whole picture. The singer must choose a light scale of colours in his voice, which he must modify swiftly, according to the meaning of each phrase.

The original key is G and the tempo ♩ = 92 better than the indicated 84. The first stanza *mf*, legato and well phrased, in contrast with the *pizzicati* of the mandolin. In the second stanza, the diverse charming figures can offer different shadings. For instance 'l'éternel Clitandre', who is the bore of the party, can be emphasized, with a stress on the syllable 'ter'. In the third stanza the line 'Leurs courtes vestes de soie' can be *non legato*, and 'Leurs longues robes à queues' with an exaggerated legato. All the fourth stanza should be *pp* and mysterious, for the pink moon and the quivering breeze. Then Fauré allows himself to return to the first stanza, words and music. It must begin *mf* with a gradual *diminuendo*. It is the pianist who establishes the *ritardando*, with his scale, on the last line of the verse, and he is back in tempo for the last three bars. He should take off the pedal just on the last chord.

*

Let us now consider Fauré's settings of two poems from Verlaine's 'Ariettes oubliées' ('Forgotten Airs'). The Debussy settings may possibly be preferred.

GREEN	GREEN
Voici des fruits, des fleurs, des feuilles et des branches,	Here are fruits, flowers, leaves and branches,
Et puis voici mon cœur, qui ne bat que pour vous.	and here too is my heart that beats only for you.
Ne le déchirez pas avec vos deux mains blanches,	Do not destroy it with your two white hands,
Et qu'à vos yeux si beaux, l'humble présent soit doux!	and to your lovely eyes may the humble gift seem sweet!
J'arrive tout couvert encore de rosée	I come still covered with dew
Que le vent du matin vient glacer à mon front.	that the morning breeze has chilled on my brow.
Souffrez que ma fatigue, à vos pieds reposée,	Let my weariness, resting at your feet,
Rêve des chers instants qui la délasseront.	dream of dear moments which will bring repose.
Sur votre jeune sein laisser rouler ma tête	On your young breast let me rest my head
Toute sonore encore de vos derniers baisers;	still ringing with your last kisses;
Laissez-la s'apaiser de la bonne tempête,	let it be appeased after the good tempest,
Et que je dorme un peu puisque vous reposez.	that I may sleep a little as you rest.

Paul Verlaine

C'EST L'EXTASE...

C'est l'extase langoureuse,
C'est la fatigue amoureuse,
C'est tous les frissons des bois
Parmi l'étreinte des brises,
C'est, vers les ramures grises,
Le chœur des petites voix.

O le frêle et frais murmure!
Cela gazouille et susurre,
Cela ressemble au cri doux
Que l'herbe agitée expire...
Tu dirais, sous l'eau qui vire,

Le roulis sourd des cailloux.

Cette âme qui se lamente
Et cette plainte dormante,
C'est la nôtre n'est-ce pas?
La mienne, dis, | et la tienne,
Dont s'exhale l'humble antienne
Par ce tiède soir, tout bas?

Paul Verlaine

IT IS ECSTASY

It is languorous ecstasy,
it is loving lassitude,
it is all the tremors of the woods
in the embrace of the breezes,
it is, in the grey branches,
the choir of tiny voices.

O the frail, fresh murmuring!
That twittering and whispering
is like the sweet cry
breathed out by the ruffled grass . . .
You would say, beneath the swirling
waters,
the muted rolling of the pebbles.

This soul which mourns
in subdued lamentation,
it is ours is it not?
Mine, say, and yours,
breathing a humble anthem
in the warm evening, very softly?

These two mélodies are beautiful and subtle and a delight for the performers, provided they do not try too hard to make the marriage between the poetry and the music a love marriage as in Debussy's settings, when it seems here to be only a marriage of convenience. Given a perfect performance of the music and of the literary text (which often seems to have been adapted to the music), justice will be done to both. These two mélodies are very 'singable' and should be well 'sung'. All the dynamics are quite well indicated and should be observed. The delight comes from the refined and constantly modulating music, woven with musical themes we have already met in 'En sourdine' and 'Mandoline'. (These four songs are part of the 'Mélodies de Venise', so called only because they were partly composed in Venice.)

As always in Fauré's music, the tempo must be flawless. For 'Green' it is ♩ = 72, with a feeling of animation and youth. For 'C'est l'extase' ♪ = 120, with a feeling of tenderness and warmth.

SPLEEN

Il pleure dans mon cœur
Comme il pleut sur la ville,
Quelle est cette langueur
Qui pénètre mon cœur ?

O bruit doux de la pluie
Par terre et sur les toits !
Pour un cœur qui s'ennuie,
O le chant de la pluie !

Il pleure sans raison
Dans mon cœur qui s'écœure,
Quoi ! nulle trahison ?
Mon deuil est sans raison.

C'est bien la pire peine
De ne savoir pourquoi,
Sans amour et sans haine,
Mon cœur a tant de peine !

Paul Verlaine

SPLEEN

Tears fall in my heart
like rain upon the town,
what is this languor
that pervades my heart ?

O gentle sound of the rain
on the ground and on the roofs !
For a listless heart,
O the song of the rain !

Tears fall without reason
in my sickened heart,
What ! no perfidy ?
My sorrow has no cause.

Indeed it is the worst pain
not to know why,
without love and without hate,
my heart feels so much pain.

The title 'Spleen' was given to this mélodie by Fauré; Verlaine's poem has no title. Another poem by Verlaine called 'Spleen' has been set by Debussy (*see* page 170), as well as this same poem (*see* page 164). Indeed, this title very well suits the depressed mood of this poem, of this music, which discreetly evokes the sound of the rain on the roofs of the city, monotonous and ceaseless; while the poet sings of his sadness and weariness, in the modest range of a ninth, with no dramatic accents. Here again, the indicated *f* should be quite relative. It may not be easy to give the impression of boredom without being boring . . . but this must be achieved.

The original key is D minor and the indicated tempo, ♩ = 76/80, is quite satisfactory. A little stress can be made on the two verbs 'pleure' and 'pleut', using the 'pl' to emphasize the alliteration. No crescendo at all on the *pp* lines 'O bruit doux de la pluie Par terre et sur les toits'. 'Quoi ! nulle trahison ?' must not be too intensely expressive, and the end of the mélodie should be sung with the darkest melancholy.

PRISON

Le ciel est par dessus le toit
    Si bleu, si calme,
Un arbre par dessus le toit
    Berce sa palme;
La cloche dans le ciel qu'on voit
    Doucement tinte,
Un oiseau sur l'arbre qu'on voit
    Chante sa plainte.

Mon Dieu, mon Dieu la vie est là,
    Simple et tranquille!
Cette paisible rumeur-là
    Vient de la ville.
Qu'as-tu fait, | ô toi que voilà

    Pleurant sans cesse,
Dis, qu'as-tu fait, toi que voilà,

    De ta jeunesse?

Paul Verlaine

PRISON

The sky is above the roof
    so blue, so calm,
a tree above the roof
    rocks its branches;
in the sky that one sees, a bell
    sweetly tolls,
on the tree that one sees, a bird
    sings its plaint.

Dear God, life is there,
    simple and tranquil!
That peaceful sound
    comes from the town.
What have you done, O you who are
    there
    weeping unceasingly,
say, what have you done, you who
    are there,
    with your youth?

Verlaine was actually once in prison himself (in Brussels, after attempting to kill his friend, the great poet Arthur Rimbaud), and this poem describes his own experience and emotions. It has been set by Fauré, with a dramatic sense quite exceptional in his works.

In my personal opinion, the tempo indicated by Fauré is too fast: ♩ = 46 can give much more intensity to this mélodie. Its original key is E flat minor (the saddest of all keys), and it loses very much when transposed. All the first stanza must be sung *p*, avoiding carefully any involuntary nuances. It is extremely important to respect the exact value of each note, especially the semiquavers: 'par dessus le toit' and 'dans le ciel qu'on voit'. In this slow tempo there is plenty of time to sustain the semiquavers well, particularly those which are not on the beats. This alone can give to the first stanza all the calm and immobility required, to suggest the poet prisoner looking through the iron bars of his cell at the blue sky, listening to a bird singing, and to all the tranquil sounds of the city.

Then, all of a sudden, the piano makes a big crescendo in three beats, and brings the sad exclamation: 'Mon Dieu, mon Dieu', which is followed by a *diminuendo*. Then, it is firmly recommended to avoid singing *f* as indicated: 'Cette paisible rumeur-là Vient de la ville'. A *mf* is quite sufficient. Keep the *ff* for the dramatic outburst on: 'Qu'as-tu fait', etc. This intensity must be maintained for 'pleurant sans cesse'. On the following bars the *diminuendo* and the *p* are indicated too soon. The line 'Dis, qu'as-tu fait, toi que voilà' should be intensely desperate; 'de ta jeunesse' is *p* not *pp*, with a strong expressive stress on the semiquaver of the syllable 'jeu' [œ]. A truly pathetic expression can be given to this heart-breaking interrogation.

*

LA BONNE CHANSON (THE GOOD SONG)

This cycle of nine mélodies is quite unique from many standpoints, but firstly because it is entirely devoted to the expression of happiness and joy. It is rare in poetry and in music for a feeling of happiness not to turn very soon into sadness or melancholy. In this cycle, no! Each song, in its own way, conveys a different expression of joy or tenderness, of enthusiasm or peaceful happiness, of hope or confidence. It may be said that the successive embodiment of all these feelings by the interpreters is not easy to realize. It is certainly much easier to give oneself up to the expression of romantic sorrow or despair than to project these subtle nuances of happiness.

Verlaine wrote these poems when he was about to marry a young girl, Mathilde Mauté, feeling convinced that he would have a normal and happy life. Although his hopes were not realized, as the marriage was a complete failure, yet at the time he was sincere in his hope and faith, and his poems give direct and poetic expression to simple human happiness. The mood is very different from those of the previous seven songs which evoke elusive and charming figures, or give expression to the poet's sadness and loneliness.

With his usual discretion and taste, Fauré has caught to perfection the joy of this series of twenty-one poems, called *La Bonne Chanson*. He chose nine of them, and without placing them in the same order as in the book, and even without setting all their stanzas, he succeeded in constructing a cycle which is varied, contrasted, with a good ascending line of expression, leading to the very short, quiet, peaceful, tender and grateful ending of the last enthusiastic mélodie.

There is a version of this cycle with string quartet and piano. In spite of the fact that it was made by Fauré himself, it is not at all successful and he recommended that it should never be used.

All the metronomic markings in this cycle are very good, and must be observed, and *kept*. It is remarkable that in the whole cycle there is only one gradual change of tempo during a mélodie—in the seventh. There are contrasted tempi in the fourth, the fifth and the ninth. This is all. In the other mélodies the tempo should be strictly maintained with no *rubato* whatsoever, not even a *ritenuto* at the end of the mélodie.

UNE SAINTE EN SON AURÉOLE...	A SAINT IN HER HALO

Une Sainte en son auréole,
Une Chatelaine en sa tour,
Tout ce que contient la parole
Humaine de grâce et d'amour;

A saint in her halo,
a chatelaine in her tower,
all that human words contain
of grace and love;

La note d'or que fait entendre
Le cor dans le lointain des bois,

the golden note that can be heard
from the horn in the distance of the woods,

Mariée à la fierté tendre
Des nobles Dames d'autrefois;

combined with the tender pride
of the noble ladies of long ago;

Avec cela le charme insigne
D'un frais sourire triomphant
Éclos dans des candeurs de cygne
Et des rougeurs de femme-enfant;

withal the rare charm
of a fresh, triumphant smile
blooming in the purity of the swan
and the blushes of a woman-child.

Des aspects nacrés, blancs et roses,
Un doux accord patricien:
Je vois, j'entends toutes ces choses
Dans son nom Carlovingien.

A pearly sheen, white and pink,
a sweet patrician harmony:
I see, I hear all these things
in her Carlovingian name.

Paul Verlaine

The poet enumerates the visions suggested by the name of his fiancée, this old 'Carlovingian name': Mathilde. As often with Fauré, the music does not try to follow exactly the meaning of the words, differentiating all the different visions. We can, however, hear (repeated F flat) the golden note of the horn in the distance of the woods. Thus, like the composer, the interpreters should not try to vary too much this long enumeration. But from the very beginning, the singer has to suggest that he is describing successive and enchanting visions, and it is only when he comes to the line 'Je vois, j'entends toutes ces choses', that by a sudden change of colour and expression, he must make it clear that this is the key to all these poetic evocations.

The dynamics only twice lead to a real *f*; and the first very quick crescendo 'de grâce et d'amour' has its climax on the B flat of 'mour' not on the E flat of 'et' as is too often heard. The tempo may seem a little fast, but is exactly right, and it is most important to maintain it until the very last bar of the mélodie. No *ritardando* at all, for example on these bars:

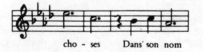

cho - ses   Dans son nom

PUSIQUE L'AUBE GRANDIT...	SINCE DAWN IS BREAKING
Puisque l'aube grandit, puisque voici l'aurore,	Since dawn is breaking, since day-break is here,
Puisqu'après m'avoir fui longtemps, l'espoir veut bien	since hope, having eluded me so long, is ready
Revoler devers moi qui l'appelle et l'implore,	to return, heeding my supplication,
Puisque tout ce bonheur veut bien être le mien,	since all this happiness is to be mine,
Je veux, guidé par vous, beaux yeux aux flammes douces,	Guided by you, lovely eyes alight with tenderness,
Par toi conduit, ô main | où trem-blera ma main,	led by you, O hand in which my own hand trembles,

Marcher droit, que ce soit par des sentiers de mousses	I will walk ahead, be it by mossy paths
Ou que rocs͜ et cailloux | encombrent le chemin;	or tracks made rough by rocks and boulders;
Et comme, pour bercer les lenteurs de la route,	and as if to beguile the slowness of the journey,
Je chanterai des͜ airs͜ ingénus, je me dis	I will sing some simple airs, I tell myself
Qu'elle m'écoutera sans déplaisir sans doute;	that no doubt she will listen without displeasure;
Et vraiment je ne veux pas √ d'autre Paradis.	and truly I wish for no other paradise.

Paul Verlaine

The three different emotions expressed in this poem: exaltation of hope; firm decision to walk straight ahead whatever life may bring; and the supreme happiness of simply walking this road with his beloved, 'singing simple airs' (that is to say writing poetry) are musically expressed in one flow of lyricism, and one immutable tempo. The final emotion of peaceful joy is given by longer values in the vocal line, and quavers instead of semiquavers in the arpeggios of the piano. The metronomic marking ♩ = 112 seems a minimum of speed, it can be 112/120, and to feel it in two instead of four gives a good impulse to the mélodie. There are many indications of dynamics and it is important to observe them; they are often very sudden and contrasted.

The voice should be young and enthusiastic. There can be a contrast between the rhythmic and the melodic phrases. For example, 'Marcher droit' is rhythmic, and 'que ce soit par des sentiers de mousse' is melodic; 'Ou que rocs et cailloux' is rhythmic.

The suddenly tranquillized third quatrain, strictly in tempo as already mentioned, must have great charm in its phrasing. The last line is difficult to accomplish. There is a big crescendo on 'Et vraiment je ne veux pas', then a very quick and expressive breath to emphasize the upbeat on 'd'autre'; afterwards there is real *diminuendo* up to the end of the mélodie, but at the same time there must be a crescendo of intensity! One must imagine that the phrase goes up, not down; and, most important, there must not be the slightest feeling of *ritardando*, especially on the word 'Paradis'.

LA LUNE BLANCHE LUIT
    DANS LES BOIS...

La lune blanche
Luit dans les bois;
De chaque branche
Part une voix
Sous la ramée...

O bien aimée.

L'étang reflète,
Profond miroir,
La silhouette
Du saule noir
Où le vent pleure...

Rêvons, c'est l'heure.

Un vaste et tendre
Apaisement
Semble descendre
Du firmament
Que l'astre irise...

C'est l'heure exquise.

THE WHITE MOON IS
SHINING IN THE WOODS

The white moon
is shining in the woods;
from each branch
comes a voice
under the boughs. . . .

O beloved.

The pool reflects,
deep mirror,
the outline
of the black willow
where the wind is weeping. . . .

Let us dream, this is the hour.

A vast and tender
peacefulness
seems to descend
from the heavens
made iridescent by the moon. . . .

This is the exquisite hour.

Paul Verlaine

Moonlight is a favourite, and sometimes a little outworn, subject of inspiration for poets and musicians from all countries, but rarely has it inspired a more beautiful poem or a more perfect musical setting. The poet describes the nocturnal landscape and, interrupting himself, he addresses his beloved, and these three interruptions are, by themselves, a short poem:

O bien aimée
Rêvons, c'est l'heure
C'est l'heure exquise

O beloved
Let us dream, this is the hour
This is the exquisite hour

This is clearly brought out in Fauré's setting. As one can expect from him, there is nothing too sweet or too sentimental.

The *tempo andantino* ($\unicode{x2669}$. = 76) discourages dragging and languishing singers, and is exactly right for the creation of the transparent atmosphere and the 'vast and tender calm' of this ecstatic love poem.

The three descriptive sections should remain in this atmosphere, rarely reaching a *mf*. (In the first line I suggest a little stress on the verb 'luit', to make it understandable, the prosody being rather bad.)

The first interruption must be marked by a change of colour, with a sudden increase of warmth and intensity, and a big lyrical crescendo. The second one, changing in colour as before, starts *pp* with a slight crescendo, and a diminuendo on 'c'est l'heure'. This time it is the piano which has the big lyrical crescendo.

'Un vaste et tendre Apaisement' should be *p* but rather broad. The last address to the beloved is, of course, the expressive climax, and should be sung with beautiful vocal quality in the *pp*. It is better to take the low F sharp not too *p*, in order to have a *diminuendo* on the top one. It is difficult . . . and the pianist, who should have kept a perfectly even pace in his important part, may perhaps just for once be a little kind and supple for the singer, for this jump of one octave.

J'ALLAIS PAR DES CHEMINS PERFIDES...

J'allais par des chemins perfides,
Douloureusement incertain.
Vos chères mains furent mes guides.

Si pâle à l'horizon lointain
Luisait un faible espoir d'aurore;
Votre regard fut le matin.

Nul bruit, sinon son pas sonore,
N'encourageait le voyageur.
Votre voix me dit: 'Marche encore!'

Mon cœur craintif, mon sombre cœur

Pleurait, seul, sur la triste voie;
L'amour, délicieux vainqueur,

Nous a réunis dans la joie.
Paul Verlaine

I FOLLOWED TREACHEROUS PATHS

I followed treacherous paths,
sadly insecure.
Your dear hands guided me.

Palely on the far horizon
gleamed a faint hope of dawn;
your eyes were the morning.

No sound, but of his own footsteps,
encouraged the traveller.
Your voice said to me: 'Walk on!'

My heart full of fear, my despondent heart
wept, alone, on the sad journey;
love, deliciously triumphant,

has united us in joy.

In this poem, the first two lines of each stanza evoke the poet's sombre fate before he met Mathilde, and the last line (at the end, the last two lines) says that now all is changed for good and joy.

The music makes this still clearer, with the contrast of a rugged and rhythmic theme in the piano part for the first two lines of each stanza, and smooth ascending scales for the third line. (These scales obviously have their origin in the theme at the end of the preceding mélodie suggesting the 'exquisite hour'.) This musical contrast can greatly help the singer to find in his voice and expression a similar change of mood: the first two lines with firm declamation and rhythm, and the third one extremely legato.

The same effect is repeated for the second stanza. The third one, the great climax, with arpeggios in the piano instead of scales, should be *f*, with strong articulation, to the end of 'Marche encore!'

Then in the fourth stanza, one finds not only the smooth scales for the poet's new state of mind, but also a theme directly issuing from the first mélodie with its vision of pure joy. The tempo here is a little faster, about ♩ = 144.

The dynamics are clearly indicated and these few musical remarks may help the singer in the interpretation of this difficult mélodie.

J'AI PRESQUE PEUR, EN VÉRITÉ...

J'ai presque peur, en vérité,
Tant je sens ma vie enlacée
A la radieuse pensée
Qui m'a pris l'âme l'autre été,

Tant votre image, | à jamais chère,

Habite en ce cœur tout à vous,
Ce cœur uniquement jaloux
De vous aimer et de vous plaire;

Et je tremble, pardonnez-moi
D'aussi franchement vous le dire,
A penser qu'un mot, qu'un sourire
De vous | est désormais ma loi,

IN TRUTH, I AM ALMOST AFRAID

In truth, I am almost afraid,
so closely do I feel my life linked
to the radiant conception
that possessed my soul last summer,

so constantly does your image, for ever dear,
dwell in this heart, all yours,
this heart whose only longing
is to love and to please you;

and I tremble, forgive me
for telling you so frankly,
when I realize that a word, a smile
from you is henceforth law to me,

Et qu'il vous suffirait d'un geste,
D'une parole ou d'un clin d'œil,
Pour mettre tout mon être en deuil
De son illusion céleste.

and that a gesture is enough,
a word or the merest glance,
to plunge me into mourning
for my celestial illusion.

Mais plutôt je ne veux vous voir,
L'avenir dût-il m'être sombre

Yet I determine to look upon you,
though the future were to be dark
   for me

Et fécond | en peine sans nombre,
Qu'à travers un immense espoir,

and full of countless afflictions,
with only immense hopefulness,

Plongé dans ce bonheur suprême
De me dire encore et toujours,
En dépit des mornes retours,
Que je vous aime, que je t'aime!

immersed in the supreme happiness
of saying to myself again and for ever,
despite returning dejection,
that I love you, that I love thee!

Paul Verlaine

The first four stanzas of this poem are the only occasion in the whole cycle when a certain feeling of anxiety and fear is expressed. The kind of fear that can arise from excess of happiness and joy. This is wonderfully expressed by the syncopated and panting piano part, while the first notes of the voice set the musical theme of the mélodie.

It should be sung with a kind of uneasiness, but legato over the staccato of the piano. In the second stanza, a little stress on the syllable 'ja' of 'jamais' and a re-attack on 'à' will help to avoid the ugly 'ge à ja'. In the third stanza the phrase 'pardonnez-moi D'aussi franchement vous le dire' is in parenthesis before the big crescendo of ten bars leading to 'Pour mettre', etc.

Then all anxiety is over, as is apparent in the poem and also in the music, which loses its panting rhythm and suddenly turns to the major. This is a favourite device of Schubert, and here it makes the same luminous effect that it makes in Schubert's own music. The voice brightens, all fear has vanished. An 'immense hope' is stronger than all the possible difficulties of life, and the end of the song is pure lyricism. The *pp subito* (*senza rallentare!*) is to emphasize the difference: 'Que je vous aime'—'que je t'aime', for the first time the poet dares to use the intimate French 'tu' and a stress of tenderness must be given on the 't'.

AVANT QUE TU NE T'EN AILLES...

Avant que tu ne t'en_ailles,
Pâle étoile du matin;
　　—Mille cailles
Chantent, chantent dans le thym!—

Tourne devers le poète,
Dont les_yeux sont pleins d'amour;
　　—L'alouette
Monte_au ciel avec le jour!—

Tourne ton regard que noie
L'aurore dans son_azur;
　　—Quelle joie
Parmi les champs de blé mûr!—

Et fais luire ma pensée
Là-bas, bien loin, oh! bien loin!
　　—La rosée
Gaîment brille sur le foin!—

Dans le doux rêve_où s'agite
Ma mie endormie encor...
　　—Vite, vite,
Car voici le soleil d'or!—

Paul Verlaine

BEFORE YOU VANISH

Before you vanish,
pale star of the morning;
　　—a thousand quails
are singing, singing in the thyme!—

Turn towards the poet,
whose eyes are full of love;
　　—the lark
rises up to the sky at daybreak!—

Turn your gaze steeped
by the dawn in its azure;
　　—what joy
among the fields of ripe corn!—

And make my thoughts shine
yonder, far away, oh! far away!
　　—the dew
gleams brightly on the hay!—

into the sweet dream
of my love who still stirs in sleep . . .
　　—quickly, quickly,
for here is the golden sun!—

Here again there are two poems together. One is the poet's request to the morning star to carry his thoughts into his beloved's dreams. The other (which is printed between dashes) expresses the successive and joyful impressions of the poet at dawn. The description of the scene is an interpolation. This could not have been set to music with more intelligence and sensitivity, with more skill and art.

When working on this mélodie, I suggest that the two different poems be performed separately, to get the perfect continuity of each of them, and especially of the address to the star, with its calm and serene legato, which must never be affected by the rhythmic and swift interruptions.

Towards the end, the two poems together become more and more intense in dynamics and exaltation as the sun rises. At this point, the extremely important piano part should be very lyrical and the singer must make allowance for that. Wait just a little before the last climax, the last note of the voice 'd'or!'—this seems to make the first ray of sun suddenly appear.

DONC, CE SERA PAR UN CLAIR JOUR D'ÉTÉ...

Donc, ce sera par un clair jour d'été;
Le grand soleil complice de ma joie,
Fera, parmi le satin | et la soie,
Plus belle encore votre chère beauté;

Le ciel tout bleu, comme une haute tente,
Frissonnera somptueux √ à longs plis

Sur nos deux fronts √ qu'auront pâlis‾
L'émotion du bonheur √ et l'attente;

Et quand le soir viendra, √ l'air sera doux
Qui se jouera, caressant, dans vos voiles,
Et les regards paisibles des étoiles
Bienveillament souriront aux époux.

Paul Verlaine

SO, IT WILL BE ON A CLEAR SUMMER DAY

So, it will be on a clear summer day;
the great sun, accomplice of my joy,
will make, clad in silk and satin,
your dear beauty lovelier still;

the blue sky, like a tall canopy,

will quiver magnificently, in long folds

above our two brows, pale
with the emotion of happiness and anticipation;

and when evening comes, the breeze will be soft
playing caressingly among your veils,

and the peaceful gaze of the stars
will smile beneficently on the married lovers.

This is the day of the wedding, a clear summer day; there could not be more sun in the music, based on the enthusiastic theme of the end of the preceding mélodie.

The semiquavers, both in the voice and the piano, must be rather rhythmic and marked, specially '<u>d'été</u>', '<u>soleil</u>', '<u>beauté</u>'. In the second stanza observe the breaths as indicated above. The diminuendo on 'qu'auront pâlis' is important, in order to begin the following crescendo effectively.

Then comes the only *ritardando* of the whole cycle; it leads to the quiet tempo and the tender and hopeful mood of the evening of this wedding day. Both singer and pianist must find the soft quality of sonority and the perfect legato that is required, always maintaining the tempo. The last line should be sung in one breath.

N'EST-CE PAS?...	IS IT NOT TRUE?
N'est-ce pas? nous_irons, gais_et lents, dans la voie⁀	Is it not true? light of heart and unhurried, we shall follow
Modeste √ que nous montre en souriant l'Espoir,	the modest path which smiling hope has shown us,
Peu soucieux qu'on nous_ignore ou qu'on nous voie.	caring little if others are aware of us or not.
Isolés dans l'amour ainsi qu'en_un bois noir,	Isolated in love as if in a dark forest,
Nos deux cœurs, √ exhalant leur tendresse paisible,	our two hearts breathing peaceful tenderness
Seront deux rossignols qui chantent dans le soir.	will be two nightingales singing at evening.
Sans nous préoccuper de ce que nous destine	Without concern about our future
Le Sort, nous marcherons pourtant du même pas,	fate, we shall walk along together
Et la main dans la main, avec l'âme⁀ enfantine	hand in hand, with the child-like soul
De ceux qui s'aiment sans mélange, n'est-ce pas?	of those whose love is unalloyed, is it not true?

Paul Verlaine

Is it possible to convey the expression of peaceful and confident happiness more perfectly than does this poem and this music? I doubt it. The quiet, but not dragging, pace of the music suggests the lovers walking gaily and calmly, hand in hand, on the roads of life.

Please watch the evenness of the quavers on 'qu'on nous ignore ou qu'on nous voie'. The lyrical and tender theme of the evening of the wedding day soon appears in the piano part. The voice expands its long and beautiful curves into a fine *bel canto* line. Then in the piano part the semiquaver rhythm returns, always exactly in the same tempo, with no agitation or dragging whatsoever, up to the very end. It is the only possible way of giving the impression of the total calm and confidence of the last question: 'Is it not true?'

<table>
<tr><td>

L'HIVER A CESSÉ...

L'hiver a cessé, la lumière est tiède
Et danse, du sol au firmament clair,

Il faut que le cœur le plus triste cède
A l'immense joie éparse dans l'air.

J'ai depuis un an le printemps dans
   l'âme
Et le vert retour du doux floréal,
Ainsi qu'une flamme entoure une
   flamme,
Met de l'idéal sur mon idéal,

Le ciel bleu prolonge, exhausse et
   couronne
L'immuable azur où rit mon amour.

La saison | est belle et ma part est bonne

Et tous mes espoirs ont enfin leur
   tour.

Que vienne l'été! que viennent
   encore
L'automne et l'hiver! Et chaque
   saison
Me sera charmante, ô Toi que décore

Cette fantaisie et cette raison!
           Paul Verlaine

</td><td>

WINTER IS ENDED

Winter is ended, the light is warm
and is dancing, from the earth up to
   the clear sky,
the saddest heart must surrender
to the immense joy spreading through
   the air.

For a year I have had springtime in
   my soul,
and the green return of maytime,
like a flame encircling a flame,

adds perfection to perfection,

the blue sky extends, rises and crowns

the unchanging azure wherein my
   love is smiling.
The season is beautiful and my destiny
   is fair
and all my hopes are realized.

Let summer come! Let come in turn

the autumn and the winter! And
   each season
will delight me, O you who are so
   blessed
with imagination and understanding!

</td></tr>
</table>

For a whole year the poet has had spring in his soul, and in this mélodie many musical themes reappear which have illustrated the various expressions of happiness. The quails and the larks of the sixth mélodie, as well as its enthusiastic ending, appear in the marvellous soaring phrases leading to the outburst: 'L'hiver a cessé!' 'La lumière est tiède' is more *p*, but so warm! The *f* is kept up to the end of the stanza.

The exaltation should not drop with the beginning of the second stanza: the word 'printemps' must be pronounced with great intensity. All the subtle, quickly changing nuances should be carefully observed throughout the song (a strong 'r' and a stress on the word 'rit' in the third stanza), particularly in the final stanza, where a contrast of expression is required between the happy summer and the possibly frightening autumn and winter of life. Then in singing of the delight that each season will bring, the theme of exalted hope of the second mélodie returns, to end abruptly before the beautiful conclusion of the whole cycle, in which the voice reintroduces the theme of the first mélodie with its idealistic vision. This must be in the same tempo: the ♪ of the $\frac{9}{8}$ equal to the ♩ of the first mélodie. In fact this tempo begins on the last beat of the $\frac{4}{4}$, and it is the singer who must establish it with his triplet on 'ô toi'. Four bars further the *istesso tempo* for the $\frac{3}{4}$ means, of course, the beat of the $\frac{9}{8}$ equal to the beat of the $\frac{3}{4}$ (and not ♪ = ♪).

Both the poet and the composer have imbued this last 'envoi' with so much tenderness and gratitude for the wonder of this happiness, that the interpreters in the sincerity of their hearts (of their art) cannot fail to express it.

*

Four more songs, belonging to the third volume of the Hamelle collection, must now have our attention.

AU CIMETIÈRE	IN THE CEMETERY
Heureux qui meurt ici, ✓	Happy he who dies here,
Ainsi	like
Que les oiseaux des champs!	the birds of the fields!
Son corps près des_amis, ✓	His body near his friends
Est mis	is laid
Dans l'herbe et dans les chants.	in the grass amid songs.

Il dort d'un bon sommeil
    Vermeil,
Sous le ciel radieux.
Tous ceux qu'il a connus,
    Venus, ✓
Lui font des longs‿adieux.
	He sleeps a good sleep
	    rosy
	under the radiant sky.
	All those whom he has known
	    are come
	to bid him a lo g farewell.

A sa croix les parents
    Pleurants, ✓
Restent‿agenouillés,
Et ses‿os sous les fleurs, ✓
    De pleurs⁀
Sont doucement mouillés.
	At his cross the relatives
	    weeping
	are on their knees
	and his bones beneath the flowers
	    with tears
	are gently moistened.

Chacun sur le bois noir,
    Peut voir
S'il était jeune | ou non,
Et peut‿avec de vrais
    Regrets, ✓
L'appeler par son nom.
	On the black wood, everyone
	    may read
	if he were young or no,
	and may with true
	    regret
	call him by his name.

Combien plus malchanceux ✓
    Sont ceux
Qui meurent‿à la mé
Et sous le flot profond ✓
    S'en vont
Loin du pays aimé!
	How much more unfortunate
	    are those
	who die at sea,
	and beneath the deep waters
	    go down
	far from the beloved country!

Ah! pauvres! qui pour seuls
    Linceuls ✓
Ont les goëmons verts,
Où l'on roule‿inconnu,
    Tout nu, ✓
Et les yeux grands‿ouverts!
	Ah! poor creatures! whose only
	    shroud
	is the green seaweed,
	where they roll unknown,
	    naked,
	with wide-open eyes!

Jean Richepin

This poem has certainly not the quality or the rarity of the Verlaine poems, and it prompted Fauré to compose a mélodie which is much simpler in style. It is divided into three parts. The first four stanzas are set in a peaceful mood, then the two following stanzas are very dramatic in expression, and Fauré concludes with a *da capo* of the first two stanzas.

The indicated tempo ♩ = 66 is perhaps a shade fast and 60 more advisable. The vocal line should be well sustained, *p*, and with almost no nuances. No romanticism, no sentimentality, but a great serenity. The modulation 'Il dort' can be a little emphasized by a *subito pp* on 'dort'. The vowels must be well stretched on 'Lui font des longs adieux'. The breaths and breaks are carefully indicated above.

The tempo can be a little more *animato* in the dramatic section. It is very demanding for the singer, who should achieve the intensity more with strong articulation and broad diction than with a constant *ff*. The more so, as he must give the impression of a constant crescendo.

Then comes the *da capo*, only a knell is added in the bass of the piano, and the singer, more *p* than at the beginning of the mélodie, should again suggest the most peaceful serenity.

LE PARFUM IMPÉRISSABLE

Quand la fleur du soleil, la rose de Lahor,
De son âme odorante a rempli goutte à goutte,
La fiole d'argile | ou de cristal | ou d'or,
Sur le sable qui brûle | on peut l'épandre toute.

Les fleuves et la mer inonderaient en vain
Ce sanctuaire étroit qui la tint enfermée,
Il garde en se brisant son arôme divin
Et sa poussière heureuse | en reste parfumée.

Puisque par la blessure ouverte de mon cœur
Tu t'écoules de même, | ô céleste liqueur,
Inexprimable amour qui m'enflammait pour elle!

THE IMPERISHABLE PERFUME

When the flower of the sun, the rose of Lahore,
has filled with its fragrant soul drop by drop,
the phial of earthenware or crystal or gold,
it can all be scattered on the burning sand.

In vain the rivers and the sea would inundate
this narrow sanctuary which contained it,
though broken it retains its divine aroma
and its happy dust remains perfumed.

Since through the open wound of my heart
likewise you pour, O celestial nectar,

inexpressible love for her that inflamed me!

Qu'il lui soit pardonné, que mon mal
    soit béni!
Par delà l'heure humaine et le temps
    infini
Mon cœur est embaumé d'une odeur
    immortelle!

Let her be forgiven, let my
    suffering be blessed!
Beyond the human span and infinity,

my heart is embalmed with an
    immortal fragrance!

Leconte de Lisle

This is the last of the Fauré mélodies with poems by Leconte de Lisle; the other two settings which have already been studied ('Lydia', 'Les roses d'Ispahan') were in a much lighter mood. This beautiful mélodie, in constant modulation, shows the evolution of the composer very markedly.

The original key is E major. The indicated tempo ($\downarrow$ = 60) is on the fast side, but it should not drag and should not change from beginning to end; the semiquavers must be carefully even.

The first two stanzas of this sonnet are objective; the voice sings legato with breadth and warmth and, following the dynamics, never reaches more than a *mf*.

All the strength and the dramatic accents should be kept for the last two stanzas, which are intensely subjective, beginning with the ascending triplet of the piano launching the outburst 'Puisque par la blessure' etc. The line 'Inexprimable amour qui m'enflammait pour elle!' is very intense and should be kept *f*, to make a contrast with the following line 'Qu'il lui soit pardonné, que mon mal soit béni!' which is *p* and, in its merciful expression, better without commencing the crescendo as indicated. Then, after an expressive breath, 'Par delà l'heure humaine' is attacked *mf* and *molto crescendo*. The difficulty is to achieve the last diminuendo, which should be observed, but at the same time should be an emotional crescendo. The end of the mélodie should not drop but, on the contrary, one should give to the word 'immortelle' all the plenitude of its meaning.

*

A few comments now on two settings of poems by Albert Samain, whose graceful and vague poetic atmosphere inspired Fauré to write two of his most beautiful mélodies.

ARPÈGE

L'âme d'une flûte soupire
Au fond du parc mélodieux;
Limpide est l'ombre où l'on respire

Ton poème silencieux.

Nuit de langueur, nuit de mensonge,
Qui poses, d'un geste ondoyant,
Dans ta chevelure de songe
La lune, bijou d'Orient.

Sylva, Sylvie et Sylvanire,
Belles | au regard | leu changeant,
L'étoile aux fontaines se mire,
Allez par les sentiers d'argent,

Allez vite, l'heure est si brève,
Cueillir au jardin des aveux
Les cœurs qui se meurent √ du rêve⏜

De mourir √ parmi vos cheveux!
Albert Samain

ARPEGGIO

The soul of a flute is sighing
deep in the melodious park;
limpid is the shadow wherein one
      breathes
your silent poem.

Languorous night, deluding night,
placing, with an undulating gesture,
in your dreamy hair
the moon, jewel of the Orient.

Sylva, Sylvie and Sylvanire,
fair ones with eyes of changing blue,
the star is mirrored in the fountains,
go follow the silvered paths,

go quickly, the hour is so short,
to gather in the garden of avowals
the hearts which are dying of the
      dream
of expiring amid your hair!

Here again we find the suggestion of a great park peopled with poetic figures, but certainly not painted by Watteau, rather by Puvis de Chavannes; this is no longer the eighteenth century, but the end of the nineteenth.

The flute heard in the distance (tempo ♩. = 66 is better than the indicated 72), very legato, tries to suggest the nocturnal silence. A little more *mp* when the flute plays under the voice: 'Nuit de langueur' etc. and there is a first little climax, not more than *mf*, on 'La lune, bijou d'Orient'. The three beauties (can you see them in their white veils?) should be delicately evoked. (There should be a little crescendo-decrescendo on 'bleu changeant'.) At the beginning of the last stanza 'l'heure est si brève' is in parenthesis, and the crescendo culminates *mf* on 'se meurent' before the decrescendo to the end. The breaths are indicated above. The whole song must be handled with extreme delicacy, as in a silvery mist.

SOIR

Voici que les jardins de la nuit vont
    fleurir
Les lignes, les couleurs, les sons
    deviennent vagues;
Vois! le dernier rayon | agonise à tes
    bagues,
Ma sœur, | entends-tu pas quelque-
    chose mourir?

Mets sur mon front tes mains
    fraîches comme une eau pure,
Mets sur mes yeux tes mains douces
    comme des fleurs,
Et que mon âme où vit le goût
    secret des pleurs,
Soit comme un lys fidèle et pâle | à
    ta ceinture!

C'est la pitié qui pose ainsi son doigt
    sur nous,
Et tout ce que la terre a de soupirs
    qui montent,
Il semble qu'à mon cœur enivré, √ le
    racontent √
Tes yeux levés au ciel, √ si tristes |
    et si doux!

Albert Samain

EVENING

Now the gardens of the night begin
    to flower,
lines, colours, sounds become
    indistinct;
See! on your rings the last rays are
    fading,
My sister, do you not hear something
    dying?

Place on my brow your hands fresh
    as pure water,
place on my eyes your hands sweet
    as flowers,
and let my soul, where dwells the
    secret essence of tears,
be like a faithful, pale lily at your
    waist!

It is compassion which thus places its
    finger upon us,
and all the sighs that rise from the
    earth,
it seems to my impassioned heart, are
    expressed
by your eyes raised towards the sky,
    so sadly and so sweetly!

In this superb mélodie there is much more warmth and subjectivity. The poem, even though not superb in itself, has very evocative and singable words.

The original key is D flat and it should be sung in this key whenever possible; the mélodie loses much of its atmosphere in the high key, E flat. The tempo is about ♩ = 60/63, which is not very slow, but the wonderful calm of a warm evening can be suggested by rich colour in the voice and perfect legato. (All the semiquavers should be even.) The poet addresses his beloved; he addresses her more precisely on the line 'Vois! le dernier rayon agonise à tes bagues'. The subtle nuance:

entends - tu pas ———— quelquecho - se

is better when made as indicated here (*p* already on 'quelquechose').

The second stanza must be in exactly the same tempo. No hurry! There should be more intensity and clear articulation on the third line, and a crescendo to *mf* on 'à ta ceinture'.

The last stanza begins *p*, with all the soft deepness suggested by the words, and a real crescendo begins, not dramatic, of course, but broad. The *f* is maintained as indicated. The diminuendo up to the end begins only on the long note of 'triste'. There can be so much tenderness in the last 'et si doux !'

*

Now we have reached Fauré's third period of composition. As already mentioned, it consists of four cycles of mélodies. The first two are settings of poems by Charles van Lerberghe: *La Chanson d'Ève* (publisher: Heugel), ten mélodies, and *Le Jardin Clos* (publisher: Durand), eight mélodies. The size of this book does not allow us to study in detail these beautiful cycles. Fauré has now stripped away all facile seduction in his music, he has attained total purity: in the melodic line (the range of the voice is rarely more than one octave), in the prosody of the literary text, and in the rare and subtle harmonies.

It is desirable that performers should have sufficient curiosity to examine these magnificent works. If they are afraid of subjecting an average audience to these cycles in their entirety, a choice can be made from among their mélodies. From *La Chanson d'Ève*, for example, a beautiful group of five can be formed with 'Prima Verba', 'L'aube blanche', 'Veilles-tu ma senteur de soleil', 'Crépuscule' and 'O mort poussière d'étoiles'. From *Le Jardin Clos* a well-chosen group might be 'Exaucement', 'La Messagère', 'Dans la nymphée', 'Il m'est cher, Amour' and 'Inscription sur le sable'.

The third cycle is called *Mirages* (publisher: Durand), four mélodies to poems by the Baronne de Brimont, of which the mysterious and sensual atmosphere has been spiritualized by the musician with infinite taste and modesty. They are precious masterpieces.

L'HORIZON CHIMÉRIQUE (THE ILLUSORY HORIZON)

L'Horizon Chimérique is the fourth cycle (publisher Durand). After the rather esoteric and secret poems Fauré had chosen for the preceding cycles, he was inspired for his very last mélodies (1922) by the much broader and more virile poems of Jean de la Ville de Mirmont (a young poet who was killed in the First World War), and his music finds in them a new occasion for real lyricism. This cycle is best suited to a baritone voice.

The metronomic marks are excellent for these four songs. As usual the precision of the rhythms is most important and there is no *rubato* whatsoever.

LA MER EST INFINIE...

La mer est infinie et mes rêves sont
   fous.
La mer chante au soleil en battant
   les falaises,
Et mes rêves légers ne se sentent plus
   d'aise
De danser sur la mer comme des
   oiseaux soûls.

Le vaste mouvement des vagues les
   emporte,
La brise les agite et les roule en ses
   plis;
Jouant dans le sillage ils feront une
   escorte
Aux vaisseaux que mon cœur dans
   leur fuite a suivis.

THE SEA IS INFINITE

The sea is infinite and my dreams are
   wild.
The sea sings to the sun as it beats
   against the cliffs,
and my light dreams are overjoyed
   beyond words
to dance upon the sea like tipsy birds.

The vast movement of the waves
   bears them away,
the breeze tosses them and rolls them
   in its folds;
playing in the ship's track, they will
   form an escort
to the vessels whose flight my heart
   has followed.

Ivres d'air et de sel √ et brûlés par
   l'écume⏜
De la mer qui console⏝et qui lave des
   pleurs,
Ils connaîtront le large et sa bonne⏝
   amertume;
Les goëlands perdus les prendront
   pour des leurs.
       Jean de la Ville de Mirmont

Intoxicated with air and salt, and
   stung by the foam
of the sea which consoles and washes
   away tears,
they will know the open sea and its
   salutary bitterness;
the vagrant seagulls will take them
   for their own.

The poet is on the cliffs and sings in the open air. His heart and his
dreams are on the sea. This is enough to suggest the broad declamation,
the scale of dynamics and the general feeling.

Fauré's indication *mp* is just right for the first line and also the big
crescendo on the second line. The semiquavers are *marcato* on '<u>en</u>
<u>ba</u>ttant <u>les</u> <u>fa</u>laises'. Then, on the third line, *subito p* and more legato,
with the crescendo as indicated. The fourth line is again more rhythmic
and *marcato*.

The whole of the second stanza is *mf* and legato. The final stanza is
subito f and rhythmic with very strong consonants: '<u>sel</u> et brûlés',
and the voice has all its fullness on 'Ils connaîtront le large et sa bonne
amertume'. The last line is *mp* or rather *mf* with no *diminuendo*. The
distant sea-gulls must be successfully suggested and for this it is important not to make the slightest *ritardando* (especially on the rhythm:
♪. = ♪ 'pour des leurs'), as though it was not the end of the mélodie.

JE ME SUIS EMBARQUÉ...

Je me suis⏝embarqué sur un vaisseau
   qui danse
Et roule bord sur bord √ et tangue⏝et
   se balance.
Mes pieds⏝ont⏝oublié la terre⏝et ses
   chemins;
Les vagues souples m'ont⏝appris
   d'autres cadences √
Plus belles que le rythme las des
   chants⏝humains.

I HAVE EMBARKED

I have embarked on a ship which
   dances
and rolls from side to side, and pitches
   and rocks.
My feet have forgotten the earth and
   its paths;
the supple waves have taught me
   other cadences
more beautiful than the weary
   rhythm of human songs.

A vivre parmi vous, | hélas! ✓
  avais-je une âme?
Mes frères, j'ai souffert sur tous vos
  continents.
Je ne veux que la mer, je ne veux
  que le vent
Pour me bercer comme un enfant, ✓
  au creux des lames.

Hors du port qui n'est plus qu'une
  image effacée
Les larmes du départ ne brûlent plus
  mes yeux,
Je ne me souviens pas de mes
  derniers adieux...
O ma peine, ma peine, où vous ai-je
  laissée?

                    Jean de la Ville de Mirmont

To live among you, alas! Had I a
  soul?
My brothers, I have suffered on all
  your shores.
I want only the sea, I want only the
  wind
to rock me like a child in the bosom
  of its waves.

Beyond the port which is no more
  than a fading image
the tears of departure no longer
  burn my eyes,
I do not remember my last
  farewells . . .
O my suffering, my suffering, where
  have I left you?

The poet himself is now on board ship, and has left his pain on land.

The pianist's left hand gives the impulse of a firm rhythm suggesting the movement of the ship, and the singer starts *mf* and broadly. Only the words 'et ses chemins' are more *p*, to give the idea of the far-away roads of the earth; the following line is again *mf*, precise in rhythm.

The first two lines of the second stanza can be *meno f* and more legato, but the third line must be strongly rhythmic (♪♪♩ ♪♪♩) with firm consonants. Thus one can make a contrast with the cradle song: 'Pour me bercer comme un enfant, au creux des lames' which is *meno f* and legato; even the rhythm of the accompaniment ceases.

The final stanza is again introduced *p*, and the voice also begins *p* (the fading image of the distant port), but soon a crescendo commences which leads to the ample interrogation of the last line.

DIANE, SÉLÉNÉ...

Diane, Séléné, ✓ lune de beau métal,

Qui reflète vers nous, par ta face
  déserte,

DIANA, SILENE

Diana, Silene, moon of beauteous
  metal,
reflecting towards us on your
  desolate surface,

Dans l'immortel ennui du calme sidéral	in the eternal monotony of sidereal calm,
Le regret d'un soleil dont nous pleurons la perte.	the regret for a sun whose loss we mourn.
O lune, je t'en veux de ta limpidité,	O moon, I begrudge you your limpidity,
Injurieuse au trouble vain des pauvres_âmes,	humiliating to the vain striving of poor souls,
Et mon cœur, toujours las | et toujours_agité,	and my heart, ever weary and ever restless,
Aspire vers la paix de ta nocturne flamme.	yearns for the peace of your nocturnal flame.

Jean de la Ville de Mirmont

Although he has departed in pursuit of his dreams, the poet is still weary and disturbed, and he invokes the moon, aspiring to its peace and limpidity.

After the former two mélodies which are full of movement and impetus, this is a completely calm nocturne, to be played and sung with perfect tranquillity (a sidereal tranquillity!) with transparent, aerial colours, *p* and with scarcely any nuances, no *rubato*, no distortion of the rhythm (real ♪, please). It is the French counterpart of Schubert's 'Nacht und Träume'.

VAISSEAUX, NOUS VOUS AURONS AIMÉS...	SHIPS, WE HAVE LOVED YOU
Vaisseaux, nous vous_aurons_aimés | en pure perte;	Ships, we have loved you to no avail;
Le dernier de vous tous est parti sur la mer.	the last of you all has set sail upon the sea.
Le couchant | emporta tant de voiles_ouvertes	The setting sun has borne away so many spread sails
Que ce port et mon cœur sont_à jamais déserts.	that this port and my heart are for ever forsaken.
La mer vous_a rendus | à votre destinée,	The sea has restored you to your destiny,
Au delà du rivage où s'arrêtent nos pas.	beyond the shore where our steps must cease.

Nous ne pouvions garder vos‿
  âmes‿enchaînées;
Il vous faut des lointains que je ne
  connais pas.

Je suis de ceux dont les désirs sont
  sur la terre.
Le souffle qui vous grise‿emplit mon
  cœur d'effroi,
Mais votre appel, | au fond des soirs,
  me désespère,
Car j'ai de grands départs √
  inassouvis‿en moi.
          Jean de la Ville de Mirmont

We could not have held your souls
  captive;
you have need of distances unknown
  to me.

I belong to those whose desires are
  earthbound.
The breeze that elates you fills my
  heart with terror,
but your call when evening falls
  makes me despair,
For I feel within me an unappeased
  longing for great departures.

The poet must now admit that he really belongs to the earth, but he still feels unsatisfied departures in his heart.

We are back to the key of the first mélodie, and almost to the movement of the second one, but with an accent of lassitude. If this mélodie is again to be broad, the singer must spare his intensity and the strength of his voice. For example, on the two lines 'La mer vous a rendus à votre destinée' and 'Je suis de ceux dont les désirs sont sur la terre', it is possible to sing much less *f*, using the relaxation of a regretful statement. Thus he will reserve himself for a big climax on the last line, with its feeling of desperate longing.

10 | Claude Debussy
(1862–1918)

No musician of any nationality (with the possible exception of Hugo Wolf) had greater mastery in creating the mysterious alloy of music and poetry than Debussy. Not only in the prosody of the literary text and in the rhythm of speech, for which he had a prodigious instinct, but also because he attained the deepest concordance between the poetic idea and the musical idea. This for the interpreters is beyond price; too often they have to fight to make the marriage of words and music appear natural and sincere. In Debussy's vocal works there is no problem, and it is easy for the singers (as it is also their duty) to serve the musician first, without betraying the poet.

It will be of interest to give here the complete list of Debussy's mélodies, in their chronological order:

1876	Nuit d'étoiles (Th. de Banville)	COUTAREL
1877/8	Beau soir (Paul Bourget)	JOBERT
	Fleur des blés (A. Girod)	LEDUC
1880/3	La belle au bois dormant (V. Hyspa)	HAMELLE
	Voici que le printemps (P. Bourget)	HAMELLE
	Paysage sentimental (P. Bourget)	HAMELLE
	Pierrot (Th. de Banville)	JOBERT
	Pantomime (P. Verlaine)	JOBERT
	Mandoline (P. Verlaine)	DURAND
	Clair de lune (1st version) (P. Verlaine)	DURAND
1884	Apparition (Stéphane Mallarmé)	DURAND

1888	Ariettes oubliées: (P. Verlaine)	JOBERT
	C'est l'extase	
	Il pleure dans mon cœur	
	L'ombre des arbres	
	Chevaux de bois	
	Green	
	Spleen	

1887/90	Cinq Poèmes: (Charles Baudelaire)	DURAND
	Le balcon	
	Harmonie du soir	
	Le jet d'eau	
	Recueillement	
	La mort des amants	

1891	Romance (P. Bourget)	DURAND
	Les cloches (P. Bourget)	DURAND
	Les angélus (G. Le Roy)	HAMELLE
	La mer est plus belle (P. Verlaine)	HAMELLE
	Le son du cor s'afflige (P. Verlaine)	JOBERT
	L'échelonnement des haies (P. Verlaine)	JOBERT
	Dans le jardin (P. Gravollet)	HAMELLE

1892	Fêtes galantes: (1st book) (P. Verlaine)	JOBERT
	En sourdine	
	Fantoches	
	Clair de lune	

1892/93	Proses lyriques: (C. Debussy)	JOBERT
	De rêve	
	De grève	
	De fleurs	
	De soir	

1897	Chansons de Bilitis: (P. Louÿs)	FROMONT
	La flûte de Pan	
	La chevelure	
	Le tombeau des naïades	

1904	Deux Rondels de Charles d'Orléans:	DURAND
	Le temps a laissié son manteau	
	Pour ce que Plaisance est morte	
	Fêtes galantes: (2nd book) (P. Verlaine)	DURAND
	Les ingénus	
	Le faune	
	Colloque sentimental	

Of the very early mélodies, two only have been chosen for study; these would seem to be the best and the most indicative of the later development of the composer's genius.

BEAU SOIR	BEAUTIFUL EVENING
Lorsqu'au soleil couchant les rivières sont roses,	When the rivers are rosy in the setting sun,
Et qu'un tiède frisson court sur les champs de blé,	and a mild tremor runs over the cornfields,
Un conseil d'être heureux semble sortir des choses	an exhortation to be happy seems to emanate from things
Et monter vers le cœur troublé.	and rises towards the troubled heart.
Un conseil de goûter le charme d'être au monde	An exhortation to enjoy the charm of being alive
Cependant qu'on est jeune et que le soir est beau,	while one is young and the evening is beautiful,
Car nous nous en allons, comme s'en va cette onde:	for we go away, as this stream goes:
Elle | à la mer, nous | au tombeau.	the stream to the sea, we to the tomb.
Paul Bourget	

Debussy was fifteen or sixteen when he wrote this mélodie, and certainly his music is marked by the aesthetics of the period, that of

Massenet, but already he showed much better taste. 'Beau soir' is, at any rate, very well written for the voice, and its melodic line already matches the literary text admirably. It should be interpreted with lyricism and simplicity.

The original key is E major and the tempo is about ♩ = 72 but supple and *senza rigore*. (Pianists should be careful at the tenth and eleventh bars, to play the arpeggio: C, G *sharp*, E, etc. . . . By carelessness they too often play the C major chord!) At the twelfth bar there is a misprint: it is the B which is linked to the B of the following bar.

The first line of the verses should be, whenever possible, sung in one breath. Broad phrasing is required for the second line, with a slight crescendo when the voice descends to the low register. On the line 'Cependant qu'on est jeune et que le soir est beau', the *animato* and the crescendo must be built up very gradually. The F sharp on 'beau' must be attacked *mf*, the true *f* being only on the first beat of the following bar. A catch breath can be taken between 'jeune' and 'et'. One returns to the *tempo primo* for the five bars of 'Car nous nous en allons, comme s'en va cette onde', and *subito più lento*, as indicated, on 'Elle à la mer'. The two following bars for the piano must be in this same tempo *più lento*, and the words 'nous au tombeau' can be still slower. For these last two vocal phrases, one has, of course, to make an expressive pause between 'Elle' and 'à la mer', and between 'nous' and 'au tombeau'. The last four piano bars can be played *rubato*, marking a little hesitation before the pretty resolution in E major.

MANDOLINE

Les donneurs de sérénades
Et les belles écouteuses,
Échangent des propos fades
Sous les ramures chanteuses.

C'est Tircis et c'est Aminte,
Et c'est l'éternel Clitandre,
Et c'est Damis qui pour mainte
Cruelle fait maint vers tendre.

MANDOLINE

The serenaders
and the lovely listeners
exchange sweet nothings
beneath the singing branches.

It is Tircis and Aminte,
and the eternal Clitandre,
and Damis, who for many
a cruel fair one writes many a tender
verse.

Leurs courtes vestes de soie,
Leurs longues robes_à queues,
Leur élégance, | leur joie, √
Et leurs molles_ombres bleues,

Their short silken doublets,
their long trailing dresses,
their elegance, their joy,
and their soft blue shadows

Tourbillonnent dans l'extase
D'une lune rose et grise,
Et la mandoline jase
Parmi les frissons de brise.

whirl in the ecstasy
of a pink and grey moon,
and the mandoline chatters
amid the quivering of the breeze.

Paul Verlaine

When studying the first poems by Verlaine set by Gabriel Fauré, a few general comments were made which also concern Debussy's settings of the same poems (*see* page 121). In fact, Debussy set Verlaine's poems before Fauré, and he wrote no fewer than eighteen mélodies to his verses, spread over a period of twenty-five years.

'Mandoline' was probably written in 1882 or 1883, when Debussy was barely twenty or twenty-one. In this serenade he has succeeded in capturing the elegance, the wit, and the poetry of the text, three words which very well sum up the spirit of its interpretation.

The original key is C major; the indicated tempo ($\quarternote$. = 126) is probably on the fast side, but one should not depart too much from it. In this tempo the following rhythms are difficult to execute with precision:

sé —— réna - des   é —— couteu - ses

The second F on the syllable 'ré' and the E on the syllable 'cou' always tend to be too short; and this also applies to the same musical phrase in the second stanza. I suggest that it should be first practised like this:

sé - rénades   é - couteuses

the semiquaver being added afterwards.

In this mélodie there are many contrasts between *staccato* and legato, which should be carefully observed.

In the bars 'sous les ramures chanteuses', the crescendo and the *subito p* (on 'teu') must be observed, by both the voice and the piano. On the contrary in the same musical phrase in the fourth stanza: 'parmi les frissons de brise', the crescendo leads to a *f*.

It is easier in Debussy's setting than in Fauré's, to suggest the different characters: Tircis, Aminte, Clitandre, Damis. For example the crescendo and diminuendo on the word 'Clitandre', if made with some exaggeration, suggest very well this boring boy, the typical fop.

The duplets on 'Leurs courtes vestes de soie' should be very even and legato. (Watch the word 'robes': with [ɔ] and not [o].) There is a *luftpause*, as indicated between 'Leur élégance' and 'leur joie', but the breath should be taken before 'Et leurs molles ombres bleues'. The breaths are as follows for the end of the mélodie:

Of course all the 'la, la, la' should be varied in expression, using the different rhythms and tessitura. The last ones can be sung with a certain exaggeration of the 'l', to suggest the plucking of the mandoline, and *sempre diminuendo*. I recommend taking the last one off with the arpeggio chord of the piano, instead of holding the last ♩..

*

'Les Cloches' and 'Romance' are two mélodies whose manuscripts are dated 1891, but their style, their aesthetic, as well as the choice of their poems, again by Paul Bourget, would rather indicate that they belong to a period seven or eight years earlier.

LES CLOCHES	THE BELLS

Les feuilles s'ouvraient sur le bord des branches,
    Délicatement,
Les cloches tintaient, légères‿et franches,
    Dans le ciel clément.

The leaves opened on the edge of the branches,
    delicately,
the bells rang, lightly and clearly,

    in the mild sky.

Rythmique‿et fervent comme‿une antienne,
    Ce lointain‿appel
Me remémorait la blancheur chrétienne
    Des fleurs de l'autel.

Rhythmical and fervent like an anthem,
    this distant call
brought to my mind the Christian whiteness
    of the altar flowers.

Ces cloches parlaient d'heureuses‿années,
    Et dans le grand bois
Semblaient reverdir les feuilles fanées

    Des jours d'autrefois.

These bells spoke of happy years,

    and in the great forest
seemed to make green again the withered leaves
    of bygone days.

Paul Bourget

The original key of this mélodie is C sharp minor – E major. The tempo is about ♩ = 104 for it is indicated in $\frac{4}{4}$, but the phrasing can be more easily found by feeling it gently rocking in $\frac{2}{2}$. Thus the ♪♪♪ of

the voice part can be placed quite naturally. The ringing of the bells which is heard all through the mélodie either:

evokes for the poet and the musician the happy 'jours d'autrefois' (bygone days). The vocal line must be well phrased; few effects can be made with the words. The tempo: *un peu plus lent* is only a very little slower. One must be able to sing in one breath and without rushing the tempo, the beautiful curve: 'Semblaient reverdir les feuilles fanées'. The nostalgia of 'Des jours d'autrefois' can be expressed with the help of a slight *rallentando*, and a slight wait for the resolution in the major.

ROMANCE

L'âme évaporée et souffrante,
L'âme douce, l'âme odorante
Des lis divins que j'ai cueillis

Dans le jardin de ta pensée,
Où donc les vents l'ont-ils chassée
Cette âme adorable des lis?

N'est-il plus un parfum qui reste
De la suavité céleste,
Des jours où tu m'enveloppais

D'une vapeur surnaturelle,
Faite d'espoir, d'amour fidèle,
De béatitude ✓ et de paix?

Paul Bourget

ROMANCE

The evanescent and suffering soul,
the gentle soul, the fragrant soul
of the divine lilies that I have
    gathered
in the garden of your thought,
whither have the winds driven
this adorable soul of the lilies?

Is there no perfume remaining
of the celestial sweetness,
from the days when you surrounded
    me
with a sublime atmosphere
of hope, of faithful love,
of beatitude and of peace?

The very title of this mélodie, the rather flat perfume of its poem, and the Massenet-like grace of its melodious lines for the voice and the piano, indicate very clearly the style of its interpretation.

The original key is D major and the tempo about $\quad$ = 69 but *rubato* and *senza rigore*, to allow great charm and suppleness in the vocal curves. Example of phrasing: 'Cette âme adorable des lis': crescendo to 'ra' and 'ble' *p subito* and *rubato*. (The 's' of 'lis' 'lily' must be pronounced or else it sounds like 'lit': 'bed'!) The high version of the phrase 'd'une vapeur surnaturelle' is much better sung in one breath, taking plenty of time but with no rest on the top

note. Crescendo on 'd'une vapeur' and *diminuendo* to a nice *pp* on this
top note.

It is the pianist who ought to conduct the *ritenuto* of the last bars; he
must be able to bring out very quietly with a singing tone the theme of
the mélodie on its last appearance:

each quaver being regularly longer than the one before; and the
singer must follow, taking plenty of time to place the 'p' of the word
'paix', thus giving a wonderful impression of peace.

*

Most of the greatest mélodies of Debussy will now be considered,
and I want to make an important preliminary remark. If, for the early
mélodies, transpositions are quite acceptable, I completely disagree
with the use of transpositions for all the mélodies studied in the following pages, even though, for some of them, published transpositions
exist in American or (rarely) French editions. It will be a hopeless task
to try to re-create the true atmosphere of these mélodies if they are
transposed. I will always give an indication of the original key.

*

Let us first consider a very important series of mélodies, where
Debussy's strong personality suddenly breaks out with all its rarest
and most precious qualities—his first great masterpieces, *Ariettes
Oubliées* (Forgotten Airs) (1888), on poems by Verlaine.

C'EST L'EXTASE...	IT IS ECSTASY
C'est l'extase langoureuse,	It is languorous ecstasy,
C'est la fatigue amoureuse,	it is loving lassitude,
C'est tous les frissons des bois	it is all the tremors of the woods
Parmi l'étreinte des brises,	in the embrace of the breezes,
C'est, vers les ramures grises,	it is, in the grey branches,
Le chœur des petites voix.	the choir of tiny voices.

O le frêle et frais murmure!
Cela gazouille et susurre.
Cela ressemble au cri doux
Que l'herbe agitée expire...
Tu dirais, sous l'eau qui vire,

Le roulis sourd des cailloux.

Cette âme qui se lamente
En cette plainte dormante,
C'est la nôtre, n'est-ce pas?
La mienne, dis, et la tienne, √
Dont s'exhale l'humble antienne
Par ce tiède soir, tout bas?

O the frail, fresh murmuring!
That twittering and whispering
is like the sweet cry
breathed out by the ruffled grass. . . .
You would say, beneath the swirling
        waters,
the muted rolling of the pebbles.

This soul which mourns
in subdued lamentation,
it is ours, is it not?
Mine, say, and yours,
breathing a humble anthem
in the warm evening, very softly?

Paul Verlaine

In these beautiful verses the poet addresses his beloved and describes for her the warm summer evening rustling with all the delicate sounds of nature, attuned to the lovers' tender voluptuousness. The languid and sensuous music could not be more in accord with the poem, following each of its inflexions and of its intentions. Both singer and pianist must achieve the smoothest possible legato as well as the most beautiful quality of tone.

The original key is E major, the initial tempo about ♪ = 54. In the second line, 'C'est la fatigue amoureuse', one must observe the crescendo and the *subito p* on the syllable 'reu'. The following lines, 'C'est tous les frissons des bois Parmi l'étreinte des brises', are a shade faster (perhaps more in feeling than really in tempo), with a little line on each note, mysterious, almost breathy. 'Le chœur des petites voix' is '*molto* ritenuto', but very gradual: the last ♪ of the bar being about twice as slow as the first one. Then *a tempo* for four bars and a *poco a poco animato* which lasts five bars. There is *no rallentando* with the diminuendo on 'Que l'herbe agitée expire'. The *tempo animato* should be maintained also on the following lines: 'Tu dirais, sous l'eau qui vire', etc. and it is still more *animato* from 'C'est la nôtre...'. On the top A, 'la tienne', one must pronounce the 'n' only (no final [ə]) at the end of the word, and take a breath before the descending phrase: 'Dont s'exhale l'humble antienne' which should definitely be *rallentando* (the syllable 'l'hum' well settled on the G sharp) to bring back the *tempo primo* on 'Par ce tiède soir', which has to be sung with a warm colour and not too *p*, to allow a real whispered *pp* on 'tout bas'. The last four bars of the piano must be played *sempre rallentando* and with beautiful sonority.

IL PLEURE DANS MON CŒUR...	TEARS FALL IN MY HEART
Il pleure dans mon cœur	Tears fall in my heart
Comme il pleut sur la ville.	like rain upon the town,
Quelle est cette langueur	what is this languor
Qui pénètre mon cœur ?	that pervades my heart ?
Ô bruit doux de la pluie	O gentle sound of the rain
Par terre et sur les toits,	on the ground and on the roofs!
Pour un cœur qui s'ennuie,	For a listless heart,
Ô le bruit de la pluie!	O the sound of the rain!
Il pleure sans raison	Tears fall without reason
Dans ce cœur qui s'écœure.	in this sickened heart.
Quoi! nulle trahison ?	What! no perfidy ?
Ce deuil est sans raison.	This sorrow has no cause.
C'est bien la pire peine	Indeed it is the worst pain
De ne savoir pourquoi,	not to know why,
Sans amour et sans | haine,	without love and without hate,
Mon cœur a tant de peine.	my heart feels so much pain!

Paul Verlaine

The poet, in his vague and inexplicable melancholy, is at his window listening to the falling rain, and the music discreetly suggests the monotonous patter of the rain. To give the impression of tediousness, the song should be purposely kept monotonous, except for the few bars of recitative. It is difficult to give the impression of being bored without being boring—but this must be done. The expressive climax is only on the last line.

The original key is G sharp minor, the tempo about ♩ = 116 (it is often performed much too slowly).

The poet plays on the alliteration of 'pleure' (pl[œ]r) and 'pleut' (pl[ø]), and the singer can take advantage of that, marking a little these two words, especially with a strong 'pl'. If the long phrase 'Quelle est cette langueur Qui pénètre mon cœur' can be sung in one breath it is better (but not necessary) and easier too, to get a nice curve and top G. There is almost no [ə] at the end of the words 'pluie' and 'ennuie'. The recitative 'Quoi! nulle trahison?' is a little slower and freer, but certainly not dramatic at all in its expression. On the line 'Ce deuil est sans raison' it is better to take the low F on 'ce' not too *p*, to permit the high F to be much more *p*. The following four bars of piano bring back the *tempo primo* gradually and precisely on 'C'est bien la pire peine'. The last line, 'Mon cœur a tant de peine', should be *molto rallentando*. The crescendo should go only as far as 'tant', which is the expressive climax, and 'de' (on C) should already be sung *p*, with the same intensity as 'peine', where one returns exactly to the *tempo primo*.

L'OMBRE DES ARBRES...

L'ombre des_arbres dans la
    rivière embrumée
      Meurt comme de la fumée,
Tandis qu'en l'air, parmi les ramures
    réelles,
      Se plaignent les tourterelles.

Combien, | ô voyageur, ce paysage
    blême
      Te mira blême toi-même,
Et que tristes pleuraient dans les |
    hautes feuillées,
      Tes_espérances noyées.
               Paul Verlaine

THE SHADOW OF THE TREES

The shadow of the trees in the misty
    river
      dies away like smoke,
while on high, among the real
    branches,
      the doves sing their plaint.

How much, O traveller, this wan
    landscape
      wanly reflected yourself,
and in the high foliage how sadly
    wept
      your drowned hopes.

For this mélodie Debussy has quoted an epigraph by Cyrano de Bergerac, which is a good illustration of the poem: 'The nightingale, which from the top of a branch looks down at its reflection, believes it has fallen into the river. It is at the top of an oak tree and yet is afraid of being drowned.' So the hopes of the poet, crying in the high branches, are for him already drowned, while he sees himself reflected in the misty and wan landscape. Both singer and pianist have to suggest this atmosphere in the first stanza of this highly impressionistic mélodie. The second stanza, being quite subjective, reaches a truly expressive climax.

The key is C major, the tempo ♩ = 50, slow and sad, is indicated by Debussy; we may add: very soft and legato. The stress on the first beat of the fourth bar in the piano part is no more than a little weight on this chord. The small crescendo on the eighth bar in the voice part (while the piano has a diminuendo) is merely to allow the voice to rise, giving greater ease and effectiveness to the *p* on the F sharp of 'se plaignent'.

The second stanza starts *p*, but is already more intense and different in colour, the declamation is broader. Then come the four bars of crescendo and *accelerando* on 'Te mira blême toi-même'. There must be no hurry in the singer's attack of the top A sharp, which should be as *subito p* as possible, for it is important to return suddenly to the slow *tempo primo*. All the desperate feeling of the last two lines should be expressed *p* and *pp*, with beautiful vocal effects; then comes the superb piano conclusion, played very slowly and quietly, with the most subtle, almost orchestral sonorities.

CHEVAUX DE BOIS

Tournez, tournez, bons chevaux de bois,
Tournez cent tours, tournez mille tours;
Tournez souvent | et tournez toujours,
Tournez, tournez | au son des | hautbois.

L'enfant tout rouge | et la mère blanche,
Le gars | en noir et la fille en rose,
L'une à la chose et l'autre à la pose,

Chacun se paie un sou de dimanche.

MERRY-GO-ROUND

Turn, turn, fine merry-go-round,

turn a hundred times, turn a thousand times,
turn often and go on turning,

turn to the sound of the oboes.

The rubicund child and the pale mother,
the lad in black and the girl in pink,
the one down to earth, the other showing off,
each one has his Sunday pennyworth.

Tournez, tournez, chevaux de leur
   cœur,
Tandi$ qu'autour de tous vos tournois,
Clignote l'œil du filou sournois,

Tournez | au son du piston vainqueur.

C'est_étonnant comme ça vous soûle
D'aller_ainsi dans ce cirque bête,
Rien dans le ventre et mal dans la
   tête,
Du mal en masse et du bien | en foule.

Tournez, dadas, sans qu'il soit besoin
D'user jamais de nuls_éperons
Pour commander | à vos galops ronds,
Tournez, tournez, sans_espoir de
   foin.

Et dépéchez, chevaux de leur âme,
Déjà voici que sonne à la soupe
La nuit qui tombe et chasse la troupe
De gais buveurs que leur soif affame.

Tournez, tournez! Le ciel en velours
D'astres_en or se vêt lentement.
L'église tinte un glas tristement.

Tournez | au son joyeux des
   tambours.

          Paul Verlaine

Turn, turn, merry-go-round of their
   hearts,
while around all your whirling
squints the eye of the
   crafty pickpocket,
turn to the sound of the triumphant
   cornet.

It is astonishing how intoxicating it is
to ride thus in this stupid circle,
with a sinking stomach and an
   aching head,
heaps of discomfort and plenty of fun.

Turn, gee-gees, without any need
ever to use spurs
to keep you at the gallop,
turn, turn, without hope of hay.

And hurry, horses of their souls,
already the supper bell is ringing,
night falls and chases away the troop
of gay drinkers famished by their
   thirst.

Turn, turn! The velvet sky
is slowly pricked with golden stars.
The church bell tolls a mournful
   knell,
turn to merry beating of the drums.

The poet, with an aching head and an empty stomach, tries to while away his boredom, and his loneliness and poverty, by riding on a merry-go-round. The scene is a little village fair in Belgium (Paysages Belges), at the end of the nineteenth century. This is sufficient to indicate that the tempo of this mélodie must not be too fast (Debussy indicates 'allegro *non tanto*'); the merry-go-round is not one of the fast engines of our modern fairs, but one of those turned by a handle; the nasal music of its little wooden organ, which is heard in the piano prelude, should immediately give the right mood and tempo. I suggest ♩ = 88. (The original key is E major.)

There are many nuances indicated in this mélodie and they should be carefully observed. For example, the two short crescendos on 'Tournez cent tours' and 'tournez mille tours'. In the last line of the first and third stanzas, the liaisons 'tournez au son…' are optional. I personally find the liaison too refined for the character of the poem. In the second stanza, the word 'gars' is pronounced g[ɑ]—no 'r', no 's', no liaison. In the third stanza watch the *subito p* and staccato on 'clignote l'œil'— 'Discreetly' says Debussy. The fourth stanza of the poem is bitter, with a touch of coarseness; this is more difficult to express successfully in a woman's voice. It should be sung *mf*, intense, with well-marked accents, particularly on the triplet of the bar in ¼. No liaison between 'bien' and 'en'.

From the beginning of the sixth stanza, the night is gradually falling, and the long *ritenuto poco a poco* of twenty bars should also be very gradually established, ending in the tempo being twice as slow. I suggest that on the first ten bars there be very little *ritardando*, but much more on the last ten bars, particularly on the four bars of piano: the pianist should start counting in four. In the seventh stanza, the poet is seized by the beauty of the night and the tolling of the bells; but he ends, on the last line, with a kind of forced gaiety, returning to the exact *tempo primo*; all vanishes in a recall of the first theme.

GREEN

Voici des fruits, des fleurs, des feuilles_et des branches,
Et puis voici mon cœur, qui ne bat que pour vous.
Ne le déchirez pas | avec vos deux mains blanches,
Et qu'à vos_ yeux si beaux l'humble présent soit doux.

GREEN

Here are fruits, flowers, leaves and branches,
and here too is my heart that beats only for you.
Do not destroy it with your two white hands,
and to your lovely eyes may the humble gift seem sweet.

J'arrive tout couvert encore de rosée	I come still covered with dew
Que le vent du matin vient glacer à mon front.	that the morning breeze has chilled on my brow.
Souffrez que ma fatigue, à vos pieds reposée,	Let my weariness, resting at your feet,
Rêve des chers instants qui la délasseront.	dream of dear moments which will bring repose.
Sur votre jeune sein laisser rouler ma tête,	On your young breast let me rest my head
Toute sonore encore de vos derniers baisers;	still ringing with your last kisses;
Laissez-la s'apaiser de la bonne tempête,	let it be appeased after the good tempest,
Et que je dorme un peu puisque vous reposez.	that I may sleep a little as you rest.

Paul Verlaine

This beautiful mélodie can be taken as a good example of Debussy's genius in setting a poem. If we compare his setting with that of Fauré, we are struck by the contrast. Fauré's mélodie is certainly very lovely music, and creates around the poem the right atmosphere, but Debussy follows exactly every inflexion of the words, every sentiment of the poem.

The little four-bar prelude of the piano (watch the two little crescendi for the left hand) already expresses to perfection the breathlessness and the spontaneity of the young lover arriving enthusiastically with flowers in his arms. The tempo *joyeusement animé* (joyously animated) is about ♩. = 104. The key, curiously full of joy, is in the minor—A flat minor. The singer should watch the evenness of his duplets. There is only a very little *ritardando* on 'qui ne bat que pour vous'; then *a tempo* for the difficult full-tone scales. It is better on 'blanches' not to pronounce the final [ə], just the 'ch'. The arpeggio of the piano is very fluid and gradually slows down, becoming even more *ritenuto* on 'L'humble présent soit doux' (observe the indicated stresses).

This first stanza should be sung with enthusiasm and tenderness, and the same mood sustained for the second stanza. It should be the same tempo, of course. In the third and fourth bars of this second stanza, it is the left hand of the piano part which is musically important—not the coloratura of the right hand—and it should be played with a singing tone; the same applies two bars further on. The line 'Que le vent du matin vient glacer à mon front' is *non legato* more than really staccato, and the indicated crescendo–decrescendo is important. Then the mood changes with 'un peu retenu' (*poco ritenuto*), and very legato. The indications for the line 'Rêve des chers instants qui la délasseront' are not very clear. *Serrez* means *accelerando* and applies to the first two bars. One has to launch the curve of the musical phrase with a *crescendo-accelerando*; and then on 'la délasseront', *molto diminuendo* and *ritardando*. This brings in the slower tempo *Andantino* (♩. = 72) of the third stanza, in which the mood is completely different and is so well captured by Debussy. The musical theme is the same as in the first stanza, but the quiet pace of the music suggested by the poem indicates that the young lover has had his reward, and gradually the tempo becomes progressively slower up to the end of the mélodie. Debussy's indication, 'caressant', invites the singer to achieve the sweetest possible vocal line, with a beautiful (and difficult) *ritenuto* and *diminuendo* on 'de vos derniers baisers'. In the *plus lent* the note values of the voice must be even and precise up to the end. The piano sings the theme:

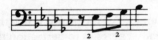

and the two lovers fall asleep.

SPLEEN

Les roses étaient toutes rouges,
Et les lierres étaient tout noirs.
Chère, pour peu que tu te bouges,
Renaissent tous mes désespoirs.

Le ciel était trop bleu, trop tendre,
La mer trop verte et l'air trop doux.
Je crains toujours, | ce qu'est
    d'attendre !
Quelque fuite atroce de vous.

SPLEEN

The roses were all red,
and the ivy quite black.
Dearest, if you so much as move
all my despair returns.

The sky was too blue, too tender,
the sea too green and the air too soft.
Always I fear, such is the consequence
    of waiting!
some pitiless abandonment by you.

Du houx | à la feuille vernie
Et du luisant buis, je suis las,

Of the holly with its glossy leaves
and of the shining box tree, I am
  weary,

Et de la campagne infinie,
Et de tout, fors de vous, hélas!

and of the boundless countryside,
and of everything but you, alas!

Paul Verlaine

This is certainly a difficult poem and a difficult mélodie, but Debussy, by his setting, once more succeeds in making the meaning of the poem clearer. The 'spleen' of the poet is expressed by his weariness of everything in nature, as can be seen in the first two lines of each stanza, with the climax in the third line of the last stanza. And why this spleen and this weariness? Because of his love and his anxiety about it, as expressed in the last two lines of the first and second stanzas and the desperate conclusion of the last line of the last stanza. These contrasts of spleen and of anxiety Debussy has expressed perfectly, with the same musical theme throughout the mélodie passing through the different moods:

The *tempo primo* is about ♩ = 52 (the key F minor). The repeated E natural of the first two lines must be sung *sotto voce* and very even in rhythm. As always with Debussy's music, one must take care never to mark the beats with the voice.

The sudden outpouring of the following two lines is *con moto*, nearly twice as fast as the *tempo primo*, with uneasiness, but without reaching more than a *mf*.

Now comes again the 'spleen' feeling, with the *tempo primo* and the dynamics *p* and *pp*. Then, beginning in slow tempo and with the musical theme, comes again the feeling of anxiety. (One has to make an expressive pause, or breath, between 'Je crains toujours' and 'ce qu'est d'attendre', which is in parenthesis.) And, expressing the poet's unbearable weariness, a big crescendo and *accelerando* begins, which leads to the great climax on the B flat. On this very note, one has suddenly to return to the very slow *tempo primo*, in total despair. And the repeated musical theme, *molto rallentando*, brings the sad and bitter conclusion: 'hélas!' intense in the *p*.

*

Two years after the *Ariettes Oubliées*, Debussy published another series of mélodies: *Cinq Poèmes de Baudelaire*, very different in their spirit and their musical writing, curiously much less typical of his personality. But it is true that the density, the sumptuousness, the broad inspiration of Baudelaire's poems demanded music much more lyrical in style, of a more symphonic texture. At that time 'Wagnerism' was dominating the whole of Western music, and Debussy shows in these mélodies the obvious influence of his two recent visits to Bayreuth, though this influence was quite brief and was followed by a violent reaction.

These mélodies are very demanding for their interpreters: the singer must have a generous voice of good range, and the pianist must suggest an orchestral accompaniment. ('Le jet d'eau' exists with Debussy's own orchestration.) Only two of these long mélodies can be studied in this book.

LE JET D'EAU

Tes beaux yeux sont las, pauvre
    amante!
Reste longtemps sans les rouvrir,
Dans cette pose nonchalante
Où t'a surprise le plaisir.

Dans la cour le jet d'eau qui jase

Et ne se tait ni nuit ni jour,
Entretient doucement l'extase
Où ce soir m'a plongé l'amour.

    La gerbe d'eau qui berce
      Ses mille fleurs,
    Que la lune traverse
      De ses pâleurs,
    Tombe comme une averse
      De larges pleurs.

THE FOUNTAIN

Your lovely eyes are tired, poor
    beloved!
Stay long without opening them,
in this languid pose
where pleasure has taken you by
    surprise.

In the courtyard the fountain that
    babbles
and is never silent night or day,
sweetly prolongs the ecstasy
into which this evening love has
    plunged me.

    The sheaf of water lulling
      its myriad flowers,
    through which the moon shines
      with its pallid light
    falls like a shower
      of big tears.

Ainsi ton âme qu'incendie
L'éclair brûlant des voluptés

S'élance, rapide et hardie,
Vers les vastes cieux enchantés.
Puis, elle s'épanche, | mourante,
En un flot de triste langueur,
Qui par une invisible pente
Descend jusqu'au fond de mon cœur.

> La gerbe d'eau qui berce
> Ses mille fleurs,
> Que la lune traverse
> De ses pâleurs,
> Tombe comme une averse
> De larges pleurs.

O toi, que la nuit rend si belle,
Qu'il m'est doux, penché vers tes
seins,
D'écouter la plainte éternelle
Qui sanglote dans les bassins!
Lune, | eau sonore, nuit bénie,
Arbres qui frissonnez autour,
Votre pure mélancolie
Est le miroir de mon amour.

> La gerbe d'eau qui berce
> Ses mille fleurs,
> Que la lune traverse
> De ses pâleurs,
> Tombe comme une averse
> De larges pleurs.

Thus your soul set ablaze
by the burning flash of sensuous
delight

darts with speed and fearlessness
towards the vast enchanted heavens.
Then, it overflows, dying,
in a wave of sorrowful languor,
which by an invisible sloping path
descends to the depths of my heart.

> The sheaf of water lulling
> its myriad flowers,
> through which the moon shines
> with its pallid light,
> falls like a shower
> of big tears.

O you, whom night so beautifies,
how sweet it is for me, leaning on
your breast,
to listen to the eternal plaint
which sobs in the marble basins!
Moon, plashing water, blessed night,
trees that quiver around us,
your pure melancholy
is the mirror of my love.

> The sheaf of water lulling
> its myriad flowers,
> through which the moon shines
> with its pallid light,
> falls like a shower
> of big tears.

Charles Baudelaire

This sensuous poem and its peculiar form and rhythm has been expressed musically with amazing intelligence and sensitivity.

The original key is C major, the tempo is ♩ = 52. The prefatory indication excellently suggests the mood: *languido* (languid) and, one might add, lingering and amorous; the legato must be extreme, almost *portamento*. In the first stanza there is scarcely any change of

dynamics. No crescendo when the voice goes up, rather the contrary.
At the end of the first stanza there is a *ritardando* in the two bars of the
piano which brings in the *più mosso* of the first refrain. (These bars are
in ⁶₈, an obviously forgotten indication.) The groups:

become in the new tempo:

so practically the ♪ of the last beat in ⁶₈ becomes the ♩ of the ³₄, and this
gives the right tempo for all the refrain. I suggest beginning the indicated *en retenant* at the end of this refrain one bar earlier, on 'larges
pleurs', with a little line on each note. The tempo is now a little slower,
but must not lose the excitement and ardour of both poem and music,
and soon an *accelerando* begins as well as a crescendo, the climax of
which is on 'cieux'. There is a diminuendo and, no doubt, a little
ritenuto on the last beat of this bar, on the word 'enchantés', or rather a
slight hesitation before the first beat on the syllable 'tés', sung really *p*.
This first beat must be immediately in *tempo primo: andantino tranquillo
languido*. A fine and really *p* attack is required on the F sharp and a
liaison for 'Puis_elle'. I suggest that the return to the fast tempo of the
refrain should be attained gradually during the bar 'La gerbe'. Again
at the end of this second refrain one can bring back the *meno mosso,
tempo rubato* with a gradual small *ritenuto* on 'larges pleurs'. One is now
back to a tempo which is about that of the line 'Ainsi ton âme qu'incendie', but this time there is no *accelerando* or crescendo, and one has
two bars (one in ³₄, one in ⁴₄) to bring back the *a tempo* indicated *più
lento* which is practically the *tempo primo*. The singer on the four

following bars has an excellent opportunity of displaying beautiful vocal effects: *pp* on the top notes, languorous phrasing, etc. And one does not have to change this slow tempo at all for the third refrain, which, in contrast to the other two, is in *tempo primo, andantino tranquillo*. The last seven bars of the mélodie are progressively slower, fading away in languorous ecstasy.

RECUEILLEMENT

Sois sage, | ô ma Douleur, et tiens-toi
    plus tranquille.
Tu réclamais le Soir; il descend; le
    voici:
Une atmosphère obscure enveloppe
    la ville,
Aux uns portant la paix, aux
    autres le souci.

Pendant que des mortels la multitude
    vile,
Sous le fouet du Plaisir, ce bourreau
    sans merci,
Va cueillir des remords dans la fête
    servile,
Ma Douleur, donne-moi la main;
    viens par ici,

Loin d'eux. Vois se pencher les
    défuntes Années,
Sur les balcons du ciel, en robes
    surannées;
Surgir du fond des eaux le Regret
    souriant;

Le Soleil moribond s'endormir
    sous une arche,
Et, ✓ comme un long linceul
    traînant à l'Orient,
Entends, ma chère, entends la douce
    Nuit qui marche.

Charles Baudelaire

CONTEMPLATION

Be still, O my sorrow, and remain
    more calm.
You called for the evening; it
    descends; it is here:
a sombre atmosphere envelops the
    town,
bringing peace to some, to others
    care.

While the base multitude of mortals

under the whip of pleasure, this
    merciless tormentor,
goes to gather remorse in the baleful
    festival,
my Sorrow, give me your hand;
    come hither,

far away from them. See the dead
    years leaning
over the balconies of the sky, in
    outdated garments;
smiling Regret rising up from the
    depths of the waters.

The dying sun goes to sleep beneath
    an arc,
and, like a long shroud trailing
    towards the east,
hear, my dear, hear the steps of the
    gentle night.

A complete contrast to the sensual atmosphere of 'Le jet d'eau'. In this magnificent poem the poet addresses his sorrow, appealing to it to go with him in the night; he even calls it 'ma chère' in the last line. The broad and dramatic tension, the sombre mood of these verses have inspired Debussy to write one of his masterpieces.

The original key is C sharp minor–major, the tempo about ♩ = 52. In the prelude the pianist must at once establish the mood. His part is quite orchestral and should suggest the timbres of different instruments, the two successive crescendos (in bars four and five) should be emphasized. The prosody of the poem is so perfect during the first two lines of introduction that the singer must respect carefully the rhythm, and especially the rests. He should use a dark, full-toned colour of voice, not too *p* (it is a big song), and it must be well sustained (no *parlando*).

Then comes a *tempo rubato* (about ♩ = 60). The piano part obviously suggests the vague sounds of a big city in the coming night. From 'pendant que des mortels...' the singer gives not only more strength to his voice but more strength to his articulation, and builds up a big crescendo and *animato*. I cannot agree with the *diminuendo molto* indicated on 'dans la fête servile'; the voice comes down to the low register and must express bitterness and scornfulness.

In the following five bars the music is the same as in the prelude, and rightly so: the two lines of verses being in exactly the same mood as the beginning of the poem. I recommend a stress on the word 'loin'.

The same slow tempo (*tempo primo*) should be maintained for the following section. The first vocal phrase is *p* up to the G sharp. I suggest this nuance in the voice for the two following bars (instead of the one indicated):

sur les balcons du   ciel, en robes   suran - né — es

'le Regret souriant' not too *p*. There is a *ritardando* on 'arche' to bring in a tempo as slow as possible for the wonderful phrase 'comme un long linceul traînant à l'Orient' which *must* be sung in one breath, suggesting the meaning of the words by *legatissimo* and stretching of the vowels. The tempo is still slower for the last bars of the mélodie. In the last phrase of the voice the climax must be a real *pp* on the G sharp. If it cannot be beautifully achieved, it is better not to sing this mélodie. If necessary, a breath can be taken before 'qui marche'. The pianist continues in this very slow tempo to the end.

*

Several mélodies composed by Debussy in 1891 have had to be omitted here, in order to proceed directly to two series of mélodies, settings of Verlaine's poems from the *Fêtes galantes*. The particular spirit of the *Fêtes galantes* has already been described in the study of the mélodies of Gabriel Fauré, and also of Debussy's 'Mandoline'. The reader will find these comments on page 121. Debussy composed two series of *Fêtes galantes*, the first one in 1891, and the second one twelve years later, in 1904. In the first series he chose two poems also set by Fauré: 'En sourdine' and 'Clair de lune'

FÊTES GALANTES I

EN SOURDINE

Calmes dans le demi-jour
Que les branches | hautes font, ✓
Pénétrons bien notre amour
De ce silence profond.

Fondons nos âmes, nos cœurs
Et nos sens extasiés,
Parmi les vagues langueurs
Des pins et des arbousiers.

Ferme tes yeux à demi,
Croise tes bras sur ton sein,
Et de ton cœur endormi
Chasse à jamais tout dessein.

MUTED

Calm in the half light
made by the tall branches,
let our love be imbued
with this deep silence.

Let us merge our souls, our hearts
and our ecstatic senses
with the vague languors
of the pines and the arbutus.

Half close your eyes,
fold your arms across your breast,
and from your sleeping heart
for ever drive away all purpose.

Laissons-nous persuader |
Au souffle berceur et doux
Qui vient_à tes pieds rider
les_ondes de gazon roux.

Let us surrender
to the soothing, gentle zephyr
that comes to ruffle at your feet
the waves of russet grass.

Et quand, solennel, le soir √
Des chênes noirs tombera,
Voix de notre désespoir,
Le rossignol chantera.

And when, solemnly, evening
falls from the dark oak trees,
voice of our despair,
the nightingale will sing.

Paul Verlaine

As usual Debussy, in setting these beautiful love poems, follows much more closely than Fauré the meaning of each line and even of each word. The original key is G sharp minor, the tempo $\quad = 48$. In the short piano prelude is heard, 'soft and expressive', the voice of the nightingale singing in the great oaks of the park (this is the musical theme of the mélodie), and it should create an atmosphere of 'profond silence'. The singer enters *p* (and in the whole song he never sings louder than a *mf*), with a warm and tender quality in his voice. The dynamics and the breath should be observed in the bar 'branches hautes font, √ Pénétrons bien', a quick breath of course, but with no hurry; the rhythm can be supple. There is a *poco a poco animato* on the line 'Fondons nos âmes, nos cœurs, Et nos sens extasiés', which is exactly counterbalanced by a *ritardando* on the three notes of 'Parmi les', leading to the exact *tempo primo* on 'vagues langueurs Des pins et des arbousiers'. N.B.: (1) The liaison must be made between 'cœurs' and 'et' in spite of the fact that they are in two different lines of the verse. (2) The 's' at the end of the word 'sens' is a hard 's', not 'z'. (3) 'Parmi les vagues langueurs Des pins et des arbousiers' should be in one breath.

Now an *animato* begins, which should be gradual. A faster tempo, about $\quad = 72$, should be reached within three bars and this tempo should continue to the *un peu plus lent* (the pianists often have a tendency to slow down their two solo bars in triplets). But this *tempo animato* should not give the slightest feeling of agitation: the two lovers remain lazily entranced.

The *un peu plus lent* is actually the *tempo primo*, with the theme of the nightingale. The singer has plenty of time to sing 'Et quand, solennel (pronounced s[ɔ]l[a]n[ɛ]l), le soir √ Des chênes noirs tombera' quite calmly and the last lines quite slowly, well phrased, with a nice *p* attack on the F sharp. The word 'désespoir' should not be emphasized; it is not truly despair, but amorous melancholy. The piano conclusion is the song of the nightingale fading away in the night.

In the original order of the French edition, 'Fantoches' follows as a scherzo between two slow movements.

FANTOCHES	MARIONETTES
Scaramouche et Pulcinella Qu'un mauvais dessein rassembla	Scaramouche and Pulcinella whom a nefarious plot brought together,
Gesticulent, noirs sous la lune.	gesticulate, black beneath the moon.
Cependant l'excellent docteur Bolonais cueille avec lenteur Des simples parmi l'herbe brune.	Meanwhile the excellent doctor from Bologna leisurely gathers medicinal herbs in the dark grass.
Lors sa fille, piquant minois, Sous la charmille ✓ en tapinois Se glisse demi-nue, en quête	Then his daughter, prettily piquant, beneath the hedge stealthily glides half naked, in quest
De son beau pirate espagnol; Dont un amoureux rossignol Clame la détresse à tue-tête. <div align="right">*Paul Verlaine*</div>	of her handsome Spanish pirate, of whom an amorous nightingale proclaims the distress at the top of its voice.

This charming little poem evokes the fanciful characters of the old Italian Comedy, and the music is a witty scherzo, about $\textstyle\quad = 126$ (the original key is A). It requires from both performers a rhythmic, almost metronomic precision, a biting articulation, and, of course, humour and elegance. Verlaine uses the Italian word 'Pulcinella' instead of the French 'Polichinelle' (Punch), so it should be pronounced in the Italian way. It is not easy, with the three 'l's, to sing it in rhythm:

Pulcinel - la

The rhythm:

- sein rassembla

is also difficult. Rhythmic precision is required on the la, la, la, with the contrasts of quavers, semiquavers and triplets, and also of staccato and legato. Throughout the whole mélodie, these la, la, la, should have their appropriate meaning. The first ones suggest the gesticulation of the two droll figures; attack *mf* and there is an exaggerated crescendo-diminuendo on the triplets. Careful stress and nuances for 'Cependant l'excellent docteur Bolonais', 'cueille avec lenteur Des simples' is *subito pp* and very legato. Very fast crescendo to a real *f* on 'parmi l'herbe brune'. (There is a misprint in certain editions: the flat of the A on 'parmi' is obviously forgotten.) Not too *p* on 'Lors sa fille' and more *p* on 'piquant minois'. A little *portamento* (without anticipating the 'l'!) for the big jump 'Sous la charmille'. 'En tapinois' is *pp*, then the dynamics are difficult in tempo: 'se' is *molto crescendo* and *porta-mento*, but 'glisse' is *p subito*. The following 'la, la, la' suggest the naughty girl going secretly to meet her lover: they should be light, staccato, with a big crescendo–diminuendo. Do not miss the Spanish music in the left hand when the Spanish pirate is evoked. The wonderful effect of a big crescendo on 'Clame la détresse à tue-<u>tê</u>te', with climax on the attack of 'tê' and diminuendo to *pp* on the top A should be made without the slightest *rubato*. For the last

la   <u>la</u> ——   <u>la</u> ——

the dynamics and stresses must be carefully observed. Last pirouettes of the two mischievous characters, they can suggest the disappearance —the first one of Scaramouche, the second one of Pulcinella.

CLAIR DE LUNE	MOONLIGHT
Votre âme est un paysage choisi	Your soul is a chosen landscape
Que vont charmant masques et bergamasques,	to which maskers and bergamasks bring delight,
Jouant du luth, et dansant, et quasi	playing the lute and dancing, and almost
Tristes sous leurs déguisements fantasques.	sad beneath their fanciful disguises.
Tout en chantant sur le mode mineur	While singing in the minor key
L'amour vainqueur et la vie opportune,	of victorious love and the propitious life,
Ils n'ont pas l'air de croire à leur bonheur	they do not seem to believe in their happiness
Et leur chanson se mêle au clair de lune.	and their song mingles with the moonlight,
Au calme clair de lune triste et beau,	with the calm moonlight, sad and beautiful,
Qui fait rêver les oiseaux dans les arbres	which brings dreams to the birds in the trees
Et sangloter d'extase les jets d'eau,	and makes the fountains sob with ecstasy,
Les grands jets d'eau sveltes parmi les marbres.	the tall slender fountains among the marble statues.

Paul Verlaine

The three quatrains of this poem have been set by Debussy in a most subdued light, a most poetic atmosphere, quite different from Fauré's graceful minuet. The four bars of piano prelude are like a lazy improvisation (the original key is G sharp minor), and can create the right mood for the singer. I mean by this, that listening to them will inspire him to find the right colour for his first phrase. And also, of course, the right tempo, about ♪ = 100.

The first quatrain remains in this very slow tempo, in the same dynamics: *p*, and with perfect legato. The second quatrain, *poco più animato* but not too much (about ♪ = 112), again maintains its tempo for its eight long bars. The singer must be able to sing each line of the verses in one breath. The slight crescendo indicated should not reach more than a *mf*, but there should not be too much diminuendo on

'Et leur chanson se mêle au clair de lune', to give effectiveness to the contrast: *p subito* and *subito tempo primo*, on the first line of the last quatrain. There can be a slight *ritardando* on the last beat before this *tempo primo*, which should give the impression of perfect calm, the pianist playing with a singing tone the little theme:

and the singer avoiding any involuntary nuance, his voice being evenly *p* from top F sharp to low E. One cannot take a breath in the line 'Et sangloter d'extase les jets d'eau'. The little crescendo on this line should not go further than the word 'extase'; then a slight diminuendo on 'les jets', with a slight suppleness in the tempo, prepares the *pp* on 'd'eau'. The last phrase in this slow tempo is almost impossible without a breath between 'sveltes' and 'parmi'. The little theme in the left hand of the last bars of piano must be well 'sung'. It is certainly difficult to succeed in creating, both vocally and expressively, the picture of the quiet moonlight, in the great park, with its fountains and marble statues: 'à la française'.

*

FÊTES GALANTES II

The second series of *Fêtes galantes*, written twelve years later, shows the evolution of Debussy's style. These three mélodies are perhaps (with the three *Poèmes de Mallarmé*) the most subtle he ever wrote. A kind of mysterious haze seems to blur these three pictures. Therefore one must beware of giving them too tangible a reality.

LES INGÉNUS	THE INGENUOUS ONES
Les hauts talons luttaient avec les longues jupes,	The high heels contended with the long skirts,
En sorte que, selon le terrain | et le vent,—	so that, according to the ground and the wind,—

Parfois luisaient des bas de jambes,
    trop souvent✓
Interceptés!—et nous‿aimions ce jeu
    de dupes.

Parfois‿aussi le dard d'un‿insecte
    jaloux
Inquiétait le col des belles sous les
    branches,
Et c'était des éclairs soudains de
    nuques blanches.
Et ce régal comblait nos jeunes‿yeux
    de fous.

Le soir tombait, un soir équivoque
    d'automne:
Les belles, se pendant rêveuses‿à nos
    bras,
Dirent‿alors des mots si spécieux,
    tout bas,
Que notre‿âme depuis ce temps ✓
    tremble et s'étonne.

one caught an occasional glimpse of
    the lower part of legs, too often
intercepted!—and we loved this
    dupe's play.

At times also the sting of a covetous
    insect
troubled the neck of the fair ones
    under the branches,
and there were sudden flashes of
    white necks,
and this was a feast for our doting
    young eyes.

The evening descended, an uncertain
    evening of Autumn:
the fair ones, dreamily hanging on
    our arms,
softly murmured then such specious
    words
that our souls ever since tremble and
    are amazed.

Paul Verlaine

    This mélodie, with its uncertain and changing tonality, pictures very well the wavering characters of the young Watteau figures, in the mist of a warm autumnal night, feeling confusedly their first sensual perplexity.

    The original key is rather ambiguous but begins as follows:

the tempo about ♪ = 108 and precise. The vocal line, with all the repeated notes, must be sung with a sustained legato, not *parlando*. There is a slight *rallentando* on the bar 'interceptés', then immediately *a tempo*. (C, D, E in the piano part are important.) Now begins a *poco a poco animato* and crescendo of nine bars, followed by one bar of marked *rallentando* and *diminuendo*, leading to a very slow tempo, correctly indicated 'twice as slow' as the *animato* previously reached. Five bars later this tempo slows down quite noticeably and arrives at a really very slow tempo for the last bars. They should not give the impression of a conclusion; a strange atmosphere should be created: uncertain, confused, interrogative. . . .

LE FAUNE	THE FAUN
Un vieux faune de terre cuite	An old terra-cotta faun
Rit au centre des boulingrins,	laughs in the centre of the lawns,
Présageant sans doute une suite	doubtless presaging a sequel
Mauvaise à ces instants sereins	less happy to these serene moments
Qui m'ont conduit | et t'ont conduite,	which have led me and you,
—Mélancoliques pélerins,—	—melancholy pilgrims—
Jusqu'à cette heure dont la fuite ✓	to this hour whose flight
Tournoie au son de tambourins.	whirls to the sound of the
Paul Verlaine	tambourines.

The two lovers have left the feast, of which the tambourines are heard in the distance, and they have come to a lonely part of the park where there is the statue of a faun, and one of them expresses the transience of their happiness.

The descending patterns of a flute, the constant rhythm of the tambourine (the original key is D minor, the tempo $\downarrow = 69$) are enough to set the scene, and the voice sings its part very simply, with scarcely any nuances. Only the 'presence' of the performer can give life to this highly poetic picture. The two lines 'Présageant sans doute une suite Mauvaise à ces instants sereins' must be sung in one breath. There is a *poco animato* (very little) on four bars: 'Qui m'ont conduit', etc. (no liaison between 'conduit' and 'et'), but soon the monotonous *tempo primo* returns.

COLLOQUE SENTIMENTAL	SENTIMENTAL COLLOQUY
Dans le vieux parc solitaire et glacé	In the old, deserted, frosty park
Deux formes ont tout à l'heure passé.	two forms have just passed.

Leurs_yeux sont morts | et leurs
lèvres sont molles,
Et l'on_entend_à peine leurs paroles.

Their eyes are dead and their lips are
weak,
and their words can scarcely be heard.

Dans le vieux parc solitaire_et glacé
Deux spectres ont_évoqué le passé.

In the old, deserted, frosty park
two ghosts have recalled the past.

—Te souvient-il de notre_extase_
ancienne ?
—Pourquoi voulez-vous donc qu'il
m'en souvienne ?

—Do you remember our past
ecstasy ?
—Why do you want me to
remember it ?

Ton cœur bat-il toujours à mon seul
nom ?
Toujours vois-tu mon_âme_en rêve ?
—Non.

—Does your heart beat always just
to hear my name ?
Do you always see my soul in your
dreams ?—No.

—Ah ! les beaux jours de bonheur
indicible
Où nous joignions nos bouches !—
C'est possible.

—Ah ! the rapturous days of inexpressible happiness
when our lips met !—Possibly.

—Qu'il était bleu le ciel, ✓ et grand,
l'espoir !
—L'espoir a fui, | vaincu, ✓ vers le
ciel noir.

—How blue the sky was, and how
high our hopes !
—Hope has flown, vanquished,
towards the dark sky.

Tels_ils marchaient dans les_avoines
folles,
Et la nuit seule | entendit leurs paroles.
Paul Verlaine

Thus they walked in the wild oat
grass,
and the night alone heard their words.

This is one of the most beautiful of Debussy's mélodies, but one of
the most difficult and subtle. Edward Lockspeiser says that it is like a
Latin counterpart of the Germanic Schubert's 'Doppelgänger'. But
here there is nothing frightening about the ghosts of the two lovers
coming back to the cold, deserted park. They show that there is a
background of poetic melancholy in all these poems of the *Fêtes
galantes*, which may often seem only frivolous and elegant. (The
original key is A minor. Never to be transposed !)

This mélodie can be divided into three parts: (1) The introduction of the narrator: (2) The dialogue between the two ghosts: (3) The conclusion of the narrator. This is to say that the singer must succeed in giving three different colours to his voice: the narrator and the two ghosts.

(1) Introduction. The short piano prelude must be sufficient to suggest the frosty night and the deserted park. (Tempo about ♩ = 45.) The voice of the poet enters *p* and without any nuance (no crescendo when the voice goes up), legato, stretching the vowel sounds (no *parlando*), and with perfect evenness of the quavers or triplets. There is a *ritenuto* only in the last two bars of the introduction. Nothing should be dramatic in the expression, but objective and mysterious. The liaisons are optional in the two lines 'Deux formes ont tout à l'heure passé' and 'Deux spectres ont évoqué le passé'. It is more singable with the liaison and more expressive without.

(2) Dialogue. In the piano part is heard expressive, melancholy and distant, the song of the nightingale, to which the lovers at the height of their love were listening in the 'profond silence' of 'En sourdine', the first mélodie of the first series of *Fêtes galantes*. This time it comes as a remote remembrance, to bring back to earth the ghosts of the two lovers. It seems obvious, from the tessitura and the writing of the music, that the first one to speak is the woman. She asked: 'Te souvient-il de notre extase ancienne?' With a clear voice, very simple and quite confident. But he replies, in a slower tempo, with a darker timbre (which should not be overdone), and with a cold and indifferent expression: 'Pourquoi voulez-vous donc qu'il m'en souvienne?' Back to the tempo for the nightingale theme, she asks with more insistence: 'Ton cœur bat-il toujours à mon seul nom? Toujours vois-tu mon âme en rêve?' Exactly in tempo; no *ritardando* on 'rêve'; the first beat of the following bar must come abruptly. And now the terrible 'Non'. It must drop down (with a strong 'n') exactly in tempo, with all the weight of indifference and fate. Then, in a desperate climax, the poor woman-ghost tries to evoke the rapture of their past love. It is expressed in the music with five bars of a marked *animato* and *crescendo poco a poco*. 'Ah! les beaux jours de bonheur indicible' (It is better to take a good breath after 'Ah!'). There should be a sudden *p* and a gradual *ritardando* on

'où nous joignions nos bouches'. This *ritardando* has to be kept up *to the end* of its second bar. No hurry. Now comes, exactly in tempo, the flat, the ruthless: 'C'est possible', almost *parlando*, stress on the syllable 'si'. In the following bar the piano sings expressively (E, D) and building up a crescendo, piano and voice express the total despair of 'Qu'il était bleu le ciel, et grand, l'espoir!' The arpeggio chord on the next bar is *subito p*, cold, and then comes the appalling last statement of the man-ghost, who evidently is beyond all human passion: 'L'espoir a fui, vaincu, √ vers le ciel noir.' Then three bars of quasi silence; the theme of the introduction is faintly heard to lead to the

(3) Conclusion. The narrator speaks again with exactly the same voice as in the introduction and in the same tempo: 'Tels ils marchaient dans les avoines folles'. Then, more slowly, comes the last line: 'Et la nuit seule entendit leurs paroles'. Three times descending, the song of the nightingale is heard before it vanishes for ever.

This is the kind of song one can work on for a lifetime. . . .

*

PROSES LYRIQUES (LYRICAL PROSE)

One year after the first series of *Fêtes galantes*, Debussy wrote another important set of four mélodies, completely different in spirit and musical writing: the *Proses lyriques*. They are much more lyrical and, in many ways, closer to the *Poèmes de Baudelaire*. Here again is found an accompaniment quite orchestral in style, but all the same very well written for the piano, and the vocal line is very demanding. The texts are by Debussy himself and unfortunately one must admit that they are not very good in their rather toilsome obscurity. They are written in the style of the symbolist poets whom Debussy was constantly meeting in Stéphane Mallarmé's circle. One can see that he was trying to achieve a synthesis of words and sounds in a single creative endeavour. (For instance, in the first mélodie, the same words always come on the same music.)

DE RÊVE...

La nuit | a des douceurs de femme

Et les vieux arbres sous la lune d'or,

Songent!
A celle qui vient de passer la tête
    emperlée,
Maintenant navrée, à jamais navrée,

Ils n'ont pas su lui faire signe...

Toutes! elles ont passé:
les Frêles, les Folles,
Semant leur rire au gazon grêle,

aux brises frôleuses la caresse
    charmeuse
des | hanches fleurissantes.
Hélas! de tout ceci, plus rien qu'un
    blanc frisson...
Les vieux arbres sous la lune d'or
pleurent leurs belles feuilles d'or!

Nul ne leur dédiera plus la fierté des
    casques d'or
Maintenant ternis, ✓ à jamais ternis.
Les chevaliers sont morts
Sur le chemin du Graal!
La nuit | a des douceurs de femme,

Des mains semblent frôler les âmes,
mains si folles, si frêles,
Au temps | où les épées chantaient
    pour Elles!
D'étranges soupirs s'élèvent sous les
    arbres.
Mon âme c'est du rêve ancien qui
    t'étreint!

Claude Debussy

OF DREAMS...

The night has the sweetness of
    woman
and the old trees under the golden
    moon
are dreaming!
To her who has just passed with head
    bepearled,
now heartbroken, for ever
    heartbroken,
they did not know how to give her a
    sign . . .
All! they have passed:
the Frail Ones, the Foolish Ones,
casting their laughter to the thin
    grass,
and to the fondling breezes the
    bewitching caress
of hips in the fullness of their beauty.
Alas! of all this, nothing is left but a
    pale tremor. . . .
The old trees under the golden moon
are weeping their beautiful golden
    leaves!
None will again dedicate to them the
    pride of the golden helmets
now tarnished, tarnished for ever.
The knights are dead
on the way to the Grail!
The night has the sweetness of
    woman,
hands seem to caress the souls,
hands so foolish, so frail,
in the days when the swords sang for
    them!
Strange sighs rise under the trees.

My soul you are gripped by a dream
    of olden times!

The poem, evoked by a mild autumnal night, tries to express the nostalgic dream of days long past.

This *mélodie* (in the original key the first note is F sharp) is constructed on two different tempi. The first one, *moderato*, is about ♩. = 52. It should be played and sung very legato. As is usual in Debussy's music, one must take care not to mark the beats with the voice. For instance, in the following phrase, the stresses must be: 'Et les vieux arbres sous la lune d'or'.

et les vieux arbres sous la lune d'or

After five bars, the second tempo, *andantino*, enters (about ♩ = 80) with the second musical theme. (Stress on 'navrée'.) After twelve bars which are still more *animato*, one gradually returns during five bars, with all the sadness of regret, to the first tempo, *moderato*, and to the first musical theme. This warms up a little during six bars, and leads to a real *f* and *marcato*, where the horn theme, which has so much importance in the whole end part of the *mélodie*, and which evokes the Knights of the Grail, now appears. There is again a definite slowing down before once more returning very briefly, for two bars only, to the first theme and tempo, like a remembrance. Here the second theme and tempo returns, the indication of which has obviously been forgotten in the score. The tempo becomes progressively livelier, and culminates in a top A for the voice. Then the piano, with the horn theme, has five bars of definite *diminuendo* but very little *ritardando*, to return to the first tempo *moderato* finding again the theme of the *andantino*, which this time is played *moderato* (*tempo primo*), for the nostalgic ending: 'Mon âme c'est du rêve ancien qui t'étreint'. The horn theme fades away. . . . The whole interpretation of this *mélodie* requires true lyricism.

DE GRÈVE...

Sur la mer les crépuscules tombent,
Soie blanche effilée.
Les vagues comme des petites folles
Jasent, petites filles sortant de l'école,

Parmi les froufrous de leur robe,
Soie verte irisée!
Les nuages, graves voyageurs,
Se concertent sur le prochain orage,
Et c'est un fond vraiment trop grave

A cette anglaise aquarelle.
Les vagues, les petites vagues,
Ne savent plus où se mettre,
Car voici la méchante averse,
Froufrous de jupes envolées,
Soie verte affolée.
Mais la lune, compatissante à tous!

Vient apaiser ce gris conflit.
Et caresse lentement ses petites amies
Qui s'offrent comme lèvres aimantes
A ce tiède et blanc baiser.
Puis, plus rien....
Plus que les cloches attardées des
    flottantes églises!
Angélus des vagues,
Soie blanche apaisée!

OF THE SHORE...

Over the sea twilight falls,
frayed white silk.
The waves like little mad things
chatter, little girls coming out of
    school,

amid the rustling of their dresses,
iridescent green silk!
The clouds, grave travellers,
hold counsel about the next storm,
and it is a background really too
    solemn

for this English water-colour.
The waves, the little waves,
no longer know where to go,
for here is the annoying downpour,
rustling of flying skirts,
panic-stricken green silk.
But the moon, compassionate
    towards all!

comes to pacify this grey conflict.
And slowly caresses his little friends
who offer themselves like loving lips
to this warm, white kiss.
Then, nothing more. . . .
Only the belated bells of the floating
    churches!
Angelus of the waves,
calmed white silk!

Claude Debussy

This is an entirely descriptive song, a true 'impressionist' mélodie, and when Debussy speaks in his poem of an 'English watercolour', there is no doubt that it is Turner he had in mind, whose painting is intensely evoked by his music. In fact there are three successive water-colours. The first is a picture of the sea at dusk. The second depicts a sudden squall, and in the third, the moon appearing appeases 'this grey conflict', and the sea is like 'smooth white silk'

The original key is D and there are no problems of tempi. The tempo *moderato* is about $\quad\downarrow = 76$, and is maintained for the whole of the first part of the song, but with suppleness and always with a feeling of agitation. The indication in the piano part is 'very even and very muffled'. The voice enters *p* and there are no nuances until 'Les vagues comme des petites folles' where a crescendo builds up, but diminuendo again on 'Soie verte irisée'. The next two lines must be extremely legato: 'Les nuages, graves voyageurs, Se concertent sur le prochain orage', with the dynamics well emphasized. 'Et c'est un fond vraiment trop grave A cette anglaise aquarelle' is *p* and much less legato. But suddenly the squall comes and it can be quite a serious one! Soon the weather clears up during two bars of piano, and the moon appears, which in four bars (*calmando*) completely calms the little waves. The tempo *più lento* is about ♩ = 66, and it slows down to ♩ = 56 ('Puis, plus rien...') to the end of the mélodie. Again the vocal part is very lyrical, and it requires great mastery to achieve the contrast between the precise and sparkling first part of the song and its soft and appeased ending.

DE FLEURS...

Dans l'ennui | si désolément vert √ de
  la serre de douleur,
Les fleurs‿enlacent mon cœur √ de
  leurs tiges méchantes.
Ah! quand reviendront √ autour de
  ma tête
Les chères mains (√) si tendrement
  désenlaceuses?
Les grands‿Iris violets
Violèrent méchamment tes yeux
En semblant les refléter,
Eux, qui furent l'eau du songe où
  plongèrent mes rêves

Si doucement‿enclos | en leur
  couleur;
Et les lys, blancs jets d'eau de pistils‿
  embaumés,
Ont perdu leur grâce blanche
Et ne sont plus que pauvres malades
  sans soleil!

OF FLOWERS...

In the tedium so desolately green of
  the hothouse of grief,
the flowers entwine my heart with
  their wicked stems.
Ah! when will return around my
  head
the dear hands so tenderly
  disentwining?
The big violet irises
wickedly ravished your eyes
while seeming to reflect them,
they, who were the water of the
  dream into which my dreams
  plunged
so sweetly enclosed in their colour;

and the lilies, white fountains of
  fragrant pistils,
have lost their white grace
and are no more than poor sick
  things without sun!

Soleil! ami des fleurs mauvaises,	Sun! friend of evil flowers,
Tueur de rêves! Tueur d'illusions!	killer of dreams! Killer of illusions!
Ce pain béni des_âmes misérables!	This consecrated bread of wretched souls!
Venez! Venez! Les mains salvatrices!	Come! Come! Redeeming hands!
Brisez les vitres de mensonge,	Break the window-panes of falsehood,
Brisez les vitres de maléfice,	Break the window-panes of malefice,
Mon_âme meurt de trop de soleil!	my soul dies of too much sun!
Mirages! Plus ne refleurira la joie de mes_yeux	Mirages! the joy of my eyes will not flower again
Et mes mains sont lasses de prier,	and my hands are weary of praying,
Mes_yeux sont las de pleurer!	my eyes are weary of weeping!
Eternellement ce bruit fou des pétales noirs de l'ennui	Eternally this maddening sound of the black petals of tedium
Tombant goutte_à goutte sur ma tête	falling drop by drop on my head
Dans le vert de la serre de douleur!	in the green of the hothouse of grief!

Claude Debussy

This poem, very 'modern-style-1900', has inspired Debussy to write a superb mélodie, which makes extreme demands on its interpreters.

The original key is C major; the *tempo primo* about ♩ = 58, not faster. Perfect legato, of course. A little expressive stress on the first syllable of 'l'ennui'. If possible no breath in the phrase 'Les fleurs enlacent mon cœur de leurs tiges méchantes'. (A breath is, however, possible after 'cœur'.) The same thing for the phrase 'les chères mains si tendrement désenlaceuses' (with a possible breath after 'mains'). Immediately after the modulation into E major, an *animando poco a poco* of nine bars begins, compensated by a *ritenuto poco a poco* of three bars returning quietly to the *tempo primo*. Obviously an important indication is missing on the two bars 'Et ne sont plus que pauvres malades sans soleil', which should be *accelerando* and crescendo to reach the *animato* (double bar—three flats) which should be about ♩ = 100 (singer: *f* with strong consonants), and six bars later still more *animato*: ♩ = 120. This tempo should be maintained, if the pianist can achieve it, up to the big tremolo in E flat minor. After the up-beats of the preceding bar, the pianist must take a broad breath before attacking, with a strong stress, the first beat of this tremolo.

(Debussy used to do this.) The line 'Mon âme meurt de trop de soleil' is already in a broader tempo, slowing down and *molto diminuendo*, to bring back the slow *tempo primo* ♩ = 58 (Mirages) *p*, the left hand being played with singing tone. There is plenty of time for the great arpeggio in C major and a breath before beginning again in tempo the phrase 'Mes yeux sont las de pleurer', which is very lyrical, and after that all the end of the mélodie is quite peaceful, with a good legato and timbre in the voice, slowing down to allow for the very quiet placing of all the up-beats of the last bars.

DE SOIR...	OF EVENING...
Dimanche sur les villes,	Sunday in the towns,
Dimanche dans les cœurs!	Sunday in the hearts!
Dimanche chez les petites filles	Sunday for the little girls
chantant d'une voix | informée	singing with immature voices
des rondes obstinées où de bonnes Tours	persistent rounds where good Towers
n'en ont plus que pour quelques jours!	will last only for a few days!*
Dimanche, les gares sont folles!	Sunday, the stations are frenzied!
Tout le monde appareille pour des banlieux d'aventure	Everyone sets off for the suburbs of adventure
en se disant adieu avec des gestes éperdus!	Saying good-bye with distracted gestures!
Dimanche, les trains vont vite,	Sunday, the trains go quickly,
dévorés par d'insatiables tunnels;	devoured by insatiable tunnels;
Et les bons signaux des routes	and the good signals of the tracks
échangent d'un œil unique	interchange with a single eye
des impressions toutes mécaniques.	purely mechanical impressions.
Dimanche, dans le bleu de mes rêves,	Sunday, in the blue of my dreams,
où mes pensées tristes de feux d'artifices manqués	where my sad thoughts of abortive fireworks
Ne veulent plus quitter le deuil	will no longer cease to mourn
de vieux Dimanches trépassés.	for old Sundays long departed.
Et la nuit, | à pas de velours,	And the night, with velvet steps,
vient endormir le beau ciel fatigué,	sends the beautiful, tired sky to sleep,
et c'est Dimanche dans les avenues d'étoiles;	and it is Sunday in the avenues of stars;

* The girl who is the tower in the centre of the round will soon be replaced by another girl.

la Vierge | or sur argent
laisse tomber les fleurs de sommeil!
Vite, les petits_anges, dépassez les
    hirondelles
afin de vous coucher, forts
    d'absolution!
Prenez pitié des villes,
Prenez pitié des cœurs,
Vous, la Vierge or sur argent!

the Virgin, gold upon silver,
lets the flowers of sleep fall!
Quickly, the little angels, overtake
    the swallows
to put you to bed, blessed by
    absolution!
Take pity on the towns,
take pity on the hearts,
You, Virgin gold upon silver!

Claude Debussy

This poem has two contrasted parts. In the first one Debussy 'poet' describes a joyful summer Sunday; the children playing in the city parks; the citizen trying to escape from town in crowded trains. And in the second part he evokes the Sundays that are gone, and he ends with a prayer to the Virgin Mary begging her to have pity for the towns and pity for the hearts.

The contrast has been well observed by Debussy 'composer'. The bells of Sunday morning are heard in one of his favourite keys, G sharp. They ring throughout the mélodie, in different keys, speeds, moods and variations. First they are full of life and joy: the tempo is ♩ = 69, precise and rhythmic, even for the voice, which must be *marcato* for the first two phrases, but more legato on 'Dimanche chez les petites filles', etc. Here, a theme in the piano part, is a popular tune to which all little French girls make a singing game, one of them representing the tower, while the others turn around her:

la   tour prends garde la   tour prends garde de   te   laisser   abat - tre

and this explains the literary text.

The initial joyful carillon is heard again but after two bars the voice is *subito p* and more legato, building up a big crescendo of eight bars. The piano alone makes another very quick crescendo during two bars, and two bars later there is another one for both voice and piano. Then

a new ringing of the bells begins, which continues during all the
second part of the mélodie:

It must be kept in exactly the same tempo. The even triplets in the
voice can give the 'impressions toutes mécaniques'.

Now begins the second part of the mélodie, suddenly *p* and poetic.
A great contrast in the shading of the voice and in the mood can be
achieved. But I insist that exactly the same tempo should be maintained on 'Dimanche, dans le bleu de mes rêves', and also on 'où mes
pensées tristes de feux d'artifices manqués Ne veulent plus quitter le
deuil De vieux dimanches trépassés'. It is only after this phrase that
the piano slows down the ringing of the bells to about ♩ = 60, and the
voice, *pp* and well phrased, evokes the velvety night. A *ritenuto* can be
made when the Virgin lets the flowers of slumber fall, with the bells
in up-beats. Suddenly, for the little angels (with precise articulation),
there are a few bars in a faster tempo, about ♩ = 80. The last prayer
to the Virgin, 'Prenez pitié des villes' and 'Prenez pitié des cœurs',.is
almost twice as slow (♩ = 80). Notice that the rhythm is different for
these two lines, as well as the nuances. The bells fade away in the
distance.

*

CHANSONS DE BILITIS (SONGS OF BILITIS)

These three mélodies were completed in 1897. The prose poems were
supposed to be Greek poems translated by Pierre Louÿs, but they are
really original works of this close friend of Debussy. They form a little
triptych: in the first mélodie the very young Bilitis sings of the first
emotion of the awakening of first love; in the second one, this love
has reached its height; and in the third, winter has come and passion
has dimmed.

LA FLÛTE DE PAN

Pour le jour des Hyacinthies
il m'a donné une syrinx
faite de roseaux bien taillés,
unis avec la blanche cire
qui est douce à mes lèvres comme le
   miel.
Il m'apprend à jouer, assise sur ses
   genoux;
   mais je suis un peu tremblante.
Il en joue après moi,
   si doucement que je l'entends à
   peine.
Nous n'avons rien à nous dire,
tant nous sommes près l'un de l'autre;
   mais nos chansons veulent se
   répondre,
et tour à tour nos bouches
   s'unissent sur la flûte.
Il est tard;
   voici le chant des grenouilles vertes
qui commence avec la nuit.
Ma mère ne croira jamais
que je suis restée si longtemps
à chercher ma ceinture perdue.

Pierre Louÿs

THE FLUTE OF PAN

For Hyacinthus day
he has given me a pipe
made of well-cut reeds,
bound with white wax
that is sweet to my lips
   like honey.
He teaches me to play, sitting on his
   knee;
   but I am a little tremulous.
He plays it after me,
   so softly that I scarcely hear it.

We have nothing to say,
so close are we to each other;
   But our songs wish to respond

and from time to time our mouths
   join upon the flute.
It is late;
here is the song of the green frogs
that begins at nightfall.
My mother will never believe
that I have stayed so long
to look for my lost girdle.

The original key is B, the tempo about ♪ = 84. (But counting in four.)

The flute of the boy is heard, playing rather freely: 'Slow and with no rigour in the rhythm' writes Debussy. Actually it is mostly the ascending scale patterns which have to be launched rather freely each time they appear. And if the rhythm is supple, the singer must be precise enough to let the piano play its two bars of introduction again, in exactly the same way under the first phrase of the voice. Bilitis should choose a clear, pure colour in her voice, with nothing passionate in it. It is better to sing in one breath 'unis avec la blanche cire Qui est douce à mes lèvres comme le miel', but as a *ritenuto* must be made on the three last words, a breath is possible before them. *A tempo* for the following phrase. Observe the little crescendo and the *subito p* on 'si doucement'.

The flute is heard again playing rather freely, but in the following bars the singer must be careful of her rhythm (triplets), different from the rhythm of the piano. The *ritenuto* comes only on 'bouches s'unissent sur la flûte', not sooner. All these last bars must be sung with lyricism, to permit a wonderful contrast of expression. Suddenly the piano must give an impression of immobility, imitating the little sounds of the evening, and the girl realizes all at once that it is late. She is worried and says 'Il est tard' almost like speech. The piano goes on playing very regularly, starting to imitate the frogs, and the girl listens to them. The precise rhythm of these two bars is seldom heard:

voici le chant des grenouilles vertes qui com - mence avec la nuit

and yet when it is properly achieved (especially the four against three in the second bar), it can give an extraordinary impression of evening calm.

The piano, *poco più lento*, continues its imitative music, and then comes the last, very difficult phrase for the singer; begun regularly with the piano triplets, it is quite without rigour of rhythm. Debussy had to write it somehow, and one can understand what he wanted: a faster and faster delivery. This is why the indication to accelerate a little has to be observed, and continued up to the end. No *rallentando* on 'chercher ma ceinture perdue', and no rest on the A of 'cher<u>cher</u>'. It is the only possible way to give the right expression to this fleeting phrase. Above all one should try not to be childish, or to give any double meaning to that phrase. *No.* The simpler it is, the better it will be.

LA CHEVELURE	THE TRESSES OF HAIR
Il m'a dit:	He said to me:
'Cette nuit, j'ai rêvé,	'Tonight I dreamed,
J'avais ta chevelure autour de mon cou.	I had the tresses of your hair around my neck.

J'avais tes cheveux comme un collier noir	I had your hair like a black circlet
autour de ma nuque et sur ma poitrine.	around the nape of my neck and on my breast.
Je les caressais, | et c'était les miens;	I caressed it and it was my own;
et nous étions liés pour toujours ainsi,	and we were united for ever thus,
par la même chevelure la bouche sur la bouche,	by the same tresses mouth upon mouth,
ainsi que deux lauriers n'ont souvent qu'une racine.	like two laurels that often have but one root.
Et peu à peu, il m'a semblé,	And little by little, it seemed to me,
tant nos membres étaient confondus,	so intermingled were our limbs,
que je devenais toi-même	that I became part of you
ou que tu entrais en moi comme mon songe.'	or you entered into me like my dream.'
Quand il eut achevé,	When he had done,
il mit doucement ses mains sur mes épaules,	he put his hands gently on my shoulders,
et il me regarda d'un regard si tendre,	and he looked at me with so tender a look,
que je baissai les yeux | avec un frisson.	that I lowered my eyes with a shiver.

Pierre Louÿs

The original key is G flat.

From the very beginning it must be understood that after 'Il m'a dit'. (He said to me), to 'Quand il eut achevé' (When he had done), it is the boy's dream that the girl tells. So one should have two different feelings, and two different basic tempi in this mélodie. A slow tempo for the first two bars and the last eight bars, and a tempo definitely less slow for the rest of the song. One being about ♩ = 44 and the other one ♩ = 66.

The first piano bar should be as legato as possible. 'Il m'a dit' quite simple and straightforward; then the pianist must establish the second tempo very clearly, and the girl begins to describe the dream: 'very expressive and passionately concentrated', says Debussy; therefore there must be intensity in the *p*. There is a first crescendo starting from 'J'avais tes cheveux...' for three bars. (If the singer wants to breathe, it is possible between 'nuque' and 'et'.) Then again *p*; 'Je les caressais...'

in order to build up the big *crescendo ed animato*. (A breath is possible, but not desirable, between 'chevelure' and 'la bouche'.) Then 'ainsi que deux lauriers...' is *subito p* and in tempo (but of course tempo 2, not tempo 1), and the singer must take care not to break the meaning of the literary phrase: 'by the same tresses, mouth upon mouth like two laurels that often have but one root'. Then another *crescendo ed animato* begins, with a very broad climax. Full voice for the singer, with an expressive breath before 'comme mon songe'. On this last bar, there should be a little *diminuendo* in the up-beat repeated seconds of the piano, but only for the second half of the bar. There is a wonderful effect of pedal and sonority bringing back tempo 1. The *fermata* should not be too long. Now comes the difficult conclusion for the singer; difficult and yet simple if the music is performed exactly as it is written. Precision of rhythm, legato in the voice. One has plenty of time to sing each note, especially the notes which are not on the beats, respecting the evenness of the quavers or the triplets. No *fermata* on 'tendre'; and the last phrase is exactly in tempo, with a break before 'avec un frisson'. Above all no 'frisson' (shiver), Debussy used to say. A perfectly even triplet will give the effect. Indeed, it is not easy to express in the last part of this mélodie all its subtle sensuality. There should be just enough, but not too much.

(There is a misprint in many editions, in the piano part, three bars before the end. On the first beat it should be G natural, not G flat.)

LE TOMBEAU DES NAÏADES

Le long du bois couvert de givre, je marchais;
mes cheveux, devant ma bouche,

THE TOMB OF THE NAIADS

Along the wood covered with frost, I walked;
my hair, hanging down before my mouth,

se fleurissaient de petits glaçons,
et mes sandales_étaient lourdes
de neige fangeuse et tassée.
Il me dit: 'Que cherches-tu?'
—'Je suis la trace du satyre.
Ses petits pas fourchus_alternent
comme des trous dans_un manteau
    blanc.'
Il me dit: 'Les satyres sont morts.
Les satyres_et les nymphes_aussi.
Depuis trente ans | il n'a pas fait_un
    hiver aussi terrible.
La trace que tu vois | est celle d'un
    bouc
Mais restons_ici, où est leur tombeau.'

Et | avec le fer de sa houe
il cassa la glace de la source où jadis
    riaient les naïades.
Il prenait de grands morceaux froids,
et les soulevant vers le ciel pâle

il regardait_au travers.

was bespangled with little icicles,
and my sandals were heavy
with muddy, packed snow.
He said to me: 'What do you seek?'
—'I follow the track of the satyr.
His little cloven hoof marks alternate
like holes in a white mantle.'

He said to me: 'The satyrs are dead.
The satyrs and the nymphs too.
For thirty years there has not been so
    terrible a winter.
The track that you see is that of a
    buck.
But let us stay here, where their
    tomb is.'

And with the iron of his spade
he broke the ice of the spring where
    formerly the naiads had laughed.
He took some big, cold pieces,
and raising them towards the pallid
    sky
he looked through them.

Pierre Louÿs

The very slow tempo of this mélodie, about ♩ = 50, gives, from the beginning, the impression of the girl heavily trudging in the snow. Her slow, and should one dare to say, weary pace, can be felt in the rhythm. She sings 'softly and wearily'. The *pp* on 'et mes sandales' must not be emphasized; the triplets well sustained. Then comes the dialogue. The two voices should be suggested, but with no exaggeration. A crescendo on 'La trace que tu vois est celle d'un bouc', helps the pianist with his little climax on the bar in $\frac{2}{4}$, followed by a *molto diminuendo*, certainly *poco rubato*. (In certain editions a B natural is forgotten on the last semiquaver.) The last words of the boy, 'Mais restons ici, où est leur tombeau', are soft but serious. Then a contrast (she admires him very much), crescendo as the voice goes up. There is no good place to breathe in this phrase; the least bad place is between 'source' and 'où'. The last phrases not too *p*, with a crescendo on 'au travers' and a beautiful *diminuendo* on the last D. The piano ending is very important and quite orchestral. The even movement of the semi-quavers of the flute should not be disturbed by the stresses of the rest of the orchestra, especially on the first beat of the last bar.

*

From now on, Debussy finds inspiration for new mélodies only in the works of the old French poets of the fifteenth and seventeenth century (with the exception of the three poems of Stéphane Mallarmé), and it is interesting to notice how his music is in accord with the character, the style, the feeling of the poems, and undoubtedly evokes the period without any pastiche of old music.

In some of these old French poems there are problems of pronunciation. In my opinion, the singer should try to make the texts as understandable as possible, modernizing the pronunciation of many words. As the old French spelling is in the music score, in the text given here the spelling has been modernized where necessary to aid the pronunciation.

DEUX RONDELS DE CHARLES D'ORLÉANS
(TWO RONDELS OF CHARLES D'ORLÉANS)

These were first published and are still published in a series called *Trois Chansons de France* (publisher: Durand), with a third mélodie, 'La Grotte', to a poem by Tristan L'Hermite, which is the first mélodie of *Le Promenoir des Deux Amants* (*see page 203*).

LE TEMPS A LAISSÉ SON MANTEAU...

Le temps | a laissé son manteau
De vent de froidure et de pluie
Et s'est vêtu de broderie,
De soleil rayant, clair et beau.

Il n'y a bête ni oiseau
Qui en son jargon ne chante ou crie:

Le temps | a laissé son manteau.

THE SEASON HAS CAST ITS CLOAK

The season has cast its cloak
of wind and cold and rain
and is dressed in embroidery,
in clear and lovely shining sun.

There is not a beast nor a bird
that does not sing or cry in its own
    tongue:
the season has cast its cloak.

Rivière, fontaine et ruisseau	River, fountain and stream
Portent en livrée jolie	wear as a charming livery
Gouttes d'argent d'orfaverie.	drops of silver jewellery.
Chacun s'habille de nouveau.	Each one is newly clad.

Le temps | a laissé son manteau!	The season has cast its cloak.
Charles d'Orléans	

The poet, together with the whole of nature, welcomes the coming spring, and Debussy's setting is a joyful hymn to its glory.

The original key is C sharp, the tempo ♩ = 132. It should be performed very rhythmically by both singer and pianist, and the articulation must be precise. The mélodie is made up of four successive crescendos. The first one leading to 'De soleil rayant, clair et beau', climax on 'beau' with a strong 'b'. The second one up to 'en son jargon ne chante ou crie'. Then '*subito p*', but intense, on 'Le temps a laissé' with a very fast crescendo and a clear, definite *ritenuto* on 'son manteau'. There is a short piano interlude: the same bar twice, once *f*, once *p* echo. Then begins a last long crescendo to the end of the mélodie. The last refrain with a broad *ritardando*, which, in my opinion, should begin on:

and slow down regularly to the last chord. The voice ends *f* and cuts off on this chord.

POUR CE QUE PLAISANCE EST MORTE...   BECAUSE PLAISANCE IS DEAD

Pour ce que Plaisance est morte	Because Plaisance is dead
Ce mai, suis vêtu de noir;	this May, I am attired in black;

C'est grand pitié de véoir	it is pitiful to see
Mon cœur qui s'en déconforte.	my heart which is so discomfited.
Je m'habille de la sorte	I dress in the manner
Que dois, pour faire devoir,	that is befitting,
Pour ce que Plaisance est morte	because Plaisance is dead
Ce mai, suis vêtu de noir.	this May, I am attired in black.
Le temps ces nouvelles porte	The elements proclaim the news
Qui ne veut déduit avoir;	and will allow no diversion;
Mais par force du plouvoir	but by means of the rain
Fait des champs clore la porte.	close the door of the meadows.
Pour ce que Plaisance est morte.	Because Plaisance is dead.

Charles d'Orléans

The original key is D minor, the tempo about $\dotseq = 48$.

This is a quiet pavane which suggests noble figures in rich fifteenth-century mourning clothes. The poet's lament is sung over this dance without ever disturbing its rhythm; the feeling is deeply sad, but must be simple, discreet and dignified.

In the tenth bar there is a *rallentando* that should be maintained for three bars, up to the return of the *tempo primo*. Two bars further on is a *molto ritenuto*, really *molto* for two bars. Then one bar *a tempo* and the *molto ritenuto* to the end should not be too slow.

*

LE PROMENOIR DES DEUX AMANTS
(THE WALK OF THE TWO LOVERS)

Six years later (1910) Debussy published (Durand) *Le Promenoir des Deux Amants*, a set of three mélodies to fragments of a long poem by Tristan L'Hermite, a poet of the beginning of the seventeenth century; this exquisite poem is characteristic of the tender preciosity of the period, wonderfully captured by Debussy, in this short cycle of extraordinary refinement.

AUPRÈS DE CETTE GROTTE SOMBRE...

Auprès de cette grotte sombre
Où l'on respire un air si doux,
L'onde lutte avec les cailloux
Et la lumière avecque l'ombre.

Ces flots, ✓ lassés de l'exercice
Qu'ils ont fait dessus ce gravier,
Se reposent dans ce vivier
Où mourut autrefois Narcisse...

L'ombre de cette fleur vermeille
Et celle de ces joncs pendants
Paraissent être là-dedans
Les songes de l'eau qui sommeille.

Tristan L'Hermite

CLOSE TO THIS DARK GROTTO

Close to this dark grotto
where one breathes such sweet air,
the water contends with the pebbles
and the light with the shade.

These ripples, spent with the exertion
that they have made over the shingle,
come to rest in this pool
where once on a time Narcissus
died. . . .

The reflection of this crimson flower
and of these drooping reeds
seem to be therein
the dreams of the sleeping water. . . .

This descriptive poem can itself evoke the dark and humid atmosphere of the poetic grotto; but how much Debussy has added to it with his liquid and mysterious music! The performers must deal with this precious work with velvety fingers and a smooth voice.

The original key is G sharp minor, the tempo about ♪ = 72.

A liquid arpeggio begins the first bar, leading to the E sharp, and starts the little rhythmic pattern: 𝅘𝅥𝅮𝅘𝅥𝅮𝅘𝅥 which fills the whole mélodie with its soft pulsation. The second bar, with a change of harmony, is the same, but introduces a purely melodic theme, as though played by another instrument. There is a little *fermata* on the third beat, but the last semiquaver must be in tempo introducing the first bar of the voice. It enters *p*, as if whispering so as not to disturb the silence, but with a rich and sombre colour and, I must insist, extremely legato. (For instance, the four semiquavers:

cette   grotte

must be very even, sustaining the two weak syllables.) In the word 'sombre' no final [ə], and take a breath before 'ou'. A little stress on '<u>lu</u>tte' to have the D more *p* than the B. Breath before 'et'. Expressive breath after 'ces flots' to give the idea of the word 'lassés' (tired), with a little *portamento* (and no double 's'!). Small crescendo on 'se reposent dans ce vivier'; and 'Où mourut autrefois Narcisse' a shade slower, especially the last two quavers, to prepare the modulation. Then tempo again, the piano playing with a singing tone. In the beautiful curve of the voice:

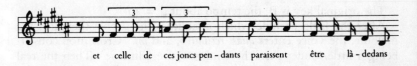

no *diminuendo* coming down. This makes it possible, after a quick deep breath, to be more mysterious in speaking of the dreams of the water that slumbers: 'Les songes de l'eau qui sommeille'. A little stress on '<u>so</u>nges', *ppp* the G of '<u>so</u>mmeille' and of course only one 'm'—I should like to say half an 'm'. It is a long phrase for the breath, but please, no hurry. In the last bar of the piano the mysterious instrument heard in the second bar of the mélodie is heard again, playing its semiquaver without haste.

*

No love poems could be more delicate, elegant, rare, than the two following poems. Both are indeed tender, but they have been set by Debussy in quite differing moods. The first one is sprightly, light and gay, and the other, soft, deep and yearning.

CROIS MON CONSEIL, CHÈRE CLIMÈNE...	TAKE MY COUNSEL, DEAR CLIMÈNE...
Crois mon conseil, chère Climène;	Take my counsel, dear Climène;
Pour laisser_arriver le soir, |	to await the coming of evening,
Je te prie, ✓ allons nous_asseoir	I beg you, let us go to sit
Sur le bord de cette fontaine.	on the margin of this fountain.

N'ouis-tu pas soupirer Zéphire,
De merveille et d'amour atteint,
Voyant des roses sur ton teint
Qui ne sont pas de son empire?

Do you not hear Zephyrus sighing,
stricken with amazement and love,
seeing roses on your cheeks
which are not of his dominion?

Sa bouche d'odeur toute pleine
A soufflé sur notre chemin,
Mêlant un esprit de jasmin
A l'ambre de ta douce haleine.
                    Tristan l'Hermite

His mouth, so full of fragrance,
has breathed on our path,
mingling an essence of jasmine
with the amber of your sweet breath.

The original key is B, the tempo about ♩ = 46.

After the little prelude which establishes the supple theme of the mélodie, the voice enters *quasi recitativo*, and *mf*. 'Crois mon conseil' being a little louder than the tender 'chère Climène'. Then the real tempo begins and the voice sings in a charming mood, quite engagingly. Break after 'soir', breath after 'je te prie'. A little *ritardando* (very little) and *a tempo* again, *p*, whispering and interrogative: 'N'ouis-tu pas soupirer Zéphire?' with a little stress on the E natural of 'Zé'. Then a warm crescendo–*accelerando* begins, always interrogative. After a diminuendo for the piano, one is back to the *tempo primo*, and the voice sings the delicate poem with great charm and elegance. The last two triplets of the voice part must be *ritenuto* but very regular, to fit precisely with the semiquavers of the piano part. And the final arpeggio of the piano comes with a smile.

JE TREMBLE EN VOYANT TON VISAGE...

I TREMBLE WHEN I SEE YOUR FACE...

Je tremble en voyant ton visage
Flotter avecque mes désirs,
Tant j'ai de peur que mes soupirs
Ne lui fasse faire naufrage.

I tremble when I see your face
floating with my desires,
so much do I fear that my sighs
may cause it to sink.

De crainte de cette aventure
Ne commets pas si librement
A cet infidèle élément
Tous les trésors de la Nature.

For fear of this hazard
do not trust so freely
to this uncertain element
all the treasures of Nature.

Veux-tu, par un doux privilège,
Me mettre au-dessus des humains?
Fais-moi boire au creux de tes mains,

Si l'eau n'en dissout point la neige.
Tristan L'Hermite

Will you, as a sweet privilege,
raise me above mortals?
Let me drink from your cupped hands

if the water will not melt their snow.

The original key is D flat, the tempo ♩ = 46.

The tenderness of this mélodie is in a quite different mood from the former song. From the beginning the supple phrases of the piano create a more languid atmosphere. (It is advisable to think of the first semiquaver triplet of the piano as an up-beat.) The voice begins very legato. 'Soft and sustained in the expression', writes Debussy; let us add: with warmth and concentration. No crescendo in the first quatrain (a charming *p* on the F of 'naufrage'). Then a crescendo begins to reach its climax on the F with no diminuendo coming down. In spite of this crescendo there should be almost no *accelerando* in the second quatrain and the subtle rhythm must be watched. Then a bar of *ritardando* in the piano part and a breath before attacking the following bar in tempo. 'Veux-tu' is rather intense and 'par un doux privilège' rather in parenthesis. One has to let the tone swell on 'Me mettre au-dessus des humains?' with a beautiful diminuendo on the D, to bring in the next phrase *p*, with extremely sustained tone and a nice *p* on 'creux'. These two bars, 'Fais-moi boire au creux de tes mains', still exactly in tempo, before the very gradual *rallentando* up to the end. A breath can be taken before 'la neige', as it is very low; and without loss of timbre it must be *pp*, with the sweetest possible tenderness.

*

BALLADES DE FRANÇOIS VILLON
(BALLADS OF FRANÇOIS VILLON)

In 1910 Debussy also published a very important series of three mélodies, for a baritone voice: *Ballades de François Villon*, the fifteenth-century poet, and in setting his poems, Debussy has succeeded in creating a marvellously medieval atmosphere.

BALLADE DE VILLON A S'AMIE

Fausse beauté, qui tant me coûte cher,
Rude en effet, hypocrite douceur,

Amour dure, plus que fer à mâcher;

Nommer te puis de ma deffaçon
sœur.
Charme félon, la mort d'un pauvre
cœur,
Orgueil mussé, qui gens met au
mourir,
Yeux sans pitié! ne veut droit de
rigueur,
Sans empirer, un pauvre secourir?

Mieux m'eût valu avoir été crier↑
Ailleurs secours, √ c'eût été mon
bonheur:
Rien ne m'eût su de ce fait arracher;
Trotter m'en faut | en fuite à
déshonneur.
Haro, haro, le grand et le mineur!

Et qu'est ceci? Mourrai sans coup
férir,
Ou pitié peut, selon cette teneur,

Sans empirer, un pauvre secourir?

Un temps viendra, qui fera dessécher,
Jaunir, flétrir, votre épanie fleur:

J'en risse lors, se tant peusse marcher,
Mais las! nenni: ce serait donc foleur,
Vieil je serai; vous, √ laide et sans
couleur.
Or, buvez fort, tant que ru peut
courir.

BALLAD OF VILLON TO HIS LOVE

False beauty, who costs me so dear,
heartless, in truth, with feigned
sweetness,
hard love, harder than iron to
outwear;
I name you sister of my undoing.

Treacherous charm, the death of a
poor heart,
dissembled pride, which sends men
to their death,
pitiless eyes! From such cruelty will
justice not
rescue a poor fellow, without
worsening his lot?

It had been better to have begged
for help elsewhere, it could have
meant my happiness;
nothing can tear me from this fate;
I must go on in my flight to hide my
dishonour.
Great and small are crying shame
upon me!
Now what is this? Shall I die without
striking a blow
or will pity, given these
circumstances,
rescue a poor fellow, without
worsening his lot?

A time will come, when dried up,
yellowed, faded, your full-blown
flower shall be:
I will laugh then, if I can still walk,
but alas! Nay: it would be folly,
I shall be old; you, ugly and
colourless.
Now drink deep while the brook ·
still runs.

Ne donnez pas à touṣ cette douleur,	Do not give to all this pain,
Sans empirer, un pauvre secourir.	rescue a poor fellow, without worsening his lot.
Prince amoureux, des amants le greigneur,	Amorous prince, greatest of lovers,
Votre mal gré ne voudrais | encourir;	I do not wish to incur your displeasure;
Mais tout franc cœur doit, par Notre Seigneur,	but every honest heart must, for our good Lord's sake,
Sans empirer, un pauvre secourir.	rescue a poor fellow, without worsening his lot.
François Villon	

The poet laments the harshness and the infidelity of his love, and begs for pity. Debussy's indication: 'with an expression of anguish and regret' is excellent for the beginning of the mélodie, but this changes several times.

The original key is F sharp minor, the tempo about ♩ = 52.

The piano immediately sets the little rhythmic pattern, which is like a short wail, and which continues throughout the mélodie. The singer begins *mf* or *mp*, intense, legato of course, and giving a stress on 'Fausse' to avoid marking the beat on the weak syllable. Legato, but not *portamento* between 'qui' and 'tant'. Crescendo, with a stress on 'rude en effet', and rather more *p* because of the meaning of the words, on 'hypocrite douceur'. A definite *ritardando* on 'Nommer te puis de ma deffaçon sœur'. Bitterness on the words 'charme félon' with an expressive stress on 'fé'. *Marcato*: 'yeux sans pitié', etc. Observe the crescendo on 'un pauvre secourir' and after the *ritardando* for the piano, back to *tempo primo*, for the second stanza.

The phrase 'Mieux m'eût valu avoir été crier Ailleurs secours' should be sung in one breath with a crescendo. Then breath and diminuendo on 'c'eût été mon bonheur'. Two bars later, one of Debussy's favourite expressions is seen, *en serrant*, which means simply *accelerando*, but, in my opinion, this *accelerando* should begin slightly on the preceding bar, on 'su de ce fait arracher', and of course be resumed up to the indication *a tempo primo* with a big crescendo. The music so well expresses the meaning of the words: I must run away to hide my dishonour, as everybody is crying shame upon me! Now, rather freely

and returning to the *tempo primo*, interrogative and desolate: 'Et qu'est
ceci?' Now what is this? And at the end of this second stanza, no
crescendo on 'un pauvre secourir'.

There are many indications in Debussy's hand at the beginning of
the third stanza: 'imbued and expressive' for the left hand of the
pianist; 'soft and melancholy' for the singer; but virtually in the same
tempo: 'Un temps viendra, qui fera dessécher, Jaunir, flétrir, votre
épanie fleur'. No *portamento* on 'jaunir' and 'flétrir', but an expressive
stress on the first syllable. Then an *animato* begins, with little bursts of
laughter in the piano part and a bitter irony in the voice. Sudden contrast: 'Mais las! (pronouncing the 's'). The poet realizes he will be old
himself. There is no accompaniment, but the *tempo animato* should be
maintained, observing the rests, until the *ritenuto*: 'Vieil je serai, vous,
laide et sans couleur'. (Stresses on 'vieil' and 'lai', and an expressive
breath between 'vous' and 'laide.') Brisk *accelerando*, with little bursts
of laughter in the piano, showing the intention of the poet not to
lament any longer, to drink: 'or, buvez fort!', with a *ritardando*, but
not too much diminuendo on 'tant que ru peut courir'. Then *tempo
primo*, really slow, in order to keep the phrase 'Sans empirer, un
pauvre secourir' in tempo.

The 'envoi' address to Love must be sung broadly; the irony of it is
in the piano part. But the last prayer for pity is taken seriously, with the
original feeling of anguish and regret. Very broad *ritenuto* on the last
bars, and 'un pauvre secourir' with a little stress on each note, but
legato.

BALLADE QUE VILLON FAIT A LA REQUÊTE DE SA MÈRE POUR PRIER NOTRE-DAME	BALLAD MADE AT THE REQUEST OF HIS MOTHER, FOR A PRAYER TO OUR LADY
Dame du ciel, régente terrienne.	Lady of Heaven, Regent of the earth,
Emperière des_infernaux palus,	Empress of the infernal swamps,
Recevez-moi, votre humble chrétienne,	receive me, your humble christian woman,
Que comprinse sois | entre vos_élus,	let me be numbered among your elect,
Ce nonobstant qu'onques rien ne valus.	although I am unworthy.

Les biens de vous, ma Dame | et ma
    Maîtresse,
Sont trop plus grands que ne suis
    pécheresse,
Sans lesquels biens, | âme ne peut
    mérir
N'avoir les cieux, je n'en suis
    menteresse.
En cette foi je veux vivre et mourir.

A votre Fils dites que je suis sienne;
De lui soient mes péchés abolus:

Pardonnez-moi comme à
    l'Égyptienne,
Ou comme il fit au clerc Théophilus,
Lequel par vous fût quitte et absolu,

Combien qu'il eût au diable fait
    promesse.
Préservez-moi que je n'accomplisse
    ce!
Vierge portant sans rompure encourir
Le sacrement qu'on célèbre à la messe.
En cette foi je veux vivre et mourir.

Femme je suis pauvrette et ancienne,
Qui rien ne sait, | onques lettre ne lu;
Au moutier vois, dont suis
    paroissienne,
Paradis peint | où sont | harpes et lus,

Et un enfer où damnés sont boullus:

L'un me fait peur, l'autre joie et liesse.

La joie avoir fais moi, haute Déesse,
A qui pécheurs doivent tous recourir,
Comblés de foi, sans feinte ne paresse.

En cette foi ✓ je veux vivre et mourir.
             François Villon

Your goodness, my Lady and my
    Mistress,
is far greater than my sinfulness,

without this goodness, no soul can
    merit
Heaven nor gain it. I do not speak
    falsely:
In this faith would I live and die.

Say to your Son, I am His;
through Him let my sins be swept
    away:
may He forgive me as He forgave the
    woman of Egypt,
or the priest Théophilus,
who through your intercession was
    acquitted and absolved,
although he had made a pact with the
    devil.
Preserve me from ever doing such a
    thing!
Virgin bearing without blemish
the sacrament we celebrate at Mass.
In this faith would I live and die.

I am a poor old woman,
ignorant and unlettered;
in my parish church I see

a picture of Paradise with harps and
    lutes,
and Hell where the damned are
    boiled:
the one frightens me, the other gives
    me joy and gladness.
Give me the joy, exalted Goddess,
to whom all sinners must resort,
full of faith, without insincerity or
    sloth.
In this faith would I live and die.

This superb prayer to the Virgin Mary has touched Debussy, who was not a religious man, and inspired him to write a song full of exaltation and humility.

Original key is A minor/C major, the tempo ♩ = 52.

The piano establishes the mood 'soft and simple' like a little wooden organ, perfectly even in tempo. The voice, from the very beginning absorbed in its prayer, enters *p* with no crescendo on the ascending fifth. A little insistence on 'Recevez-moi' and more *p* on 'votre humble chrétienne'. Scarcely any *ritenuto* on the bar in $\frac{2}{4}$, and *a tempo*. Perfect evenness of the triplets: 'ce nonobstant [no nasal sound on the first syllable of nonobstant] qu'onques rien ne valus'. Definite *ritenuto* on 'N'avoir les cieux'; then *a tempo*, and on the indication *pieusement* (piously) almost the same tempo. One must not feel any change of tempo in beginning the second stanza. Pianist and singer must count; the singer holding his note on C for the four beats.

The same mood for the beginning of the second stanza, *p*, with the same little insistence on 'Pardonnez-moi' and more *p* on 'comme à l'Égyptienne'. Then an *animato* of five bars begins; good stresses as indicated on the score, especially on the up-beat '<u>diable</u>', and (this is very difficult) no *rallentando* on the bar:

vierge portant sans rompure   encourir

(I recommend no crescendo in the piano part) which must return abruptly to the *tempo primo*, and the very even triplets of 'Le sacrement qu'on célèbre à la messe', slightly *parlando* but certainly not staccato, with the deep respect and contemplative mood that is implied. 'En cette foi je veux vivre et mourir' is sung again with a beautiful legato and in the same tempo as the first stanza.

Continuing in this tempo, the third stanza has the excellent indication: 'soft and humble'. One can well imagine the very simple old woman looking at the frescoes on the walls of her parish church. The singer, characterizing the old woman, must express enchantment or terror with what she sees. These very quick contrasts are not easy to realize, changing instantly dynamics, colours and expressions. I suggest that the phrase 'Et un enfer où damnés sont <u>boullus</u>' should be taken *mf* and crescendo, then a quick expressive breath, and 'L'un me fait peur' *p* with a muffled voice. Breath again, and 'l'autre joie et liesse' with a clear voice, crescendo, and broadening a very little. Then a very gradual *ritardando* begins in quite an ecstatic mood. The phrase 'Comblés de foi, sans feinte ne paresse' is rather free; and 'En cette foi je veux vivre et mourir' in this last stanza is in a slower tempo. A breath may be taken after 'foi', especially for this last phrase, as the low C has to be sustained for its four long beats.

BALLADE DES FEMMES DE PARIS	BALLAD OF THE WOMEN OF PARIS
Quoiqu'on tient belles langagières	Although they praise as fine talkers
Florentines, Vénitiennes,	Florentines, Venetians,
Assez pour être messagères,	good enough to be go-betweens,
Et mêmement les anciennes;	even the old women too;
Mais soit Lombardes, Romaines,	yet be they from Lombardy, Rome,
Genevoises, | à mes périls,	Geneva, heaven help me,
Piémontaises, Savoisiennes,	Piedmont, Savoy;
Il n'est bon bec que de Paris.	for the gift of the gab give me Paris.
De beau parlé tiennent chayères,	Those who hold professorships in loquacity
Ce dit-on, Napolitaines,	are, they say, the Neapolitans,
Et que sont bonnes caquetières	and outstanding as chatterboxes
Allemandes et Prussiennes,	are the Germans and the Prussians,
Soit Grecques, | Égyptiennes,	yet be they Greeks, Egyptians,
De Hongrie ou d'autres pays,	from Hungary or other lands,
Espagnoles | ou Castellannes,	Spaniards or Castilians,
Il n'est bon bec que de Paris.	for the gift of the gab give me Paris.
Brettes, Suisses, n'y savent guère,	The Bretons, the Swiss know nothing about it,
Ne Gasconnes et Toulousaines;	neither do they in Gascony or Toulouse;
Du Petit-Pont deux | harangères	two jabberers from the Petit-Pont
Les concluront, et les Lorraines,	would soon settle them, and also those from Lorraine,

Anglèches_ou Calaisiennes,
(Ai-je beaucoup de lieux compris?)
Picardes, de Valenciennes...
Il n'est bon bec que de Paris.

Prince, | aux dames parisiennes,
De bien parler donnez le prix;
Quoi qu'on die d'Italiennes,

Il n'est bon bec que de Paris.

England or Calais,
(have I included enough places?)
Picardy, of Valenciennes. . . .
For the gift of the gab give me Paris.

Prince, to the Parisian ladies
present the prize for good talking;
whatever they may say of the
    Italians,
for the gift of the gab give me Paris.

François Villon

This malicious ballad sings the praises of the Parisian women, who surpass all others in their chattering and prattling.

The original key is F major, the tempo ♩ = 132.

The piano begins at once its unremitting tittle-tattle, 'alert and gay', and the voice enters *mp* and *non legato*. (It is very important in this mélodie to observe the contrasts of legato and '*non legato*'.) The second phrase is legato: 'Florentines, Vénitiennes, Assez pour être messagères', and: 'Et mêmement les anciennes' *non legato* again. Quick crescendo in the two bars of repeated notes for the piano, and *subito pp*. The singer continues to observe his contrasts. Exaggerated legato on 'Romaines', crescendo with the piano on 'Piémontaises, Savoisiennes', and *subito p* to begin the big crescendo 'Il n'est bon bec que de Paris', 'bec' being rather staccato with a strong 'c'.

The second stanza begins legato and also 'ce dit-on', but 'Napolitaines' is staccato. These four bars indicated *rubato* are a little slower, with the triplets well marked in the piano part. (It is a little serenade-barcarolle for the Neapolitans.) Then *a tempo* again, always observing the contrasts.

The third stanza with very precise rhythm: 'Brettes, Suisses' with strong stresses; 'n'y savent guère' is legato; and on 'Toulousaines' there is a really exaggerated *portamento* on the syllable 'lou'. It does not matter if in doing this, the singer is a little late on the first beat; the piano must not follow. Then six bars *rubato*, and very witty on the important phrase: 'Du Petit-Pont deux harangères les conclueront'. Villon invents three more women: 'et les Lorraines, Anglèches ou

Calaisiennes' (*a tempo*), and suddenly finds himself at a loss: 'Ai-je beaucoup de lieux compris?' The interrogations of the piano and the voice must be quite free. But as soon as the piano begins its tattling again, the singer must give the impression, by breathing and holding his breath, that he has thought of some more women to cite: 'Picardes, de Valenciennes'.

The 'envoi' begins in tempo (in certain editions there is a misprint: on the syllable 'ri' of the word 'parisienne' it is an A, not a G sharp), and, with the triplets, an *animato* and *crescendo molto* begins. This *accelerando* must stop abruptly, and the pianist must take a breath before attacking his C major chord. It is very important to return to the *tempo primo* for the last 'Il n'est bon bec que de Paris'. The voice cuts off *ff* on the last staccato E of the piano.

*

In 1913, Debussy composed three mélodies on poems by Stéphane Mallarmé, which are masterpieces of concision and subtlety, and match the hermetic refinement of the poems. But the study of Debussy's mélodies has already taken a long chapter. A few words only can be said about the last song he wrote in 1915.

Unfortunately it is far from being one of the best, but admittedly it is successful. Debussy was already very ill (he died of cancer in 1918), and very upset by the tragedy of the First World War. It is this that gives this mélodie its emotion; the regrettable words were written by Debussy himself, and it is dedicated to the children of those parts of France occupied and devastated by the enemy.

NOËL DES ENFANTS QUI N'ONT PLUS DE MAISONS

Nous n'avons plus de maisons!
Les ennemis_ont tout pris,
jusqu'à notre petit lit!
Ils_ont brûlé l'école et notre maître
    aussi.

CHRISTMAS CAROL OF THE CHILDREN WHO HAVE NO HOMES

We have no homes any more!
The enemy have taken everything,
even our little bed!
They have burned the school and our
    schoolmaster too.

Ils_ont brûlé l'église et monsieur
    Jésus-Christ
et le vieux pauvre qui n'a pas pu
    s'en aller!

Nous n'avons plus de maisons!
Les ennemis_ont tout pris,
jusqu'à notre petit lit!
Bien sûr! Papa est_à la guerre,
Pauvre maman | est morte
Avant d'avoir vu tout çà.
Qu'est-ce que l'on va faire?
Noël! petit Noël! n'allez pas chez_
    eux,
n'allez plus jamais chez_eux.
    Punissez-les!
Vengez les enfants de France!
Les petits Belges, les petits Serbes,
et les petits Polonais | aussi!
Si nous_en oublions, pardonnez-nous.
Noël! Noël! surtout, pas de joujoux,

Tâchez de nous redonner le pain
    quotidien.

Noël! écoutez-nous,
nous n'avons plus de petits sabots:
Mais donnez la victoire aux_enfants
    de France!

They have burned the church and
    Mister Jesus Christ
and the poor old man who could not
    escape!

We have no homes any more!
The enemy have taken everything,
even our little bed!
To be sure! Papa is at the war,
poor Mama died
before she saw all that.
What are we going to do?
Christmas! Little Father Christmas!
    do not go to them,
never·go to them again. Punish them!

Avenge the children of France!
The little Belgians, the little Serbs,
and the little Poles too!
If we have forgotten any, forgive us.
Christmas! Christmas! above all, no
    toys,
try to give us again our daily bread.

Christmas! hear us,
we have no little clogs any more:
but grant victory to the children of
    France!

Claude Debussy

    The only difficulty of this very simple song, which is rather more a
'chanson' than a 'mélodie', is that it is supposed to be sung by a child,
and one must succeed in being neither too lyrical nor too childish. The
simpler the better.

    The original key is A major, but it can be transposed. The metrono-
mic tempo Debussy has indicated (which is rare) is ♩ = 144, 'soft and
sad', also humble and naïve. For this reason it may be better to make
no liaison between 'ennemis' and 'ont'. The nuances must not be
exaggerated. It is only from 'Bien sûr!' that the expression can be more

intense, but it must never be too dramatic. After the *animato* and *sempre* (rather *più*) *animato*', the two bars 'surtout pas de joujoux' can slow down a little, to prepare the *meno mosso* which suddenly becomes *più legato* for the singer. Then the original tune begins again; it can be taken really *pp*. The interpretation of the end of the song is quite obvious.

ERIK SATIE

Erik Satie (1866–1925) was an enigmatic, disconcerting figure, always disguising under eccentricities his real sensitivity. Full of inspiring ideas about the destiny of music, he was content to offer a kind of condensation of them. He wrote very little, but his influence was great, even on musicians such as Debussy and Ravel, the latter calling him 'a gifted but awkward precursor'.

Three mélodies, among the small number he wrote, can give a good example of his art, and are also very amusing and rewarding for their interpreters. (They are published by Salabert under the title *Trois Mélodies*.)

LA STATUE DE BRONZE

La grenouille du jeu de tonneau √
S'ennuie | le soir | sous la tonnelle;
Elle en‿a assez d'être la statue
Qui va prononcer‿un grand mot, | le
    Mot...
Elle‿aimerait mieux‿être avec les‿
    autres
Qui font des bulles de musique
Avec le savon de la lune.
Au bord du lavoir mordoré

THE BRONZE STATUE

The frog of the game of 'tonneau'
is bored at evening under the arbour;
she has had enough of being a statue
who prepares to utter an important
    word, the Word . . .
she would rather be with the others

who are blowing music bubbles
with the soap of the moon.
By the edge of the reddish-brown
    washhouse

Qu'on voit là-bas luire entre les
    branches.
On lui lance à cœur de journée,
Une pâture de pistoles
Qui la traversent sans lui profiter
Et s'en vont sonner dans les cabinets

De son piédestal numéroté.
Et le soir les insectes couchent
Dans sa bouche.

Léon-Paul Fargue

that can be seen yonder shining
    through the branches.
All day they ceaselessly throw
fodder of metal disks
that pass through her fruitlessly
and rattle down into the compart-
    ments
of her numbered pedestal.
And at night the insects go to bed
in her mouth.

It should be explained that the 'jeu de tonneau' was a garden game very popular at the end of the last century. A bronze frog with an open mouth sat on a cabinet which had numbered compartments. The players threw metal discs which fell through holes into the compartments; they aimed at the frog's mouth, which represented the highest score.

This little poem has inspired a beautiful mélodie, which should be sung with seriousness, emphasizing its poetry.

The prefatory indication 'not too fast' would seem to correspond to ♩ = 80. The first four bars of the piano part are *f*, then a *p* prepares the entrance of the voice, singing legato. A crescendo leads to 'le Mot' (strong capital 'M'!). The dynamics of the following six bars for the piano should be carefully observed. Then the indication *attendre un peu* (wait a little) really means a long breath before attacking 'Elle aimerait mieux,' etc. A crescendo on 'Avec le savon de la lune'. The puzzling indication on the following bar *Un temps* (one beat) means, according to Satie's friends, that a silent beat should be added before attacking the following very poetic phrase: 'Au bord du lavoir', etc., which is *p*, legato, and gradually *ritardando*. *A tempo mf* and a crescendo on 'On lui lance', etc., *p subito*, very quiet and sad on 'Qui la traversent', etc. Again according to Satie's friends there is a misprint in the bar:

et s'en vont sonner

which should be:

et s'en vont sonner

This phrase is *mf*, the *p* being reserved for the very placid ending.

DAPHÉNÉO

Dis-moi, Daphénéo, quel est donc cet
 arbre dont les fruits
  sont des_oiseaux qui pleurent?
Cet arbre, Chrysaline, est_un_
 oisetier.
Ah!... Je croyais que les noisetiers
 donnaient des noisettes, Daphénéo.

Oui, Chrysaline, les noisetiers
 donnent des noisettes, √ mais
  les_oisetiers donnent des_
   oiseaux qui pleurent.
Ah!...

M. God

DAPHÉNÉO

Tell me, Daphénéo, what is that tree
 which has for fruit
  birds who weep?
That tree, Chrysaline, is a bird-tree.★

Ah!... I thought that hazel trees†
 had hazel nuts,
  Daphénéo.
Yes, Chrysaline, the hazel trees have
 hazel nuts, but
  the bird-trees have birds who
   weep.
Ah!...

★ *un oisetier*—a bird-tree
† *un noisetier*—a hazel tree

This crazy little dialogue between Chrysaline and the boy Daphénéo is based on the play on words produced by the liaison 'un_oisetier' which makes 'oisetier' (a word which does not really exist and would mean 'bird-tree') sound like 'noisetier', which means 'hazel tree'.

The *tranquille* tempo should not be too slow: ♩ = 72 is about right. The naïve Chrysaline asks her question *p* and very evenly; Daphénéo answers *mf* and straight-forwardly with, of course, a good liaison 'un_oisetier'! Chrysaline is very surprised, and after a silence utters: 'Ah!'. A little glottal attack may give the right effect. Then comes Daphénéo's explanation: to make it clear, the indication *ralentir* should come on 'mais les_oisetiers', emphasizing the liaison. *A tempo* up to the indication *très retenu* (*molto ritenuto*) in the piano part, to give plenty of time for Chrysaline *to think* before uttering her last: 'Ah!' with still more surprise, giving the impression of not being quite sure that she has understood.

LE CHAPELIER	THE MAD HATTER
Le chapelier s'étonne de constater	The hatter is astonished to find
Que sa montre retarde de trois jours,	that his watch is going three days slow,
Bien qu'il ait_eu soin de la graisser toujours	although he has always taken care to grease it
Avec du beurre de première qualité.	with butter of the best quality.
Mais_il a laissé tomber	But he has allowed
Des miettes de pain dans les rouages,	some breadcrumbs to fall into the works,
Et il a beau plonger sa montre dans le thé,	and even if he tries dipping his watch in the tea,
Ça ne la fera pas_avancer davantage.	it will not make it go any faster.
René Chalupt	

This little nonsense text is after 'Alice in Wonderland', and Satie's setting is a kind of pastiche of an operatic aria: *Genre Gounod* is his malicious indication, and the musical theme recalls the 'Chanson de Magali' in the opera *Mireille*. Thus the singer knows the appropriate style of singing. (Allegretto ♩. = 69.) A little *portamento* on 'retarde', and very even in one breath the long descent to the low register. The second stanza should be, for fun, more dramatic, and the big climax is *molto ritardando*. No diminuendo on 'dans le thé' and *p subito*, *rallentando*, for the last phrase, sung with excessive charm!

ANDRÉ CAPLET

André Caplet (1879–1925) was undoubtedly a great musician; he unfortunately died too soon, before he was able to accomplish the works of his maturity which would have won him international fame. He was also a great conductor and a wonderful pianist. He was a close friend of Debussy and collaborated with him in 'Le Martyre de St. Sébastien'. His music, in which the influence of Debussy's aesthetic is obvious, is, however, highly personal. This is proved by the following

mélodies. He wrote about thirty-five (published by Durand). They all
have very important and difficult piano parts, often suggesting orchestral effects, with the different timbres and colours of the instruments. They need extreme subtlety in their interpretation, but the
composer being himself a performer has fortunately written a great
many indications on his scores, and when these are very carefully observed they are of great help to the interpreters. They indicate constant
changes of tempi, of dynamics, breaths and silences, which are very
important and often emphasized by the sign ⊓, meaning a short pause.
The voice part is at times quite lyrical and vocally demanding, with
many contrasts of shading, and also subtle effects of declamation, the
marvellous prosody exceptionally well emphasizing the literary text.

LA CROIX DOULOUREUSE	THE CROSS OF AFFLICTION
Hélas! √ si vous l'aviez voulu, √ Seigneur,	Alas! had it been your will, Lord,
elles ne couleraient pas de mes‿yeux	from my eyes would not be flowing
ces larmes brûlantes	these burning tears
que je répands	en votre présence;	that I am shedding in your presence;
si vous l'aviez voulu,	had it been your will
ils vivraient	et seraient‿encore près de moi,	they would have lived and would still be beside me,
ces‿êtres tendrement‿aimés,	those beings so tenderly loved,
dont la mort	a brisé mon cœur.	whose death has broken my heart.
Mais √ j'adore votre volonté,	But I adore your will
dont les desseins sont‿impénétrables,	of which the purposes are inscrutable,
èt qui est toujours miséricordieuse	and always merciful
jusque dans ses rigueurs‿apparentes;	even in apparent severity;
j'essaye de m'y soumettre sans murmurer;	I try to submit without complaint;
je courbe la tête,	I bow my head,
et j'accepte,	ô mon Dieu,	and I accept, O my Lord,
en l'unissant‿à la Vôtre,	in uniting with yours
la croix dont Vous m'accablez.	the cross with which you overwhelm me.
Je vous conjure seulement √	Only I beseech you
de m'aider √ à la porter.	to help me to bear it.
R. P. Lacordaire	

This beautiful text is by the Reverend Father Lacordaire, who was an eminent preacher; its subtitle is 'Prayer of the souls in mourning'.

The piano prelude (♩ = 60), which is quite orchestral, establishes a broad and dramatic mood, with sharp contrasts of dynamics and colours. The voice (mezzo-soprano or baritone) enters freely in tempo but precisely in rhythm. It is important, after all the *ritenuto* or *accelerando* indicated in this mélodie, to return to the initial tempo. At the indication *douloureusement* the tempo is the same, and there is no *accelerando* towards the big climax on 'la croix'. Then the *a tempo* should be anticipated by one bar and begin on 'dont vous m'accablez'.

The emotion aroused by the text and the excellence of the setting can easily suggest to the interpreters the right expression, but they must avoid being too dramatic or too sentimental, never forgetting that this is a prayer.

*

The two following mélodies are taken from a set of four called 'Quatre poèmes de Remy de Gourmont: Le vieux coffret'.

SONGE

Je voudrais t'emporter dans‿un
   monde nouveau
Parmi d'autres maisons | et d'autres
   paysages,
Et là, | baisant tes mains, ✓ contem-
   plant ton visage,
T'enseigner‿un amour | délicieux | et
   nouveau,

Un amour de silence, d'art ✓ et de
   paix profonde :
Notre vie serait lente ✓ et pleine de
   pensées,
Puis, | par hasard, ✓ nos mains | un
   instant rapprochées
Inclineraient nos cœurs ✓ aux caresses
   profondes.

DREAM

Would that I could bear you away
   to a new world
among other houses and other
   landscapes,
and there, kissing your hands,
   gazing at your face,
teach you a new, delightful love.

A love imbued with silence, with art
   and profound peace:
our life would be leisurely and full of
   thought,
then, by chance, our hands drawing
   close for a moment
would dispose our hearts to deeply
   felt caresses.

Et les jours passeraient, ✓ aussi beaux que des songes,
Dans la demi clarté d'une soirée d'automne,
Et nous dirions | tout bas, ✓ car le bonheur étonne:
Les jours d'amour sont doux ✓ quand la vie ✓ est un songe.

And the days would pass, as beautiful as dreams,
in the half-light of an autumn evening,
and we would say, very softly, for happiness astonishes:
the days of love are sweet when life is a dream.

R. de Gourmont

After four bars of D flat pedal with a big crescendo and decrescendo-*ritardando*, the piano launches an ascending motif which is caught, with enthusiasm, by the voice (there is hardly any *ritenuto* on 'monde nouveau'), and a rather fast tempo (♩ = 100) is set; the second bar of this tempo has been thus modified by the composer:

A *rallentando* leads to a 'slow and calm' tempo about ♩ = 58, very supple, which expresses 'Notre vie serait lente et pleine de pensées', and from 'nos mains' starts an *animato poco a poco* of nine bars, in spite of which the diminuendo and *p* in 'profondes' should not be missed, '-fondes' being, of course, in crescendo with the piano.

The last stanza of the poem is very quiet and slow, observing the numerous indications of nuances and tempi, which magnify so well all the intentions of the poet.

FORÊT

O Forêt, toi qui vis passer bien des
    amants
Le long de tes sentiers, sous tes
    profonds feuillages,
Confidentes des jeux, | des cris, | et
    des serments,
Témoin | à qui les âmes | avouaient
    leurs orages.

O Forêt, souviens-toi de ceux qui sont
    venus
Un jour d'été √ fouler tes mousses et
    tes herbes,
Car ils ont trouvé là des baisers
    ingénus
Couleur de feuilles, couleur d'écorces,
    couleur de rêves.

O Forêt, tu fus bonne, √ en laissant le
    désir
Fleurir, √ ardente fleur, √ au sein de
    ta verdure.
L'ombre devint plus fraîche: un
    frisson de plaisir
Enchanta les deux cœurs √ et toute la
    nature.

O Forêt, souviens-toi de ceux qui sont
    venus
Un jour d'été √ fouler tes herbes
    solitaires
Et contempler | distraits, tes arbres
    ingénus
Et le pâle océan de tes vertes
    fougères.

R. de Gourmont

FOREST

O forest, you who have seen many
    lovers pass
along your footpaths, beneath your
    deep foliage,
confidante of games, of cries, and of
    vows,
witness to whom souls confess their
    passions.

O forest, remember those who came
    one summer day to tread upon
    your moss and your grasses,
for they found there ingenuous kisses
    the colour of leaves, the colour of
    bark, of dreams.

O forest, you were kind to allow
    desire
to blossom, passionate flower, in the
    bosom of your verdure.
The shadows grew cooler: a thrill of
    pleasure
enchanted the two hearts and the
    whole of nature.

O forest, remember those who came
    one summer day to tread upon your
    lonely grasses
and to gaze, abstractedly, at your
    simple trees
and the pallid ocean of your green
    ferns.

This is one of the most beautiful mélodies of all the French concert
repertoire: a perfect alloy of poem and music, the lyricism as well as

the refinement of the music make its interpretation a delight for the performers.

In the four-bar introduction comes the first invocation to the forest. It should be slow, broad and *senza rigore*; intense but simple in expression, and for the most part without sadness, rather with gratitude. (Please read the poem carefully.) Then a tempo *sans lenteur*, about ♩ = 66, begins, which seems to be the basic tempo of the mélodie, with, however, a great many changes! In this tempo the poem should be sung simply, but all the subtle indications of nuances should be observed. This leads to the second invocation: 'O Forêt', which is more intense than the first one (not too *p* the word 'forêt'), initiating *a tempo* a tune which will return as a kind of refrain in the final stanza. Observe the silences: 'couleur de feuilles' ⊓ 'couleur d'écorces' longer ⊓, and slower 'couleur de rêve'—then immediately *a tempo*. The third 'O Forêt' can be more discreet, and here a *tempo più animato* begins for four bars, which continues in the piano part, until it slows down to bring in the phrase 'L'ombre devint plus fraîche' ('devint' and not 'devient' as printed by mistake) which should be *a tempo*, clear and transparent. A sudden *accelerando* of the piano leads to a strong accent on the first beat of the tremolo. *A tempo* for two bars and a very big *allargando* on 'et toute la nature'. Then *più animato* a great exultation of the piano part begins, leading to the last invocation to the forest: climax of lyricism. The piano brings back the refrain and the whole end of the mélodie remains quieter; the last phrase must be sung in one breath, so the piano must not drag.

*

Three more mélodies, taken from *Cinq Ballades de Paul Fort*, are now considered, in which the piano parts are of predominant importance, and are very difficult to play. The vocal line, with all its subtleties of rhythm and declamation, should never disturb the playing of the pianist.

CLOCHE D'AUBE	BELL OF DAWN
Ce petit air de cloche, | errant dans le matin,	This little bell tune, roving in the morning,

a rajeuni mon cœur |
à la pointe du jour.
Ce petit_air de cloché, |
au cœur frais du matin,
léger, proché, | et lointain,
a changé mon destin.
Quoi! vais-je après cette heure
survivre à mon bonheur,
ô petit_air de cloché
qui rajeunis mon cœur?
Si lointain, monotone |
et perdu, si perdu,
petit_air, petit_air, |
au cœur frais de la nue,
tu t'en vas, reviens, sonnés,
errant comme l'amour,
tu trembles sur mon cœur
à la pointe du jour.
Quoi! la vie pourrait_être...
monotone et champêtré |
et doucé, et comme est proché
ce petit_air de cloche?
douce et simple et lointaine aussi
comme est lointain
ce petit_air qui tremblé √
au cœur frais du matin?

has rejuvenated my heart
at daybreak.
This little bell tune
in the fresh heart of the morning,
light, near, and distant,
has changed my destiny.
What! after this hour
shall I survive my happiness,
O little bell tune
which rejuvenates my heart?
So distant, monotonous
and lost, so lost,
little tune, little tune,
in the fresh heart of the sky,
you depart, return, ring,
roving like love,
you tremble upon my heart
at daybreak.
What! life could be ...
unvaried and pastoral
and sweet, and near
as this little bell tune?
Sweet and simple and distant too
as distant as
this little tune which trembles
in the fresh heart of the morning?

Paul Fort

This charming poem immediately evokes a clear and transparent atmosphere, which is perfectly suggested by the music; pianist and singer should choose the freshest colours of their palette.

As always, in Caplet's scores, all the dynamics, nuances, changes of tempi, etc., are precisely indicated. The general tempo is about ♩ = 72. The accuracy in the voice part must be perfect, and the contrast between rhythmic and *non legato* phrases, with melodic and legato phrases, emphasized. The tempo *più lento* on the bar 'a changé mon destin' must be maintained for four bars, and then, four bars of *accelerando* bring back the *tempo primo*. After the 'crescendo-*accelerando*' before 'Quoi!' there is a sudden silence ⌐, and 'Quoi! la vie pourrait être...monotone et champêtre et douce' is in a much slower tempo, but in the bar after 'douce' the *tempo primo* begins again: this indication is obviously omitted.

LA RONDE	THE DANCING RING
Si toutɇɇ les fillɇɇ du mondɇ	If all the girls in the world
voulaient s'donner la main	would join hands
tout_autour de la mer	all around the sea
ellɇɇ pourraient faire unɇ rondɇ.	they could make a ring.
Si tous les gaɇɇ du mondɇ	If all the boys in the world
voulaient bien_êtɇ' marins	would become sailors
ils f'raient_avec leurs barquɇɇ	they could make with their ships
un joli pont sur l'ondɇ.	a pretty bridge over the water.
Alors... on pourrait faire	Then . . . one could make
une rondɇ ✓ autour du mondɇ	a ring around the world
si tous les gens du mondɇ	if everyone in the world
voulaient s'donner la main.	would join hands.

Paul Fort

This is a brilliant little mélodie, which suggests the style of a folk-song. The tempo is well indicated, ♩. = 128, and should be unremitting to the final phrase of the voice.

The first quatrain must be very gaily sung with firm rhythm, but more legato on the third and fourth line, and a strong *sforzando* on the attack of 'ronde'. The indication *à toute volée* in the piano part could be translated: ringing a full peal.

The second quatrain is marked *rude* (rough) to suggest the lads, but again the third and fourth lines must be more legato, with a diminuendo to 'l'onde' which is *p*, on the *pp* of the piano part. *A peine effleuré* means: scarcely touched.

'Alors...' is *pp* and mysterious, with the stress on the ♪ of 'A'. 'On pourrait faire une ronde autour du monde' is *ff*, crescendo and *marcato*, with a strong 'd' at the end of 'monde'. Then a silence must precede the attack of the following chord, and the singer, almost in tempo (with even quavers in the bar in $\frac{3}{4}$), and *p*, must express how Utopian this human fraternity could be.

L'ADIEU EN BARQUE	THE FAREWELL IN A BOAT
C'est l'heure où le château s'endort,	This is the hour when the castle goes to sleep,
l'heure où les rames sont si belles,	the hour when rowing is so beautiful,
où l'hirondelle entraîne l'or du soir	when the swallow carries the gold of evening
jusqu'au plus bleu du ciel,	up to the bluest blue of the sky,
où je cache le paysage ✓	when I hide the countryside
à mes yeux tout remplis d'amour.	from my eyes so full of love.
Je m'en vais, ✓ pleurs de mon visage.	I go away, my face covered with tears.
Quittons ces rames pour toujours!	Let us leave these oars for ever!
Paul Fort	

This mélodie is a beautiful piano piece on which the vocal line expressing the mysterious poem is laid. This perfect blending creates an extremely poetic atmosphere.

The general tempo is about ♩. = 56, and its alterations are, as usual, very well indicated. The words *très enveloppé* on the first phrase for the voice means 'with a veiled voice'. The indication one bar earlier for the piano—'*très effacé*'—means 'unobtrusive'.

To do full justice to this mélodie, the pianist must display wonderful effects of sonorities, as well as warm impulses of lyricism; the singer must sing with beautiful legato and phrasing. Interpreters cannot fail to be moved by the beauty of this poetic evocation.

12 | Albert Roussel
(1869–1937)

Albert Roussel was chiefly a symphonist, but he also wrote chamber music and about thirty-five mélodies. His style is entirely personal. Among the French composers of the period, Roussel was the most polyphonic in his writing. As his biographer, Arthur Hoerée, says: 'In the midst of Debussyism he maintained intact the structural, contrapuntal tradition.'

In his mélodies he combines great harmonic refinement with a marked diversity of rhythms; these are of paramount importance. In most of the songs, the singer will also find a characteristic difficulty: the singing line is often interrupted by long silences that the interpreter will need to fill by his 'presence'.

LE JARDIN MOUILLÉ

La croisée est ouverte; il pleut
Comme minutieusement,
A petit bruit | et peu à peu,
Sur le jardin frais et dormant.

Feuille à feuille la pluie éveille
L'arbre poudreux qu'elle verdit,
Au mur on dirait que la treille
S'étire d'un geste engourdi.

GARDEN IN THE RAIN

The casement is open, it is raining
as though meticulously,
quietly and gradually,
on the fresh, sleeping garden.

Leaf by leaf the rain awakens
the dusty tree that it turns green,
the vine on the wall seems
to be stretching itself with a sleepy
    movement.

L'herbe frémit, √ le gravier tiède⌒ Crépite, √ et l'on croirait là-bas Entendre sur le sable⌣et l'herbe	The grass trembles, the warm gravel crackles, as though yonder could be heard on the sand and on the grass
Comme d'imperceptibles pas.	imperceptible steps.
Le jardin chuchote⌣et tressaille	The garden is whispering and quivering
Furtif et confidentiel, L'averse semble maille⌣à maille Tisser la terre⌣avec le ciel.	stealthily and confidentially, stitch by stitch the shower seems to be weaving the earth to the sky.
Il pleut, et les yeux clos, j'écoute, De toute sa pluie à la fois Le jardin mouillé qui s'égoutte Dans l'ombre que j'ai faite⌣en moi.	It rains, and with closed eyes, I listen, as with all its rain at once the wet garden flows into the secret silence of my mind.

Henri de Régnier

This pretty poem has inspired the musician to write a very beautiful mélodie of exquisite subtlety, published by Salabert, which is rewarding for both interpreters, who should be able to achieve an extremely poetic atmosphere. There are scarcely any changes of dynamics in this mélodie; it should remain *p* or *mp*, attempting to give an impression of the kind of silence it evokes. The delicate and very well-written piano part suggests the falling rain on the gravel paths and on the lawns. The moderate tempo is about ♩ = 72. The vocal line, which seems at the beginning to be quite 'near-speech', with the perfection of its prosody and its very small range, should, however, be sung legato and be precise in rhythm. It is quite objective and descriptive in a poetic way.

The second quatrain is a very little more *animato*, and the *poco ritenuto* returning to the *tempo primo* can begin on the word 'S'étire'. With the third quatrain, a little *poco a poco animato* of six bars begins, which slows down on 'Comme d'imperceptibles pas' to return to *tempo primo*. The last bar of the fourth quatrain is slightly *ritenuto*; this makes the charming vocal phrase easier. The piano brings back the first musical theme and tempo. The rain is still falling on the garden, but the singer must have a different expression: he is now quite sub-

jective, and must convey the emotion of the poet listening to the rain
falling in the secret silence of his mind.

*

For several of his mélodies, Roussel has set very ancient Chinese
poems (adapted by H. P. Roché from the English translation of Herbert
Giles). This is not surprising; the taste for exoticism is noticeable in
many of his works. Three of these settings, the first two published by
Salabert, the third by Durand, are now considered; they tell three little
love stories.

A UN JEUNE GENTILHOMME	TO A YOUNG GENTLEMAN
N'entrez pas, Monsieur, s'il vous plaît,	Don't come in, Sir, please,
Ne brisez pas mes fougères,	don't crush my ferns,
Non pas que cela me fasse grand' peine,	not that that would very much grieve me,
Mais que diraient mon père et ma mère?	but what would my father and mother say?
Et même si je vous aime,	And even if I love you,
Je n'ose penser | à ce qui arriverait.	I dare not think what would happen.
Ne passez pas mon mur, Monsieur, s'il vous plaît,	Don't climb over my wall, Sir, please,
N'abîmez pas mes primevères,	don't spoil my primulas,
Non pas que cela me fasse grand' peine,	not that that would very much grieve me,
Mais, mon Dieu, que diraient mes frères?	but, heavens, what would my brothers say?
Et même si je vous aime,	And even if I love you,
Je n'ose penser | à ce qui arriverait.	I dare not think what would happen.
Restez dehors, Monsieur, s'il vous plaît,	Stay outside, Sir, please,
Ne passez pas mon paravent,	don't come through my shutter,
Non pas que cela me fasse grand' peine,	not that that would very much grieve me,
Mais, mon Dieu! qu'en diraient les gens?	but, heavens, what would people say?
Et même si je vous aime,	And even if I love you,
Je n'ose penser | à ce qui arriverait.	I dare not think what would happen.

H. P. Roché

A Chinese lady sees her lover trying to enter her house; of course she does not mind if he spoils her flowers, being completely captivated, but she is terrified of what people will say. However, in each stanza of the poem she sees him coming nearer and nearer, and this should be perceptible in the interpretation. The initial tempo is about ♩ = 96, but it is very supple. In each stanza on the same line, the same alteration of tempo takes place: 'Non pas que cela me fasse grand'peine' always demands a *ritenuto*, and the following line is *subito a tempo* and *mf*, before the *senza rigore* and *p*, on 'Et même si je vous aime'. In each stanza this phrase, which cleverly rises a semitone each time, can be more and more expressive and tender. In the last stanza, the final line is really whispered. 'What would happen' is rather 'what will happen . . .'. The little piano interludes and the ending are in a very fast and free tempo.

AMOUREUX SÉPARÉS

Dans le royaume de Yen, un jeune
    galant réside,
Dans le royaume de Chao, une belle
    demoiselle habite.
A vrai dire, ces royaumes ne sont pas
    très distants,
Mais une chaîne de monts à pic les
    sépare bel et bien.
'Vous, nuages, sur vos fortes
    poitrines, emportez-moi,
Vents, soyez mes chevaux, et
    galopez!'
Les nuages du ciel n'écoutent pas la
    voix,
La brise changeante s'élève et
    retombe,
Je reste dans l'amertume de mes
    pensées,
Songeant à la bien-aimée que je
    n'atteindrai pas.

SEPARATED LOVERS

In the kingdom of Yen, a young
    gallant resides,
in the kingdom of Chao, a lovely
    maiden dwells.
Truth to tell, these realms are not
    very far apart,
but a range of mountain peaks
    completely separates them.
'You, clouds, carry me on your
    strong breasts,
winds, be my steeds and gallop!'

The clouds in the sky do not hear the
    voice,
the changeful breeze rises and falls
    again,
I am left with the bitter sorrow of my
    thoughts,
dreaming of the beloved whom I
    will never reach.

H. P. Roché

Roussel's music follows this little poem very closely, and makes its interpretation quite obvious. The suggestion of Chinese music in the piano part (about ♩ = 96) immediately creates the right style for the first two lines, and the way the crescendo is built up easily suggests the fatal fact of the separation. The three tempi, always increasing in speed, with galloping rhythms perfectly suited to the words, must be *f* and *marcato*. The return to the initial rhythm suggests the right expression of disappointment for 'Les nuages du ciel n'écoutent pas la voix', and with the changing breeze, the voice 's'élève et retombe' with a crescendo–decrescendo, and a slight *portamento*. Now, in a slower tempo, the young lover laments his solitude with a florid *rallentando* phrase on the evocation of his 'bien-aimée', and much slower still, comes the statement of his cruel fate.

RÉPONSE D'UNE ÉPOUSE
SAGE

REPLY OF A VIRTUOUS WIFE

Connaissant, seigneur, mon état
    d'épouse,

Knowing, Sir, my married state,

Tu m'as envoyé deux perles
    précieuses,

you have sent me two precious pearls,

Et moi, comprenant ton amour,

and I, understanding your love,

Je les posai froidement sur la soie de
    ma robe.

coldly placed them upon the silk of
    my dress.

Car ma maison | est de haut lignage,

For my house is of high lineage,

Mon époux, capitaine de la garde du
    Roi.

my husband, captain of the King's
    Guard.

Et un homme comme toi devrait
    dire:

And a man such as yourself ought to
    say:

'Les liens de l'épouse ne se défont
    pas.'

'The bonds of matrimony are not to
    be broken.'

Avec les deux perles je te renvoie
    deux larmes,

With the two pearls I send you back
    two tears,

Deux larmes pour ne pas t'avoir
    connu plus tôt.

two tears that I did not meet you
    sooner.

H. P. Roché

A very dignified Chinese lady must be portrayed from the very first note of this *mélodie*, with complete outward calm but with secret emotion, except when she proclaims her high rank.

For once, in Roussel's mélodies, the metronomic tempi are very precisely indicated: ♩ = 92, 112, 120 and then back to 92; but there is not one dynamic indication in the voice part. However, the literary text and the indications in the piano part are sufficient. There are no reasons for any particular effect of dynamics, except, of course, for the big crescendo to the top A. The key to the interpretation of the song is the touching impassivity of the lady. She must affirm with great nobility: 'Les liens de l'épouse ne se défont pas', thus confirming herself in her intransigent attitude; and the heartrending conclusion of her answer, so full of desperate regret, can, avoiding any sweet sentimentality, be extremely moving.

*

The charming and often witty poet René Chalupt has also inspired Roussel to write several mélodies. Three of them, published by Durand, now follow:

LE BACHELIER DE SALAMANQUE	THE BACHELOR OF SALAMANCA
Où vas-tu, toi qui passes si tard	Where are you going, you who pass by so late
Dans les rues désertes de Salamanque,	in the deserted streets of Salamanca,
Avec ta toque noire et ta guitare,	with your black hat and your guitar,
Que tu dissimules sous ta mante ?	which you are hiding under your cloak ?
Le couvre-feu est déjà sonné	The curfew has already sounded
Et depuis longtemps dans leurs paisibles maisons	and long since in their peaceful houses
Les bourgeois dorment à poings fermés.	the citizens have been fast asleep.
Ne sais-tu pas qu'un édit de l'alcade	Do you not know that an edict of the mayor
Ordonne de jeter en prison	decrees that prison shall be the punishment
Tous les donneurs de sérénade,	for all those who serenade,
Que les malandrins couperont ta chaîne d'or,	that the brigands will cut your golden chain,

Et que la fille de l'Almirante,
Pour qui vainement tu te tourmentes,
Se moque de toi, derrière son
    mirador ?

René Chalupt

and that the Admiral's daughter
for whom you vainly sigh,
is laughing at you behind her
    mirador ?

No more Chinese music! but a clever and sprightly pastiche of Spanish music. ♩ = 144 is the lively tempo, and the ironical apostrophe of the singer can be rather *f*, except 'Que tu dissimules sous ta mante ?' which should be more *p* to underline the meaning of the words. In a tempo around ♩ = 104 *sforzato*, the horn of the night-watchman is soon heard in the piano part: B double flat or A. The line 'Les bourgeois dorment à poings fermés' is *poco allargando* and *portamento*, with no diminuendo coming down, and a mocking expression. Back to the *tempo primo*, the many words must be made clearly understandable. After a short breath come five bars of very languid music (about ♩ = 72), but always with the ironical theme in the left hand; they should be sung with a rather exaggerated legato. There is a sudden return to the *tempo primo*. 'Derrière son mirador' can be unhurried, but the rhythm which is excellent for the prosody must be maintained; and there should be laughter in the voice.

SARABANDE

Les jets d'eau dansent des sarabandes
Sur l'herbe parfumée des boulingrins;
Il y a des rumeurs de soie dans le
    jardin
Et de mystérieuses présences.
Sur le marbre rose d'une margelle,
Trois tourterelles se sont posées,
Comme sur tes lèvres trois baisers;
Leurs plumes s'éffeuillent dans le
    bassin.
Les fleurs fraîches des marronniers
Neigent lentement sur tes seins

Et font frissonner ta chair nue,
Car tu es nue sous ton manteau.

SARABAND

The fountains are dancing sarabands
on the fragrant grass of the lawns;
there are sounds of rustling silk in the
    garden
and of mysterious presences.
On the pink marble rim of a fountain
three doves have alighted,
like three kisses on your lips;
their feathers flutter down into the
    basin.
The fresh flowers of the chestnut tree
fall slowly like snow upon your
    breast
making your bare skin shiver,
for you are naked under your cloak.

Et c'est pour toi que les jets d'eau	And it is for you that the fountains
Dansent de sveltes sarabandes,	are dancing slender sarabands,
Que le parc est plein de présences,	that the park is full of presences,
Et que les tourterelles blanches,	and that the white doves,
Comme de vivantes guirlandes,	like living garlands,
Viennent fleurir au bord de l'eau.	are flowering on the edge of the
René Chalupt	water.

Roussel's setting of these free, poetic verses is, in my opinion, his most beautiful mélodie. He gives perfect expression to the lovely spring night, when a young lover addresses his beloved in an exquisite garden, surrounded by marble fountains and white turtle doves.

The difficult piano part, played with as much fluidity as possible, depicts the 'slender saraband' of the fountains. ♩ = 76 seems to be the best tempo. The voice starts *mf* with perfect legato and phrasing; then, on the third and fourth line, a subito *pp*, almost whispered, expresses 'rumeurs de soies' and 'mystérieuses présences'. A second tempo is introduced, about ♩ = 84, and the piano imitates the cooing of the doves. The *poco ritenuto* on the words 'sur tes lèvres trois baisers' must be well observed, before immediately picking up the second tempo again. The indication *en pressant un peu (poco animando)* must be anticipated by one bar, beginning on the words 'plumes s'effeuillent dans le bassin'. It continues to the indication *a tempo*, which is definitely the second tempo (♩ = 84). The singer has enough silences to fill. . . . A *ritenuto* on 'Car tu es nue sous ton manteau' brings back the *tempo primo*, *mf*, and a *pp* suggests again the mysterious presences. I never quite understood the indication *pp* on 'Viennent fleurir'; in my opinion one must reserve the possibility of more diminuendo for the end of the mélodie, with the *rallentando*.

CŒUR EN PÉRIL

Que m'importe que l'Infante de
  Portugal
Ait le visage rond | ou bien ovale,
Et une cicatrice sous le sein droit,
Qu'elle ait l'air d'une fille de roi |

HEART IN DANGER

What do I care whether the Infanta
  of Portugal
has a round or an oval face,
and a scar on her right breast,
whether she has the manner of a
  king's daughter

Ou d'une gardeuse d'oies,   or of a goose girl,
Que m'importe?   what do I care?

Peu me chaut que la Princesse de   It matters little to me if the Princess
   Trébizonde   of Trebizond
Soit rousse, châtaine ou blonde,   be red-haired, chestnut-haired or fair,
Qu'elle ait l'humeur prompte et le   if she be quick-tempered and
   verbe haut,   dictatorial,
Peu me chaut.   it matters little to me.

Point n'ai souci que la marquise de   I do not care at all that the Marchion-
   Carabas   ess of Carabas
Soit veuve | et veuille reprendre mari,   is a widow and wishes to marry again,
Pour faire ici-bas son paradis!   to create her paradise here on earth!
Point n'ai souci!   I do not care at all!

Mais il suffit, | jeune étourdie,   But it needs no more, young scatter-
                                                brain,
Du seul clin d'un de vos yeux   than one glance from your mocking
   moqueurs | eyes
Aux reflets irisés,   with their iridescent light,
Pour que mon pauvre cœur   to make my poor heart
Batte | à se briser.   beat hard enough to break.

                    René Chalupt

A sprightly little mélodie which, though less interesting musically,
can make an effective end to a group by Roussel. A young man tries
to allure his beloved by telling her, with a certain waggish humour,
how little he cares about the great and brilliant ladies of the world, but
(in the final stanza) how much he cares about her. . . .

It is a serenade, and ♩ = 116 is just right, with only a supple *allargando*
on 'Ait le visage rond ou bien ovale', a discreet *subito p* on 'une cicatrice
sous le sein droit', an obvious crescendo on 'Qu'elle ait l'air d'une
fille de roi' and legato with no breath before 'Ou d'une gardeuse
d'oies', short quaver on the last word and a breath on the quaver rest.

In the second stanza, there is again a supple *allargando* on 'châtaine ou
blonde'. The piano must be very rhythmic in the third stanza (it is
better to break between 'veuve' and 'et') and the supple *allargando* is
on 'Pour faire ici-bas son paradis'.

The final stanza is in a quieter tempo and very legato for the voice (break between 'suffit' and 'jeune'). The bar 'clin d'un de vos yeux moqueurs' can be freely detailed, and the serenade continues *rallentando* to the end. (It is better to break between 'batte' and 'à se briser'.) The last two lines can be quite touching, in a light mood.

13 | Maurice Ravel
(1875–1937)

In comparison with Ravel's total output, the number of his mélodies is very small. There are thirty-nine in all; and among these, eleven are harmonizations of folksongs and traditional songs, but adapted with such personality and genius, that they are worthy of being listed among his original works. Here is a complete list:

1895	Un grand sommeil noir (Verlaine)	DURAND
1896	Sainte (Stéphane Mallarmé)	DURAND
1898	Deux Épigrammes de Clément Marot:	ESCHIG
	D'Anne qui me jecta de la neige	
	D'Anne jouant de l'espinette	
1903	Manteau de fleurs (P. Gravollet)	HAMELLE
	Shéhérazade: (Tristan Klingsor)	DURAND
	Asie	
	La flûte enchantée	
	L'indifférent	
1905	Le Noël des jouets (M. Ravel)	SALABERT
1906	Les grands vents venus d'outre-mer (H. de Régnier)	DURAND
	Histoires naturelles: (Jules Renard)	DURAND
	Le paon	
	Le grillon	
	Le cygne	
	Le martin-pêcheur	
	La pintade	

1907	Sur l'herbe (P. Verlaine)	DURAND
	Vocalise en forme de habanera	LEDUC
	Cinq mélodies populaires grecques:	DURAND
	Le réveil de la mariée	
	Là-bas vers l'église	
	Quel galant!	
	Chanson des cueilleuses de lentisques	
	Tout gai!	
1910	Chants populaires:	DURAND
	Chanson espagnole	
	Chanson française	
	Chanson italienne	
	Chanson hébraïque	
1913	Trois poèmes de Stéphane Mallarmé: (piano, quartet, 2 flutes, 2 clarinets)	DURAND
	Soupir	
	Placet futile	
	Surgi de la croupe et du bond	
1914	Deux mélodies hébraïques:	DURAND
	Kaddisch	
	L'énigme éternelle	
1924	Ronsard à son âme	DURAND
1925/26	Chansons madécasses (Evariste Parny) (flute, violoncello, piano)	DURAND
	Nahandove	
	Aoua!	
	Il est doux...	
1927	Rêves (L. P. Fargue)	DURAND
1932	Don Quichotte à Dulcinée: (Paul Morand)	DURAND
	Chanson romanesque	
	Chanson épique	
	Chanson à boire	

*

SHÉHÉRAZADE

'These three poems for voice and orchestra,' writes Ravel, 'where Debussy's spiritual influence is at least fairly obvious, date from 1903. In them, I have succumbed again to the profound fascination which the

East has held for me since childhood.' They are settings of poems by Tristan Klingsor, who, the same year, had published a book called *Shéhérazade*, and here is what he writes: 'Ravel immediately wanted to set some of my poems. His love for difficulty made him choose, together with 'La flûte enchantée' and 'L'indifférent', one, the long narrative of which made it appear quite unsuitable for his purpose: 'Asie'. For at that time, he was engaged in a study of spoken verse, and was aiming at emphasizing accents and inflexions, and magnifying them by melodic transposition. To fix his conception firmly, he insisted on my reading the lines aloud.'

These two quotations are enough to explain why Ravel was attracted and inspired by these poems.

They were originally written for voice and orchestra, and 'Asie' is hardly possible to perform with piano accompaniment. 'La flûte enchantée' and 'L'indifférent', although not as good with piano, are, however, possible. 'La flûte enchantée' can be sung with flute and piano.

ASIE	ASIA
1 Asie, Asie, √ Asie,	Asia, Asia, Asia,
Vieux pays merveilleux des contes de nourrice, √	ancient, marvellous country of fairy tales,
Où dort la fantaisie comme une impératrice, √	where fantasy sleeps like an empress
En sa forêt tout emplie de mystère.	in her forest full of mystery.
2 Asie,	Asia,
Je voudrais m'en aller avec la goëlette √	I would like to go with the schooner
Qui se berce ce soir dans le port, √	which is rocking this evening in the port
Mystérieuse et solitaire,	mysterious and solitary,
Et qui déploie enfin ses voiles violettes,	and which finally spreads its violet sails
Comme un immense oiseau de nuit dans le ciel d'or.	like a huge bird of night in the golden sky.

3 Je voudrais m'en‿aller vers des‿
    îles de fleurs,
En‿écoutant chanter la mer
    perverse,
Sur un vieux rythme‿ensorceleur.

I would like to go away to the
    islands of flowers,
while listening to the song of the
    wayward sea,
with its old, bewitching rhythm.

4 Je voudrais voir Damas et les
    villes de Perse,
Avec des minarets légers dans
    l'air.
Je voudrais voir de beaux
    turbans de soie,
Sur des visages noirs | aux dents
    claires.

I would like to see Damascus and the
    cities of Persia,
with airy minarets in the sky.

I would like to see beautiful, silken
    turbans
above black faces with shining teeth.

5 Je voudrais voir des‿yeux
    sombres d'amour,
Et des prunelles brillantes de joie,
En des peaux jaunes comme des‿
    oranges.
Je voudrais voir des vêtements de
    velours
Et des habits‿à longues franges.

I would like to see eyes dark with
    love
and pupils sparkling with joy,
in skins yellow as oranges.

I would like to see garments of velvet

and robes with long fringes.

6 Je voudrais voir des calumets,✓
    entre des bouches⌢
Tout‿entourées de barbe
    blanche.
Je voudrais voir d'âpres
    marchands‿aux regards
    louches,
Et des cadis, | et des vizirs⌢
Qui de seul mouvement de leur
    doigt qui se penche,✓
Accordent vie | ou mort, ✓ au
    gré de leur désir.

I would like to see calumets, held
    between lips
fringed with white beards.

I would like to see avaricious
    merchants with shifty glances,

and cadis, and viziers
who with a single movement of their
    bending finger,
decree life or death, just as they wish.

7 Je voudrais voir la Perse,‿et
    l'Inde,‿et puis la Chine,
Les mandarins ventrus sous les‿
    ombrelles,
Et les princesses‿aux mains fines,

I would like to see Persia, and India,
    and then China,
the portly mandarins beneath their
    sunshades,
and the princesses with their delicate
    hands,

	Et les lettrés qui se querellent	and the scholars who dispute
	Sur la poésie ✓ et sur la beauté.	over poetry and beauty;
8	Je voudrais m'attarder_au palais_enchanté,	I would like to linger in the enchanted palace,
	Et comme un voyageur étranger	and like a foreign traveller
	Contempler_à loisir des paysages peints	gaze at leisure upon countrysides painted
	Sur des_étoffes ✓ en des cadres de sapin,	on materials in pinewood frames,
	Avec un personnage au milieu d'un verger.	with a figure in the midst of an orchard.
9	Je voudrais voir des_assassins souriant	I would like to see assassins smiling
	Du bourreau qui coupe un cou d'innocent,	at the executioner who cuts off an innocent head
	Avec son grand sabre courbé d'Orient.	with his great curved oriental sabre.
	Je voudrais voir des pauvres_et des reines,	I would like to see beggars and queens,
	Je voudrais voir des roses | et du sang,	I would like to see roses and blood,
	Je voudrais voir mourir d'amour ✓ ou bien de haine.	I would like to see death for love or else for hate.
10	(Interlude)	(Interlude)
11	Et puis m'en revenir plus tard	And then returning later,
	Narrer mon_aventure | aux curieux de rêves,	to narrate my adventure to those interested in dreams,
	En_élevant comme Sindbad ma vieille tasse_arabe	while raising like Sinbad my old Arabian cup
	De temps_en temps jusqu'à mes lèvres,	from time to time to my lips,
	Pour interrompre le conte_avec art...	to interrupt the tale with artistry. . . .

Tristan Klingsor

This long enumerative mélodie is divided musically into eleven sections (which are indicated above for the convenience of study), each one evoking a different picture. It is most important to settle precisely all the successive tempi. In the most recent Durand score for voice and piano, all the metronomic markings are indicated according to the orchestral score.

SECTION 1 (♩ = 40) is the mysterious introduction. On the quivering of the violins, the oboe introduces a theme that will reappear several times, particularly at the conclusion. The voice enters *p*, the poet repeating three times 'Asie', this word representing for him a whole world of dreams. In a big crescendo phrase, the first two 'Asie' are legato, and a deep expressive breath should be taken before the third. After two sparkling bars of orchestra there is a short recitative, but *sung* legato and in time. Two breaths can be taken as indicated above.

SECTION 2. (♪ = 96) The beautiful orchestral prelude suggests the 'ship rocking in the port', which will take the poet to his dream country 'spreading its violet sails in the golden sky'. The breaths indicated above do not correspond to Ravel's indications, but are much preferable and are customary.

SECTION 3 (♩. = 50) with its rhythmic pattern, and its broad harp *glissandi*, introduces

SECTION 4 (♩. = 76) with its Persian music, and the return of the initial theme, over which 'Je voudrais voir de beaux turbans de soie', etc., should be very legato.

A *rallentando* introduces SECTION 5, again based on the initial theme. This section according to the different editions is written:

je voudrais voir des yeux sombres d'amour etc. - -

je voudrais voir des yeux sombres d'amour etc. - -

the tempo is ♪ = 60, or ♩ = 60; the long values, as in the orchestral score, increase the impression of the great calm and poetic atmosphere requested.

SECTION 6 (♩ = 72) has much more intensity. Observe the indicated breaths. There is a *rallentando* on the bar 'Vie ou mort, au gré de leur désir', and then *a tempo* for two bars and again *rallentando* on 'Je voudrais voir la Perse, et l'Inde, et puis la Chine', to bring in:

SECTION 7 (♩ = 120) with its charming Chinese music, over which the singer's articulation must be very precise. But soon a *rallentando* leads to:

SECTION 8 (♩ = 40) In this *rallentando*, a slight *portamento* should be made on 'Je voudrais', and the whole section sung as in a peaceful dream.

Sharp contrast with the difficult SECTION 9. The indicated tempo (♩ = 72) is certainly a little too slow and the usual tempo is ♩ = 92. In the low tessitura of the beginning, the singer is advised to sing rather *f* with very strong articulation. (There are a few variations in the rhythm of the voice part, according to the different editions, but they are not very important.) A catch breath can be taken between 'souriant' and 'du bourreau'. It is much more dramatic to avoid a liaison between 'des roses' and 'et du sang'. At the end of the word 'haine' on the top B flat the 'n' should just be pronounced, but there should be no final [ə].

Then comes SECTION 11, a glorious orchestral interlude (♩. = 40), again suggesting the ship with its 'violet sails in the golden sky', but this time bringing the poet back from his dream country; therefore it slows down after seven bars to ♪ = 80, introducing the final

SECTION 12 (♩ = 40) where the poet in conclusion says that he will narrate his adventure, 'to those interested in dreams'. These lines are sung legato with a break between 'aventure' and 'aux curieux de rêve', the last two words *diminuendo*. Two violins *soli* play the initial theme, and a subtle little recitative ends the poem. The prosody could not be better and it should be kept exactly in rhythm and tempo, except for a hardly perceptible *rallentando* on the last triplet. The first two bars should be sung in one breath. The final [ə] in 'comme' is not pronounced, and the word 'Sindbad' has no nasal sound: S[i]n̲db[a]d.

This is a difficult but exciting mélodie, best suited to a mezzo-soprano, or a soprano with a good low register.

LA FLÛTE ENCHANTÉE

L'ombre est douce et mon maître
  dort
Coiffé d'un bonnet conique de soie,

Et son long nez jaune en sa barbe
  blanche.
Mais moi, je suis éveillée encor √
Et j'écoute au dehors⌐
Une chanson de flûte √ où
  s'épanche⌐
Tour à tour la tristesse √ ou la joie.
Un air tour à tour langoureux ou
  frivole√
Que mon amoureux chéri joue.
Et quand je m'approche de la
  croisée, √
Il me semble que chaque note
  s'envole⌐
De la flûte vers ma joue, √
Comme un mystérieux baiser.

                    Tristan Klingsor

THE ENCHANTED FLUTE

The shade is soft and my master is
  sleeping
with his conical silken cap on his
  head,
and his long yellow nose in his white
  beard.
But I, I am still awake
and I hear outside
the melody of a flute pouring forth

sadness and joy in turn.
An air now languorous, now gay,

that my darling lover plays.
And when I draw near the casement,

it seems as though each note flies

from the flute towards my cheek
like a mysterious kiss.

Here one has to imagine a kind of oriental Rosina, but so much more sensual than the Spanish one! The flute of her lover is heard softly in the narrow street ($\downdownarrows$ = 36) and comes through her lattice-window. She looks at her old master already asleep, and describes him to herself, *pp*, as if afraid of awakening him. Please keep the rhythm very precise. The flute plays a brillant cadenza, which brings in 'Mais moi, je suis éveillée encor' (very wide awake indeed!) ($\downdownarrows$ = 120). As the phrase descends, there is a very definite *rallentando* on 'Tour à tour la tristesse', but do not begin it before these words. On the octave 'ou la joie' a good crescendo must give the impulse to the strings of the orchestra to play excitedly. If performed with piano, the pianist will do the best he can. . . . He must take a definite breath on the double bar before the $\frac{5}{4}$ measure. Here the flute begins to play again, but in a slower tempo, which is really the *tempo primo*. On 'Que mon amoureux chéri joue', one must make a broad and very gradual *rallentando* (with a little line

over each note of 'chéri'), which is continued by the flute. The following very slow tempo should not, however, be too slow, as it is most
important that the singer should be able to sing *in one breath*: 'Il me
semble que chaque note s'envole De la flûte vers ma joue'—and with
most beautiful phrasing! One should not be afraid of a little *portamento*
between the F and the D; then a quick breath and a good *rallentando* on
'Comme un mystérieux baiser', which is not only 'mysterious' but
so tender!. . .

L'INDIFFÉRENT	THE INDIFFERENT ONE
Tes yeux sont doux comme ceux d'une fille,	Your eyes are gentle like those of a girl,
Jeune étranger, et la courbe fine	young stranger, and the delicate curve
De ton beau visage de duvet ombragé,	of your handsome face, shaded with down,
Est plus séduisante encore de ligne.	is still more attractive in its contour.
Ta lèvre chante sur le pas de ma porte	On my doorstep your lips chant
Une langue inconnue et charmante,	an unknown, charming tongue,
Comme une musique fausse.	like false music.
Entre! Et que mon vin te réconforte...	Enter! And let my wine refresh you . . .
Mais non, tu passes,	But no—you pass by,
Et de mon seuil je te vois t'éloigner,	and I see you departing from my threshold
Me faisant un dernier geste avec grâce,	gracefully waving farewell to me,
Et la hanche légèrement ployée	your hips lightly swaying
Par ta démarche féminine et lasse...	with your languid, feminine gait . . .
Tristan Klingsor	

Here is another oriental girl even more adventurous. . . . She is on
the threshold of her small house and is attracted by a young passer-by.
The poem expresses her feelings, and the whole scene is mute. Even
when she tries to allure him—it may have been by a little movement
of the head, an engaging smile. . . . But no . . . obviously he can feel
no interest in her charms, and he steps away. The singer must not be
afraid of creating, in this beautiful mélodie, a very sensuous atmosphere,

so well suggested by the poem and expressed by the music, more especially in its orchestral version.

The tempo is *very* slow: ♪ of the $\frac{6}{8}$ = 60. (Beautiful with an orchestra, it is hardly possible with a piano accompaniment.) The prelude should be as soft as possible, with the wonderful melody of the flute and the clarinet, one octave apart, suggesting the languid and feminine image of the young stranger. The voice enters *pp* with great tenderness, and sings admiringly, with very precise rhythm. (In the phrase 'De ton beau visage de duvet ombragé', according to the rule, there should be no liaison between 'duvet' and 'ombragé'; however, in this very particular case, a poetic and musical licence makes a very soft 't' acceptable.) On the phrase:

est plus sédui - sante

the tempo is very free and supple, and there are some rather exaggerated *portamenti* to express the irresistible fascination of the boy. On the phrase 'Ta lèvre chante...' the slowing down of the tempo is well indicated in the orchestra score: ♪ = 54.

Now comes the mute scene, but as she sings to herself, how engaging she can be! 'Entre!' with a little *portamento*. And after the pizzicato of the orchestra, how disappointed she can be! 'Mais non' should be rather flat and almost spoken, emphasizing the 'n' of 'non'. 'Tu passes' is more sung (long [ɑ], no double 's' of course, and almost no final [ə]). 'Et de mon seuil je te vois t'éloigner' well sustained. Some editions have the following phrase in one bar, but in the orchestral score it is in two bars, the value of each note being doubled. Then the following $\frac{3}{4}$ can be in about a similar tempo, but somewhat slower and slowing down a little towards the end. These last three lines should be sung with the same expression as the first one and with a certain feeling of regret. . . . However, one must be careful not to have the last line sound: 'par ta démarche féminine, hélas!' Thus, one must link 'féminine et' and make a *portamento* between 'et' and 'lasse', with a strong 'l' and a stress on the first syllable of the word 'lasse' (long [ɑ], no double 's', and very little final [ə]).

*

HISTOIRES NATURELLES (NATURAL HISTORIES)

This series of five mélodies was composed in 1906. They are settings of prose texts by Jules Renard. 'The direct, clear language, the profound and latent poetry [the underlining is mine] of the Histoires Naturelles has long tempted me,' writes Ravel, 'even the text itself demands from me a particular kind of declamation, closely linked to the inflexions of the French language.' This declamation is quite unique in French vocal literature. It involves daring elisions of the final weak syllables (final[ə]) which must be observed. But one must make no mistake: if these mélodies are, in Ravel's mind, a study of French declamation, they must be *sung*, not spoken. The contrast with some sentences which really are 'near-speech' then becomes striking. The musicologist Roland-Manuel once had these mélodies played by a violinist; the result was beautiful pieces for violin and piano.

It is the very important and difficult piano part which sets the scene and suggests the different characters of the animals, and from this, the singer can find the appropriate colour and expression.

The first duty for the two interpreters of these mélodies is to perform them with the most minute musical precision: not the slightest liberty can be taken towards all the rhythmic subtleties; there can be no *rubato* or alterations of tempo other than those indicated in the score. Only when this precision is achieved can the interpreters try to give the impression of improvising their texts, which should be the final effect. These descriptive texts—the literary and the musical—are often humorous and ironical; but these expressions should never be over-emphasized. I cannot stress this point enough. Nothing can be more contrary to Ravel's idea (I was lucky enough to work on these mélodies with him), and certainly contrary to the idea of Jules Renard, than to exaggerate the dry humour of these mélodies, to imply a 'tongue in the cheek' attitude. It is always, I insist, their 'profound and latent poetry' that must come to the fore.

LE PAON

Il va sûrement se marier aujourd'hui.
Ce devait être pour hier.
En habit de gala, il était prêt.
Il n'attendait que sa fiancée.
Elle n'est pas venue.
Elle ne peut tarder.
Glorieux, | il se promène avec une
   allure de prince indien
      et porté sur lui les riches
      présents d'usage.
L'amour avive l'éclat de ses couleurs
   et son aigrette tremble
      comme une lyre.
La fiancée n'arrive pas.
Il monte au haut du toit et regarde
   du côté du soleil.
Il jette son cri diabolique : Léon!
Léon!
C'est ainsi qu'il appelle sa fiancée.
Il ne voit rien venir | et personne ne
   répond.
Les volailles habituées ne lèvent
   même point la tête.
Elles sont lasses de l'admirer.
Il redescend dans la cour, si sûr
   d'être beau
      qu'il est incapable de rancune.
Son mariage sera pour demain.

Et, ne sachant que faire du reste de la
   journée,
      il se dirige vers le perron.

Il gravit les marches, comme des
   marches de temple,
      d'un pas | officiel.
Il relève sa robe à queue toute
   lourde des yeux
      qui n'ont pu se détacher d'elle.
Il répète encore une fois la cérémonie.

Jules Renard

THE PEACOCK

He will certainly be married today.
It should have been yesterday.
In his gala attire he was ready.
He was only waiting for his fiancée.
She has not come.
She cannot be long.
Magnificent, he walks with the
   demeanour of an Indian price
      bearing about him the customary
      rich gifts.
Love enhances the brilliance of his
   colours
      and his crest trembles like a lyre.
The fiancée does not come.
He mounts to the top of the roof and
   looks towards the sun.
He utters his fiendish cry : Léon! Léon!

It is thus that he calls his fiancée.
He sees nothing coming and no one
   replies.
The fowls who are accustomed to
   him never even raise their heads.
They are tired of admiring him.
He descends again to the courtyard,
   so sure of his beauty
that he is incapable of resentment.
His marriage will take place
   tomorrow.
And not knowing what to do for the
   rest of the day,
      he turns towards the flight of
      steps.
He ascends as though they were the
   steps of a temple,
      with an official tread.
He spreads open his tail, heavy with
   all the eyes
      that could not leave it.
Once more he repeats the ceremony.

Sans hâte et noblement (with no haste and with nobility) is Ravel's excellent indication, ♩ = 56 seems about right. The long piano prelude depicts the peacock's stupid pomposity. Thus the singer has plenty of time to visualize it approaching with the big crescendo, and moving away with the gradual diminuendo. (The *p* comes only one bar before the voice.) It is the singer's imagination of the scene that suggests to him his humorous and poetic remarks. During the whole mélodie he must thus give the impression, not of being the peacock himself!—but of constantly watching the beautiful bird, while his remarks gradually come to his mind. It is the only way to keep the tension and the intensity.

On the first phrase for the voice with the indication 'solemn', the dynamic *mp* seems preferable to the indicated *p*, in this low register. Immediately the singer meets the special prosody of the mélodies with the complete elision of the final [ə]. All these elisions are indicated in the above text. The liaison 'marier aujourd'hui' can be left to the taste of the singer: it is more colloquial and simpler without a liaison. A broad *mf* is important on 'En habit de gala il était prêt', to get the contrast of *p* on the straightforward 'Il n'attendait que sa fiancée'; and again *mf* very legato on the even triplets of 'Elle n'est pas venue', better with no diminuendo, with the long note on the last syllable; then *subito p* on the confident 'Elle ne peut tarder'. The following phrase is *mf* broad and legato; the piano part remaining rather *p*, with a *subito crescendo* on its solo bar, after the voice and before its *p molto espressivo* under the exaggerated lyricism of the phrase 'L'amour avive', etc., which underlines the sudden 'near-speech' of 'La fiancée n'arrive pas'. The same contrast should be made between 'Il monte au haut du toit,' etc. and the very simple statement 'C'est ainsi qu'il appelle sa fiancée'. The following phrases should be well sustained again. (The final [ə] must be carefully avoided even on the word 'tête', the C and the F being sung on [ɛ] with a *portamento*.) There is the same effect for 'rancune', B flat and F sung on [y]. 'Son mariage sera pour demain' is affirmed rather *marcato*, and the following sentences are sung with a certain pomposity. The piano makes a big diminuendo and suddenly, the singer is absolutely amazed: with a shivering of its feathers, the peacock spreads out its tail: 'Il relève sa robe à queue toute lourde des yeux qui n'ont pu se détacher d'elle'; this phrase should be intensely poetic. Then after two bars of piano, of caricatured majesty, the last phrase of the voice is very simple, precise in rhythm, with a little emphasis on the major A natural. (17th bar: The B is natural on the syllable "in".)

| LE GRILLON | THE CRICKET |

C'est l'heure | où, las d'errer, l'insecte nègre revient de promenade |

This is the hour when, tired of wandering, the nigger-brown insect returns from his outing

et répare avec soin le désordre de son domaine.

and carefully tidies the disorder of his home.

D'abord il ratisse ses étroites allées de sable.

First he rakes his narrow sandy paths.

Il fait du bran de scie qu'il écarte au seuil de sa retraite.

He makes some sawdust which he spreads on the threshold of his retreat.

Il lime la racine de cette grande herbe propre à le harceler.

He files the root of this tall grass likely to annoy him.

Il se repose.

He rests.

Puis il remonte sa minuscule montre.

Then he rewinds his tiny watch.

A-t-il fini ? est-elle cassée ?

Has he finished ? Is it broken ?

Il se repose encore un peu.

He rests again for a moment.

Il rentre chez lui et ferme sa porte.

He goes inside and shuts the door.

Longtemps | il tourne sa clef dans la serrure délicate.

For a long time he turns the key in the delicate lock.

Et | il écoute :

And he listens:

Point d'alarme dehors.

Not a sound outside.

Mais il ne se trouve pas en sûreté.

But he does not feel safe.

Et comme par une chaînette dont la poulie grince, |

il descend jusqu'au fond de la terre.

And as though by a little chain with a creaking pulley,

he lets himself down into the bowels of the earth.

On n'entend plus rien.

Nothing more is to be heard.

Dans le campagne muette, les peupliers se dressent

comme des doigts en l'air et désignent la lune.

In the silent countryside, the poplars rise

like fingers in the air pointing at the moon.

Jules Renard

In the preceding mélodie the interpreters suggest the peacock by giving the impression of constantly *watching* it; in the second mélodie, it is by *listening* in their imagination to all the little sounds made by the cricket that they will seem to be improvising their text. They must be, as it were, careful not to frighten or disturb the little insect, thus the dynamics are *p* or *pp* for the whole mélodie. The singer should choose a clear colour in his voice, with the most precise diction.

Ravel's indication *Placid* suggests the tempo ♩ = 58 (easily found by playing the first bar of the section which is in five flats). This tempo is immutable until the *lento* of the last phrase of the mélodie. It is better to make a little glottal attack between 'heure' and 'ou', and between 'promenade' and 'et'. A long rest on the bar ⌢𝅝 must give the impression of the sudden silence of the little cricket. One should also wait and observe a good silence after the chord 𝅘𝅥𝅮 (this bar being completely free), or else the singer cannot ask 'A-t-il fini?' and, anxiously, 'est-elle cassée?' Then after another good silence, being reassured: No! he only takes a little rest: 'Il se repose encore un peu'. Now back exactly to the tempo. The values of the rests are extremely important in the whole end of this mélodie. After the *ppp* 'On n'entend plus rien' and a long rest on the following *fermata*, the piano attacks *pp*, but with sonority, the extraordinarily poetic conclusion (about ♩ = 48), which is extremely legato for the voice; now even the final syllables are sung as indicated above. Thus the silent landscape under the blue moonlight will be easily suggested.

LE CYGNE	THE SWAN
Il glisse sur le bassin, comme un traîneau blanc, de nuage en nuage. Car il n'a faim que des nuages floconneux qu'il voit naître, | bouger, | et se perdre dans l'eau.	He glides on the lake, like a white sleigh, from one cloud to another. For the only hunger he feels is for the fleecy clouds that he sees appearing, moving, and vanishing in the water.

C'est l'un d'eux qu'il désire.
Il le vise du bec, et il plonge tout à
    coup son col vêtu de neige.

Puis, | tel un bras de femme sort
    d'une manche, il le retire.
Il n'a rien.
Il regarde : les nuages effarouchés |
    ont disparu.
Il ne reste qu'un instant désabusé, car
    les nuages tardent
      peu à revenir, et là-bas, où
        meurent les ondulations
      de l'eau, en voici un qui se
        reforme.
Doucement, sur son léger coussin de
    plumes, le cygne rame et
    s'approche.
Il s'épuise à pêcher de vains reflets,
    et peut-être qu'il mourra
      victime de cette illusion, avant
        d'attraper un seul
      morceau de nuage.
Mais qu'est-ce que je dis ?
Chaque fois qu'il plonge, il fouille
    du bec la vase nourrissante |
      et ramène un ver.
Il engraisse comme une oie.

Jules Renard

It is one of these that he wants.
He takes aim with his beak, and
    suddenly plunges his snowy neck
    into the water.
Then, like a woman's arm emerging
    from a sleeve, he draws it back.
He has caught nothing.
He looks: the startled clouds have
    disappeared.
He is disillusioned only for a moment,
    for the clouds are not slow
      to return, and yonder, where the
        undulations of the water are
      dying away,
      there is one which is re-forming.
Softly, upon a light cushion of
    feathers, the swan paddles and
    draws near.
He is exhausted by fishing for empty
    reflections and perhaps he will die
      a victim of this illusion, without
        having caught a single
      piece of cloud.
But what am I saying?
Each time he plunges in, he burrows
    in the nourishing mud
    and brings out a worm.
He is growing as fat as a goose.

This is a very lyrical mélodie. The poet, and the musician, are sincere in their poetic description of the swan; it is only on the last four bars of the mélodie that they suddenly mock their own sensitivity.

The tempo is $\quad = 52$. The piano part should be as fluid as possible. The voice part sung with a beautiful legato (it is therefore better to sing the final [ə] of 'glisse'), soft and calm as indicated. After the short *ritenuto* of the seventh bar, one should be *a tempo* for 'C'est l'un d'eux qu'il désire', and precise in rhythm and diction for 'Il le vise du bec'. There is a *subito pp* and a real *portamento* on 'plonge'. The wonderfully evocative phrase: 'Puis tel un bras de femme sort d'une manche il le retire' requires also a *portamento* on 'manche'. The following recitative: 'Il n'a rien. Il regarde: les nuages éffarouchés ont disparu', although 'near-speech' must not be too dry, above the staccato of the piano. (Watch the rhythm!) Then comes a very slow episode, about twice as slow as the *tempo primo*, and always legato for the voice and the piano. In the bar in $\frac{3}{2}$, with a crescendo and decrescendo, the piano brings back the *tempo primo*. On the sentence: 'Il s'épuise à pêcher de vains reflets, et peut-être qu'il mourra victime de cette illusion', the interpreters must be very expressive, and a big *ritenuto* must be established, counting the last two bars of $\frac{3}{4}$ in six, then *very* slow and *rallentando* on 'avant d'attraper un seul morceau de nuage'. The ♩ of the bar in $\frac{2}{4}$ remains in the very slow tempo. And suddenly the first chord, staccato, of the *Modéré* (♩ = 80) breaks the charm, and almost *parlando*, but extremely precise, with no *rallentando* to the end (check the [ə] as indicated in the above text), the singer ceases to be poetical about the swan and mocks his too imaginative vision of it.

LE MARTIN-PÊCHEUR

Ça n'a pas mordu ce soir, mais je
　　rapporte une rare émotion.
Comme je tenais ma perche de
　　ligne tendue,
　　　　un martin-pêcheur est venu s'y
　　　　poser.
Nous n'avons pas d'oiseau plus
　　éclatant.
Il semblait une grosse fleur bleue au
　　bout d'une longue tige.
La perche pliait sous le poids.
Je ne respirais plus, tout fier d'être
　　pris pour un arbre
　　　　par un martin-pêcheur.
Et je suis sûr qu'il ne s'est pas envolé
　　de peur,
　　　　mais qu'il a cru qu'il ne faisait
　　　　que passer
　　　　d'une branche à une autre.
　　　　　　　　　Jules Renard

THE KINGFISHER

Not a bite this evening. but I had a
　　thrilling experience.
As I was holding out my fishing rod,

　　　　a kingfisher came and perched
　　　　on it.
We have no bird more brilliant.

He seemed like a big blue flower on
　　the end of a long stalk.
The rod bent under the weight.
I held my breath, quite proud to be
　　taken for a tree
　　　　by a kingfisher.
And I am sure that he did not fly
　　away out of fear,
　　　　but believed that he was only
　　　　passing
　　　　from one branch to another.

This is the most difficult mélodie of the set, both musically and in its interpretation, but also perhaps the most beautiful. An extraordinary impression of poetry can emanate from Ravel's musical treatment of this short poem.

It must be admitted that Ravel's indication: *on ne peut plus lent* (one cannot be slower) does not precisely indicate anything, and moreover the same tempo *cannot* be maintained for the last six bars of the mélodie. Ravel admitted the fact.

The tempo is about ♪ = 60; one must definitely count in six. In this slow tempo the singer has plenty of time to sing *mp* the text recalling his beautiful and rare emotion. (I suggest an expressive *p subito* on 'rare'.) When he has sung 'Un martin-pêcheur est venu s'y poser', and after the following piano attack, he must give the impression of being completely motionless, singing *mezza voce*, as if afraid of frightening the bird away. Ravel even agreed that it is better not to make any crescendo on 'Nous n'avons pas d'oiseau plus éclatant' in spite of his indication. The following *très calme* in $\frac{7}{8}$ is exactly in the tempo: ♪ = 60. The indications are clear for the following two bars of the piano part. The singer begins to sing again, whispering, and precise in rhythm. A little break should be made between 'plus' and 'tout'. The slight *portamento* on the word 'arbre' is difficult because of the two rolled 'r's and the absence of final [ə]. The bar in $\frac{2}{4}$ is kept in tempo. But from the $\frac{3}{4}$, the tempo is definitely faster, about ♪ = 72; it is better to *count* in three. From there the bird has obviously flown away, the singer can relax and sings the end of his story with the same expression he had at the beginning of the mélodie. If possible sing the last phrase in one breath.

LA PINTADE	THE GUINEA-FOWL
C'est la bossu¢ de ma cour.	She is the hunchback of my courtyard.
Ell¢ ne rêv¢ que plai¢¢ | à caus¢ de sa boss¢.	She thinks of nothing but fighting because of her hump.
Les poul¢¢ ne lui dis¢n̸t rien:	The fowls say nothing to her:
Brusquement, ell¢ se précipit¢ | et les <u>harcèl</u>¢.	suddenly she sets on them and harasses them.

Puis_elle baiss¢ la têt¢, pench¢ le
   corps, et de tout¢ la vitess¢
    de ses patt_es maigr¢s, ell¢ court
      frapper de son bec dur,
        just¢_au centr¢ de la roue d'un_e
          dind¢.
Cett¢ poseus¢ l'agaçait.
Ainsi, la têt¢ bleuie, ses barbillons_à
   vif,
      cocardière, ell¢ rag¢ du matin au
        soir.
Ell¢ se bat sans motif, peut-êtr¢
    parc¢ qu'ell¢ s'imagin¢ toujours
      qu'on se moqu¢ de sa taill¢, de
        son crân_e chauv¢
      et de sa queue bass¢.
Et ell¢ ne cess¢ de jeter_un cri
   discordant
      qui perc_e l'air comm_e un¢
        point¢.
Parfois | ell¢ quitt¢ la cour | et
   disparaît.
Ell¢ laiss_e aux volaill¢s pacifiqu¢s | un
   moment de répit.
Mais_elle revient plus turbulent_e et
   plus criard¢.
Et, frénétiqu_e, ell¢ se vautr¢ par terr¢.

Qu'a-t-ell¢ donc ?
La sournois¢ fait_un¢ farc¢.

Elle_est allée pondr¢ son œuf à la
   campagn¢.
Je peux le chercher si ça m'amus¢.
Et ell¢ se roul¢ dans la poussièr¢
   comm_e un¢ _bossue.

Jules Renard

Then she lowers her head, leans
   forward, and with all the speed
of her skinny feet, she runs and smites
   with her hard beak
the exact centre of a turkey's tail.

This poseur provoked her.
Thus, with her head bluish, her
   wattles lively,
      fiercely aggressive, she rages
        from morning to night.
She fights for no reason, perhaps
    because she is always imagining
      that they are laughing at her
        figure, at her bald head,
      and her mean low tail.
And incessantly she utters her dis-
   cordant cry
      which pierces the air like a
        needle point.
At times she leaves the courtyard and
   disappears.
She gives the peace-loving fowls a
   moment of respite.
But she returns more boisterous and
   more peevish.
And in a frenzy, she wallows in the
   earth.
Whatever is the matter with her ?
The crafty creature has played a
   prank.
She went to lay her egg in the open
   country.
I may look for it if I like.
And she rolls in the dust like a
   hunchback.

The guinea-fowl's stupid wickedness is marvellously suggested by
the music. Initial tempo is ♩ = 112. The piano attacks with rage *ff*,
even with an ugly sound, and there should be no diminuendo with the

rallentando. The following four bars are in a more moderate tempo. ('ne rêve que plaies et bosses' exactly translated means 'to dream only of wounds and bumps'; but it is a colloquial expression meaning 'to think of nothing but mischief or fighting'. Thus Renard's sentence is a play on words.) *A tempo primo* again, the left hand very staccato and *marcato*. The crescendo for the voice goes to 'harcèle' with a stress on on the first syllable, as well as on 'précipite'. Then there is a big *rallentando* for the piano, this time with a diminuendo, but remaining *extremely staccato*. *A tempo* again, and one must observe the *subito p* before the big crescendo. 'Cette poseuse l'agaçait' is *mf*, moderate in tempo but precise in rhythm. *A tempo* again, and the pianist should not miss the nuance of each bar, with a dry stress on the fourth beat. The voice is crescendo up to 'rage', with biting articulation. From 'Elle se bat sans motif' suddenly definitely slower ($\downarrow$ = 76) with a *rallentando* on the fourth bar. (Observe 'taille' and 'chauve' with no final [ə] carrying the voice on [ɑ] and [o].) The words 'Et elle ne cesse de jeter un cri discordant' *accelerando* bring back the *tempo primo* and the shrillness of the piano. Then the pianist, legato, takes a very slow tempo—the tempo he will need five bars later: $\downarrow$ = 76. A sudden impression of relaxation and relief should be given by both interpreters, while the tiresome bird is away. But on the fifth bar, with the *pppp* repeated notes in the top register of the piano, one can already hear it in the distance, coming back! No change of tempo with the big crescendo; only the two bars in $\frac{4}{4}$ are suddenly twice as fast: $\downarrow$ = 76. The second being *accelerando* to the *tempo primo*: $\downarrow$ = 112, but only for six beats, because a very gradual and big *rallentando* must be made on 'La sournoise fait une farce. Elle est allée pondre son œuf à la campagne.' Thus, 'Je peux le chercher si ça m'amuse' is in a quiet tempo, and a shrug expresses the regret and the irritation of the singer. The last bars, in tempo, must be performed with perfect rhythmic precision (stress on 'roule', with a good rolled 'r', and 'bossue'), concluding the mélodie exactly as it began.

*

CINQ MÉLODIES POPULAIRES GRECQUES
(FIVE POPULAR GREEK MELODIES)

These are authentic Greek folk-songs, wonderfully harmonized by Ravel, and this is enough to underline that their style of interpretation can, and must, be much freer than that of genuine mélodies.

LE RÉVEIL DE LA MARIÉE

Réveille-toi, perdrix mignonne,
Ouvre au matin tes ailes.

Trois grains de beauté
Mon cœur en est brûlé.

Vois le ruban d'or que je t'apporte

Pour le nouer | autour de tes cheveux.

Si tu veux, ma belle, viens nous
marier!
Dans nos deux familles tous sont
alliés.

French version by M. D. Calvocoressi

THE AWAKENING OF THE BRIDE

Wake up, dear little partridge,
open your wings in the morning.

Three beauty spots
have set my heart aflame.

See the golden ribbon that I bring
you
to tie around your hair.

If you wish, my beauty, come let us
be married!
In our two families all are related.

The correct French title for this song is 'Le Réveil de la Mariée'. Not, as in certain editions, 'Chanson de la Mariée'. It is not sung by the bride, but by a young Greek peasant, who awakens his bride on the morning of the wedding by singing in front of her house, whither he has come bringing a golden ribbon for her hair. The sun is shining brightly on the scene. Over-refined vocal effects are obviously out of place; cheerfulness and virile pride should be the keynote.

The tempo is about ♩ = 88. The piano, with its persistent pedal of G, should be soft, but the singer attacks *mf*, and consistently keeps a very firm rhythm. On the lines 'Trois grains de beauté Mon cœur en est brûlé' a *subito p* can be full of the most tender meanings . . . and in 'br<u>û</u>ler' the 'r' should be strongly rolled. Then 'Vois le ruban,' etc., is back to the *mf*. The liaison 'nouer autour' would be too refined for a peasant song. On the last line there is a *rallentando poco a poco*, but not too much, and with no diminuendo. The last G of the voice can be held for three beats, up to the last chord of the piano, and *sempre f* to the end.

LÀ-BAS, VERS L'ÉGLISE

Là-bas, vers l'église,
Vers l'église Ayio Sidéro,
L'église O Vierge Sainte,
L'église Ayio Constanndino,
Se sont réunis,
Rassemblés en nombre infini,
Du monde, | O Vierge Sainte,
Du monde tous les plus braves!

French version by C. D. Calvocoressi

YONDER, NEAR THE CHURCH

Yonder, near the church,
near the church Ayio Sidéro,
the church, O Virgin Saint,
the church Ayio Constanndino,
are gathered together,
assembled in infinite numbers,
in the world, O Virgin Saint,
all the bravest in the world.

The original Greek text makes it clear that the song refers to all the brave soldiers now lying in the little cemetery behind the church.

The religious character of this song must be immediately established by the interpreters. The tempo is about ♩ = 54. I myself imagine a procession coming from a distance, and this motivates the *pp* indicated for the voice, which should not be a sweet *pp*, but give the impression of someone singing loudly in the distance. There is a gradual overall crescendo reaching a climax which is no louder than *mf*, while the piano plays its bass note four octaves lower than at the beginning. The five bars of coda are *sempre diminuendo*.

QUEL GALANT!

Quel galant m'est comparable

D'entre ceux qu'on voit passer?

Dis, Dame Vassiliki?

WHAT GALLANT!

What gallant can be compared with me

among those who are seen passing by?

Tell me, Mistress Vassiliki?

Vois, pendus à ma ceinture
Pistolets et sabre aigu...
Et c'est *toi* que j'aime.

    French version by C. D. Calvocoressi

Look, hanging on my belt
pistols and a sharp sword . . .
And it is you whom I love.

A very virile song. The tempo should not be too fast, about ♩ = 92. The singer, very proud of himself, sings *f* with a firm rhythm. The piano *ritornello* enters exactly in tempo at the end of the last bar of the voice, definitely *f* the first time, without changing the tempo at all. Do not hurry. The second stanza is also *sempre f*, as far as the rest. Then, after a silence, the piano attacks its anacrusis, and the singer, in a much slower tempo, *p*, expresses his love (stress on 'toi') with a manly and suggestive tenderness. Again the piano starts its *ritornello* exactly in tempo, but this time *pp* like an echo.

CHANSON DES CUEILLEUSES DE LENTISQUES

O joie de mon âme, joie de mon cœur,
Trésor qui m'est si cher;
Joie de l'âme et du cœur,
Toi que j'aime ardemment,
Tu es plus beau qu'un ange.
O lorsque tu parais, | ange si doux,
Devant nos yeux,
Comme un bel ange blond
Sous le clair soleil,
Hélas, tous nos pauvres cœurs
    soupirent!

    French version by C. D. Calvocoressi

SONG OF THE LENTISK GATHERERS

O joy of my soul, joy of my heart,
treasure so dear to me;
joy of the soul, and of the heart,
you whom I ardently love,
you are more beautiful than an angel.
O when you appear, angel so sweet,
before our eyes,
like a lovely, blond angel
under the bright sun,
alas, all our poor hearts sigh!

The beautiful melody of this song should be sung with no particular expression, as if sung by women at their work; even the last phrase, which is the only dynamic climax of the song. The tempo is about ♩ = 54 with care for the rhythmic subtleties.

TOUT GAI!	ALL GAY!
Tout gai,	All gay,
Ha, tout gai;	ah, all gay;
Belle jambe, tireli qui danse,	lovely leg, tireli that dances,
Belle jambe, la vaisselle danse.	lovely leg, the crockery dances.
Tra-la-la.	Tra-la-la.

French version by C. D. Calvocoressi

With completely nonsensical words, the virtue of this song lies entirely in its musical accents. The tempo is ♩ = 138 and here are the dynamics and stresses, also the contrasts between legato and staccato that I suggest:

This song can be sung with a certain triviality. The *p* on the twentieth bar of the above example can indicate a double meaning, and the stress on the 'i' four bars further on can even have some coarseness. Then the big crescendo and *accelerando* leads to a sudden and rather long *fermata*. The following bar is freely slow and *f*, but the last two notes of the voice are exactly in *tempo primo* and *subito p*, quite casual.

*

DON QUICHOTTE A DULCINÉE
(DON QUIXOTE TO DULCINÉE)

The last work of Ravel, written in 1932, these mélodies were primarily intended to be sung by Chaliapine in a film on Don Quixote, but other songs were used in the film. They are based on three rhythms of Spanish dancers: (1) guajira, (2) zorzica, (3) jota. I cannot sufficiently emphasize the importance of keeping the rhythm of these dances absolutely flawless from the beginning to the end of each mélodie (with one exception, as indicated later). It is also extremely important not to forget that it is Don Quixote himself who is singing. With this idea in mind, the singer must perforce avoid anything too sweet, or loose, or vulgar, in his interpretation. On the contrary the grand and noble figure can suggest to him virile, dignified, or even rather bombastic accents. These mélodies, of course, can only be sung by a baritone. They are orchestrated.

CHANSON ROMANESQUE	ROMANESQUE SONG
Si vous me disiez que la terre	Were you to tell me that the earth
A tant tourner vous_offensa,	offended you with so much turning,
Je lui dépêcherais Pança :	speedily would I dispatch Panza:
Vous la verriez fixe̲ et se taire.	you should see it motionless and silent.
Si vous me disiez que l'ennui͡	Were you to tell me that you are weary
Vous vient du ciel trop fleuri d'astres,	of the sky too much adorned with stars,
Déchirant les divins cadastres,	destroying the divine order,
Je faucherais d'un coup la nuit.	with one blow I would sweep them from the night.

Si vous me disiez que l'espace
Ainsi vidé ne vous plaît point,
Chevalier dieu, la lance au poing,
J'étoilerais le vent qui passe.

Were you to tell me that space
thus made empty does not please you,
god-like Knight, lance in hand,
I would stud the passing wind with
    stars.

Mais si vous disiez que mon sang |

Est plus à moi qu'à vous, | ma Dame,

But were you to tell me that my
    blood
belongs more to myself than to you,
    my Lady,

Je blêmirais dessous le blâme
Et je mourrais, vous bénissant.

I would pale beneath the reproach
and I would die, blessing you.

    O Dulcinée.

    O Dulcinea.

Paul Morand

It is, obviously, the evenness of the quavers that governs the rhythm, alternately balanced in $\frac{6}{8}$ and $\frac{3}{4}$. The indicated tempo ♩ = 208 is on the slow side, and ♩. = 76/80 in the $\frac{6}{8}$ in my opinion makes the rhythm more characteristic and the song easier to handle. The indicated scale of dynamics, going from *p* to *mf*, seems also too discreet, especially with orchestra, and *mf* to *f* more advisable. This, together with broad declamation, will make it possible to describe effectively all the impossible actions which the noble fool would be ready to accomplish to please his Dulcinée.

In the first quatrain, a stress should be made on the word 'fixe'. In the second one, the first two lines are easier when sung in one breath. Taking care over the perfect evenness of the quavers, there should not be too much diminuendo on 'Déchirant les divins cadastres', and there is a stress on the first syllable of 'faucherais' to suggest the sweeping gesture of a reaper.

In the third quatrain, the last two lines must be emphasized with very broad declamation, and a wonderful vocal effect can be made on 'le vent qui passe', to suggest the passing wind.

For the last quatrain a total change of mood, corresponding to the change of feeling in the poem, must be apparent. The tessitura being rather low, it is better to make no diminuendo and to use a rich timbre, especially to emphasize 'vous bénissant'. The sudden *p* on 'O Dulcinée' can thus be more striking, and these two words must contain all the respect and tenderness that it is possible to express; they will, of course, be exactly in tempo, as there is not the slightest *ritenuto* up to the end of the mélodie. The last two notes of the piano are like double-bass pizzicati.

CHANSON ÉPIQUE	EPIC SONG
Bon Saint Michel qui me donnez loisir	Good Saint Michael who gives me liberty
De voir ma Dame et de l'entendre,	to see my Lady and to hear her,
Bon Saint Michel qui me daignez choisir	good Saint Michael who deigns to elect me
Pour lui complaire et la défendre,	to please her and to defend her,
Bon Saint Michel veuillez descendre ✓	good Saint Michael, I pray you descend
Avec Saint Georges sur l'autel	with Saint George upon the altar
De la Madone au bleu mantel.	of the Madonna of the blue mantle.
D'un rayon du ciel bénissez ma lame	With a beam from heaven bless my sword
Et son égale en pureté	and its equal in purety
Et son égale en piété	and its equal in piety
Comme en pudeur et chasteté: Ma Dame.	as in modesty and chastity: my Lady.
(O grands Saint Georges | et Saint Michel)	(O great Saint George and Saint Michael)
L'ange qui veille sur ma veille,	the angel who watches over my vigil,
Ma douce Dame si pareille ✓	my gentle Lady so much resembling you,
A vous, | Madone au bleu mantel! Amen.	Madonna of the blue mantle! Amen.

Paul Morand

Don Quixote's prayer to St. Michael and St. George, asking them to bless his sword and his Lady, requires a fervour without sentimentality, a piety full of humility but also of grandeur. This can be attained only with a flawless legato and a perfectly even pace.

The indicated tempo is, in my opinion, a little too fast, and ♩ = 56/58 gives more scope for a beautiful line. (But beware of conductors who drag! They do not have to breathe.) The three invocations to 'Bon St. Michel' become gradually more *f*, but, as the voice also ascends gradually, not too much crescendo should be made, as indeed 'De la Madone au <u>bleu</u> <u>man</u>tel' must be only *mf*, with a little stress on 'bleu' and 'man', and strong consonants (the pianist will do his best to give the impression of the dynamics indicated in the two bars that follow), thus reserving the very big crescendo for 'D'un rayon du ciel bénissez ma lame', and the heroic *ff* on '<u>la</u>me' (the 'l' being much emphasized). On the following lines the *ff* must be continued very *marcato*, and please, with no accelerando and no *portamento* whatsoever. Thus the wonderful, the respectful, the devoted *p* on 'Ma <u>D</u>ame' will have its full value (the 'd' being much emphasized).

The tempo should be carefully maintained on the following lines. There is a stress on the syllable '<u>L'an</u>ge' to help the bad prosody. On the line 'Ma douce Dame si pareille', which *must* be sung in one breath, the voice should follow the dynamics indicated in the piano part. Then breathe, as indicated. (An eventual catch breath can be taken between 'vous' and 'Madone'.) The last 'Amen' must be a perfect *pp mezza voce*, full of devotion and confidence.

CHANSON A BOIRE

Foin du bâtard, illustre Dame,
Qui pour me perdre à vos doux yeux,
Dit que l'amour et le vin vieux
Mettent en deuil mon cœur, mon
 âme!

Je bois | à la joie!
La joie est le seul but |
Où je vais droit...
lorsque j'ai bu!

Foin du jaloux, brune maîtresse,

Qui geind, qui pleure et fait
 serment
D'être toujours ce pâle amant
Qui met de l'eau dans son ivresse!

DRINKING SONG

A fig for the bastard, illustrious Lady,
who to shame me in your sweet eyes,
says that love and old wine
will bring misery to my heart, my
 soul!

I drink to joy!
Joy is the one aim
to which I go straight...
when I am drunk!

A fig for the jealous fool, dark-haired
 mistress,
who whines, who weeps and vows

ever to be this pallid lover
who waters the wine of his
 intoxication!

Je bois | à la joie!   I drink to joy!
La joie est le seul but | Joy is the one aim
Où je vais droit...   to which I go straight...
lorsque j'ai bu!   when I am drunk!

                    Paul Morand

   More than ever in this drinking song, one must bear in mind that it
is Don Quixote who is singing, drinking, and, in fact, already drunk.
His drunkenness is certainly not that of a man of the common herd,
and this should prevent singers from exaggerating their effects and
falling into vulgarity. A sense of perfect style should never be lost.
   The indicated tempo ($\downarrow$ = 184) seems excellent. (But the cascade of
descending chords in the piano part can be a little faster.) This tempo
must be maintained exactly, even at the beginning of the refrain 'Je bois'
with the *portamento*. There is definitely a hiccup between 'lorsque j'ai'
and 'lorsque j'ai bu' but it should be made, as we said above, with no
exaggeration and in good taste; in fact it is really in the piano part.
The 'Ah! ah! ah!' must be hearty laughter, staccato, and, of course,
precisely on the notes, but real laughter. On the word 'joie', the stress
is on the short appoggiatura D, which is *on the beat*, followed by a
portamento to the C; and the same effect is made again when it comes
the second time. On 'Je bois à la joie' there should be no liaison (too
refined there), but a break between 'bois' and 'à'. The last triplet must
be *marcato* and definitely a little *allargando*. This is the only change of
tempo in these three beautiful songs of Don Quixote.

14 | Francis Poulenc
(1899–1963)

Beyond all doubt, most of Francis Poulenc's finest work was in the field of vocal composition—choral works, lyrical works, and mélodies. His inspiration never flowed more spontaneously than when stimulated by a literary text. He had an exceptional feeling for French declamatory style, and his melodic gift, which was the very essence of his music, inspired him to find the appropriate musical line to heighten the expression of the literary phrase. To quote his own words: 'The musical setting of a poem should be an act of love, never a marriage of convenience.' And again: 'I have never claimed to achieve the musical resolution of poetic problems by means of intelligence; the voices of the heart and of instinct are far more reliable.'

The mélodies selected for study here will illustrate these points extremely well, for if the clarity of his intelligent approach to his texts is evident, the inspiration that goes beyond mere intelligence can be readily discerned. It is precisely this that provoked him to say: 'One must set to music not simply the lines of the verses, but also that which lies between the lines and in the margins.'

Francis Poulenc wrote no less than 146 mélodies. They are extremely varied in character, ranging from the craziest buffoonery to the most sincere lyricism, from obvious sensuousness to poignant gravity; but they never fail to bear the mark of his personality.

A few general remarks can be given about their performance. There are seldom any rhythmical difficulties. The vocal line is often written in notes of equal value which should be observed very strictly—no shortening of any notes, even on weak syllables. Poulenc very rarely uses *parlando*; perfect legato is generally demanded, and certain *portamenti* are permissible (used with taste, of course). Poulenc, with his love of the human voice, had rather a liking for them.

There are many indications on Poulenc's scores:

Indications of tempo. There is always a metronomic indication, generally accurate (especially in his later mélodies). This tempo should be established and maintained; very few of his songs have a change of tempo. The indication *sans ralentir* (no *rallentando*) is often found, even at the end of his mélodies.

Indications of dynamics. These are always carefully marked and should be observed. It will be noticed that there are relatively few crescendo and diminuendo markings, but more often contrasted plains: one phrase being *p*, the next *f*; or *mf* and *pp*. Poulenc always asked for ample use of the pedal in the piano part. This is especially important when there are, as often, repeated chords; these should be played very softly, the repetition being only in order to prolong the harmony.

Here is a complete list of Poulenc's mélodies:

1918/19	Le Bestiaire ou Cortège d'Orphée (G. Apollinaire) (1) Le dromadaire; (2) La chèvre du Thibet; (3) La sauterelle; (4) Le dauphin; (5) L'écrevisse; (6) La carpe	MAX ESCHIG
1919	Cocardes (Jean Cocteau) (1) Miel de Narbonne; (2) Bonne d'enfant; (3) Enfant de troupe	MAX ESCHIG
1924/25	Poèmes de Ronsard (1) Attributs; (2) Le tombeau; (3) Ballet; (4) Je n'ai plus que les os; (5) A son page	HEUGEL
1926	**M** Chansons gaillardes (Anonymous seventeenth-century text) (1) La maîtresse volage; (2) Chanson à boire; (3) Madrigal; (4) Invocation aux Parques; (5) Couplets bachiques; (6) L'offrande; (7) La belle jeunesse; (8) Sérénade	HEUGEL
1927	Vocalise	LEDUC

1927/28		Airs chantés (J. Moréas)	SALABERT
		(1) Air romantique; (2) Air champêtre; (3) Air grave; (4) Air vif	
1930		Épitaphe (Malherbe)	SALABERT
1931	**F**	Trois poèmes de Louise Lalanne	SALABERT
		(1) Le présent; (2) Chanson; (3) Hier	
1931	**M**	Quatre poèmes (G. Apollinaire)	SALABERT
		(1) L'anguille; (2) Carte postale; (3) Avant le cinéma; (4) 1904	
1931	**F**	Cinq Poèmes (Max Jacob)	SALABERT
		(1) Chanson bretonne; (2) Le cimetière; (3) La petite servante; (4) Berceuse; (5) Souric et Mouric	
1934		Huit Chansons Polonaises	SALABERT
		(1) La couronne; (2) Le départ; (3) Les gars polonais; (4) Le dernier Mazour; (5) L'adieu; (6) Le drapeau blanc; (7) La Vistule; (8) Le Lac	
1935		Cinq Poèmes (Paul Eluard)	DURAND
		(1) Peut-il se reposer? (2) Il la prend dans ses bras; (3) Plume d'eau claire; (4) Rôdeuse au front de verre; (5) Amoureuses	
1935		A sa guitare (Ronsard)	DURAND
1937		Tel jour telle nuit (P. Eluard)	DURAND
		(1) Bonne journée; (2) Une ruine coquille vide; (3) Le front comme un drapeau perdu; (4) Une roulotte couverte en tuiles; (5) A toutes brides; (6) Une herbe pauvre; (7) Je n'ai envie que de t'aimer; (8) Figure de force brûlante et farouche; (9) Nous avons fait la nuit	
1937	**F**	Trois poèmes (Louise de Vilmorin)	DURAND
		(1) Le garçon de Liège; (2) Au-delà; (3) Aux officiers de la Garde Blanche	
1938		Deux Poèmes (G. Apollinaire)	SALABERT
		(1) Dans le jardin d'Anna; (2) Allons, plus vite	
1938		Miroirs brûlants (P. Eluard)	SALABERT
		(1) Tu vois le feu du soir; (2) Miroirs brûlants	
1938		Le portrait (Colette)	SALABERT
1938		La grenouillère (G. Apollinaire)	SALABERT
1938		Priez pour paix (Charles d'Orléans)	SALABERT
1938		Ce doux petit visage (P. Eluard)	SALABERT
1939		Bleuet (G. Apollinaire)	DURAND

1939	**F** Fiançailles pour rire (Louise de Vilmorin)	SALABERT
	(1) La dame d'André; (2) Dans l'herbe; (3) Il vole; (4) Mon cadavre est doux comme un gant; (5) Violon; (6) Fleurs	
1940	Banalités (G. Apollinaire)	MAX ESCHIG
	(1) Chanson d'Orkenise; (2) Hôtel; (3) Fagnes de Wallonie; (4) Voyage à Paris; (5) Sanglots	
1942	**M** Chansons villageoises (Maurice Fombeure)	MAX ESCHIG
	(1) Chanson du clair tamis; (2) Les gars qui vont à la fête; (3) C'est le joli printemps; (4) Le mendiant; (5) Chanson de la fille frivole; (6) Le retour du sergent	
1943	Métamorphoses (Louise de Vilmorin)	SALABERT
	(1) Reine des mouettes; (2) C'est ainsi que tu es; (3) Paganini	
1943	Deux Poèmes (L. Aragon)	SALABERT
	(1) C.; (2) Fêtes galantes	
1945	Montparnasse (G. Apollinaire)	MAX ESCHIG
1945	Hyde Park (G. Apollinaire)	MAX ESCHIG
1946	Le pont (G. Apollinaire)	MAX ESCHIG
1946	Un poème (G. Apollinaire)	MAX ESCHIG
1946	Paul et Virginie (Raymond Radiguet)	MAX ESCHIG
1947	Mais mourir (P. Eluard)	HEUGEL
1947	Hymne (Racine)	SALABERT
1947	Trois chansons de Garcia Lorca	HEUGEL
	(1) L'enfant muet; (2) Adelina à la promenade; (3) Chanson de l'oranger sec	
1947	Le disparu (Robert Desnos)	SALABERT
1947	Main dominée par le cœur (P. Eluard)	SALABERT
1948	Calligrammes (G. Apollinaire)	HEUGEL
	(1) L'espionne; (2) Mutation; (3) Vers le Sud; (4) Il pleut; (5) La grâce exilée; (6) Aussi bien que les cigales; (7) Voyage	
1949	Mazurka (Louise de Vilmorin) (dans: Mouvements du cœur)	HEUGEL
1950	La Fraîcheur et le Feu (P. Eluard)	MAX ESCHIG
	(1) Rayon des yeux...; (2) Le matin les branches attisent...; (3) Tout disparut...; (4) Dans les ténèbres du jardin...; (5) Unis la fraîcheur et le feu...; (6) Homme au sourire tendre...; (7) La grande rivière qui va...	

1954		Parisiana (Max Jacob)	SALABERT
		(1) Jouer du bugle; (2) Vous n'écrivez plus?	
1954		Rosemonde (G. Apollinaire)	MAX ESCHIG
1956		Le travail du peintre (P. Eluard)	MAX ESCHIG
		(1) Pablo Picasso; (2) Marc Chagall; (3) Georges Braque; (4) Juan Gris; (5) Paul Klee; (6) Joan Miro; (7) Jacques Villon	
1956		Deux mélodies 1956	MAX ESCHIG
		(1) La souris (G. Apollinaire); (2) Nuage (Laurence de Beylié)	
1956		Dernier poème (Robert Desnos)	MAX ESCHIG
1958		Une chanson de porcelaine (P. Eluard)	MAX ESCHIG
1960	F	La courte paille (Maurice Carême)	MAX ESCHIG
		(1) Le sommeil; (2) Quelle aventure!; (3) La reine de cœur; (4) Ba, be, bi, bo, bu; (5) Les anges musiciens; (6) Le carafon; (7) Lune d'Avril	

The mélodies are suitable for either male or female voices, unless marked: **M**—male voices; **F**—female voices.

A drastically limited choice has had to be made among these mélodies to remain within the bounds of this book. The chronological order—quite unimportant—will not be observed.

Four mélodies set to words by various poets will be studied first:

AIR CHAMPÊTRE

Belle source, je veux me rappeler
    sans cesse,
      Qu'un jour, guidé par l'amitié

Ravi, j'ai contemplé ton visage, | ô
    déesse,
      Perdu sous la mousse à moitié.

Que n'est-il demeuré cet ami que je
    pleure,
      O nymphe, à ton culte attaché,

PASTORAL SONG

Lovely spring, never will I cease to
    remember
      that one day, guided by friend-
      ship,

entranced, I gazed on your face, O
    goddess,
      half hidden beneath the moss.

This friend for whom I weep,
    would he had remained,
      O nymph, a devotee of your
      cult,

Pour se mêler encore au souffle qui
    t'effleure,
      Et répondre à ton flot caché.
               Jean Moréas

still to consort with the breeze which
    caresses you,
      and respond to your hidden
        waters.

One of the four *Airs Chantés*; this is among the best known and most frequently performed of Poulenc's mélodies. He was severely critical of this series of songs. He had no liking, indeed no respect for Moréas's poems; even going so far as to allow himself to cut a word in two: 'sous la mou—sous la mousse à moitié'. But he was too critical, for these mélodies are certainly successful, with their very charming melodic invention. The words are quite unimportant; the virtue of the song lies in the opportunity it gives for a beautiful display of vocal and musical qualities. It is best suited to a soprano voice. The tempo should be maintained with great precision. ♩ = 144, as indicated, is in my opinion on the fast side. The diction must be clear and accurate. The line 'Pour se mêler encore au souffle qui t'effleure' is extremely legato and well phrased. The F sharp on the syllable 'ca' of the word 'cache' should affirm the major key. The top B natural towards the end may be taken staccato if it is easier so, but in any case there should not be a nasal vowel. No *rallentando* whatsoever at the end.

AIR VIF

Le trésor du verger
Et le jardin | en fête,
Les fleurs des champs, des bois
Éclatent de plaisir.
Hélas! et sur leur tête
Le vent | enfle sa voix.

Mais toi, noble océan
Que l'assaut des tourmentes
Ne saurait ravager,
Certes plus dignement
Lorsque tu te lamentes,
Tu te prends à songer.

               Jean Moréas

LIVELY AIR

The riches of the orchard
and the festive garden,
the flowers of the fields, of the woods
burst forth with delight.
Alas! and above their head
the wind's voice is rising.

But you, noble ocean
that the assault of tempests
will not succeed in ravaging,
most certainly with more dignity
when you lament,
you lose yourself in dreams.

This is another of the *Airs Chantés*. Again the words are unimportant. The metronomic tempo ♩ = 192 is right and must be maintained to the end. For light sopranos the E flat *ff* on 'Mais toi, noble océan' can be sung an octave higher. A big crescendo–diminuendo on the last C is very effective.

PRIEZ POUR PAIX	PRAY FOR PEACE
Priez pour paix, douce Vierge Marie,	Pray for peace, gentle Virgin Mary,
Reine des cieux | et du monde maîtresse,	Queen of the skies and Mistress of the world,
Faites prier, par votre courtoisie,	of your courtesy, ask for the prayers
Saints‿et saintes, ✓ et prenez votre adresse⌐	of all the saints, and make your address
Vers votre Fils, ✓ requérant sa Hautesse.	to your Son, beseeching his Majesty
Qu'il lui plaise son peuple regarder, ✓	that he may please to look upon his people,
Que de son sang a voulu racheter,	whom he wished to redeem with his blood,
En déboutant guerre qui tout dévoie.	banishing war which disrupts all.
De prières ne vous veuillez lasser.	Do not cease your prayers.
Priez pour paix, priez pour paix,	Pray for peace, pray for peace,
Le vrai trésor de joie.	the true treasure of joy.

Charles d'Orléans

This prayer was composed in 1938, at the moment when the whole world lay under the terrifying threat of war. It uses for its text a few lines of a poem by the seventeenth century poet, Charles d'Orléans. Poulenc wrote: 'I have tried in this mélodie to give an impression of fervour and above all, of humility, which for me is the finest quality of prayer.' This should be sufficient guide to the interpretation.

This mélodie is published in two keys; the lower one, C minor, is the original and far the better. In some editions the tempo ♩ = 66 is indicated, but ♩ = 60 was the tempo usually taken by Poulenc, and the pianist should dare to take this slow tempo for the introduction. Perfect legato is needed, with a 'very soft and confident' *pp*. The breaths are indicated above. 'Saints et Saintes' is *mf*, but there is a *subito p* on 'Vers votre Fils'. (In the edition in the medium key, the indicated *f* is a misprint.)

'Que de son sang a voulu racheter' is *marcato*. (In the medium key, a flat has obviously been omitted on the first beat: E minor chord.) Then subito *mf* and legato on 'De prières ne vous veuillez lasser'. The whole end of the song is *pp*, with a slight stress on the word 'joie', and a *rallentando*.

C.	C.
J'ai traversé les ponts de Cé	I have crossed the bridges of Cé
C'est là que tout_a commencé	it is there that it all began
Une chanson des temps passés	a song of bygone days
Parle d'un chevalier blessé	tells of a wounded knight
D'une rose sur la chaussée	of a rose on the carriage-way
Et d'un corsage délacé	and an unlaced bodice
Du château d'un duc insensé	of the castle of a mad duke
Et des cygnes dans les fossés	and swans on the moats
De la prairie où vient danser	of the meadow where comes dancing
Une éternelle fiancée	an eternal betrothed
Et j'ai bu comme un lait glacé	and I drank like iced milk
Le long lai des gloires faussées	the long lay of false glories
La Loire emporte mes pensées	the Loire carries my thoughts away
Avec les voitures versées	with the overturned cars
Et les_armes désamorcées	and the unprimed weapons
Et les larmes mal effacées	and the ill-dried tears
O ma France | ô ma délaissée	O my France O my forsaken France
J'ai traversé les ponts de Cé.	I have crossed the bridges of Cé.

Louis Aragon

One of Poulenc's best-known mélodies. It is called 'C' because in French this letter is pronounced 'cé', and every line of the poem rhymes with the ending 'cé'. It recalls the dark days of 1940, and the tragic exodus of the French population as it fled before the invading forces. In a tone of extreme melancholy, the poet speaks of crossing the river Loire at a place called 'Les Ponts de Cé', and describes all that this journey through the confusion of a forsaken France brings to his mind.

It is like a touching, nostalgic old romance. The slow metronomic indication ♩ = 54 is good; both pianist and singer must achieve beauty of legato and phrasing. The diminuendo on 'Et des cygnes dans les fossés' should lead to *mp* only, to emphasize, after a good breath, the contrast of a very poetic *pp* on 'De la prairie', etc. On 'La Loire emporte mes pensées' I recommend only a *mp*, and a *p* instead of a *pp* on 'Et les armes désamorcées', reserving a very expressive *pp* for 'Et les larmes mal effacées'. The *fermata* on the top A 'délaissée' should not be too long, and after that, an immediate *a tempo* and a *rallentando* to the end.

*

Poulenc found the main source of inspiration for his mélodies in the works of two great contemporary poets—Guillaume Apollinaire and Paul Eluard. He wrote no fewer than thirty-five settings of poems by Guillaume Apollinaire. In many of these songs the interpreters find themselves faced with a problem, for their poetic melancholy is often tinged with a kind of humour which is really modesty of feeling, as though poet and musician were smiling ruefully at their own sensibility.

LE BESTIAIRE (THE BOOK OF BEASTS)

Speaking of his settings of Apollinaire's 'Le Bestiaire ou Cortège d'Orphée', Poulenc said: 'To sing *Le Bestiaire* with irony is to misunderstand completely Apollinaire's poetry and my music.' They are the first mélodies he ever wrote (in 1918), but they are already quite typical of their composer.

LE BESTIAIRE Ou Cortège d'Orphée	THE BOOK OF BEASTS or Procession of Orpheus
Le Dromadaire Avec ses quatre dromadaires Don Pedro d'Alfaroubeira Courut le monde et l'admira	*The Dromedary* With his four dromedaries Don Pedro d'Alfaroubeira roamed the world over and admired it
Il fit ce que je voudrais faire Si j'avais quatre dromadaires.	he did what I would like to do if I had four dromedaries.

Does this poem not express the unsatisfied longings for adventure that we all feel within ourselves? The prefatory indications are excellent: 'rhythmic, heavy, ♩ = 76', but with the rhythm, both interpreters must achieve perfect legato. The voice must be rather *f* on the first three lines, with a rich quality. (Don Pedro d'Alfaroubeira was a Portuguese explorer.) For the last two lines *p* is much preferable to *mf* for both singer and pianist, and the expression is nostalgic. Poulenc always made a little *rallentando* on the very last bar of the *allegro*.

La chèvre du Thibet	*The Tibetan Goat*
Les poils de cette chèvre	et même	The hair of this goat and even
Ceux d'or pour qui prit tant de peine	that hair of gold for which so much trouble was taken
Jason ne valent rien au prix	by Jason are worth nothing to the value
Des cheveux dont je suis épris.	of the hair of her I love.

This is a very happy and tender love song. The tempo (♩ = 72) should be supple but steady. (A slight stress on 'ceux' with the vowel sound a true [ø].) The fifth and sixth bars in the piano part must be very fluid; and the mélodie ends in a contented smile with a slight *rallentando* on the last bar.

La sauterelle	*The Grasshopper*
Voici la fine sauterelle	Here is the delicate grasshopper
La nourriture de Saint Jean	the nourishment of St. John
Puissent mes vers être comme elle	may my verses be likewise
Le régal des meilleures gens.	the feast of superior people.

A four-bar mélodie at a steady pace (♩ = 66), but an expressive breath must be taken by singer and pianist after the second bar. I suggest that the singer should attack the third bar only *p*, reserving the *pp* for a beautiful *diminuendo* towards the end . . . not easy to realize but essential. After the *rallentando* there can be a little pause on the last note.

Le dauphin
Dauphins vous jouez dans la mer
Mais le flot est toujours amer
Parfois ma joie éclate-t-elle
La vie est encore cruelle.

The Dolphin
Dolphins you sport in the sea
yet the waters are always briny
at times my joy bursts forth
but life is still cruel.

There should be contrasts in this mélodie according to the meaning of the poem: lines one and three *mf* and rhythmic; lines two and four *p* and legato, with an expressive stress on the syllable 'cruelle'. The indicated tempo is undoubtedly too fast and ♩ = 116 is far better. There is a *rallentando* only on the last bar.

L'écrevisse
Incertitude | o! mes délices
Vous et moi nous nous en allons
Comme s'en vont les écrevisses
A reculons à reculons.

The Crayfish
Uncertainty O! my delights
you and I we progress
just like the crayfish
backwards backwards.

The indication *assez vif* (rather fast) is not good. The tempo ♩ = 88 is preferable to 96. It should be performed in a mood of philosophical abandon. The first 'à reculons' is *f*, the second is *p*, with a big *rallentando* (*un peu*—a little—as indicated, is not enough), and there must be a long *fermata* on the final note.

La carpe
Dans vos viviers dans vos étangs
Carpes que vous vivez longtemps
Est-ce que la mort vous oublie
Poissons de la mélancolie?
                    Guillaume Apollinaire

The Carp
In your fish-ponds in your pools
carp how long you live
is it that death has forgotten you
fish of melancholy?

Using both pedals and beautiful sonority, a wonderfully liquid impression can be given by the pianist (♩ = 54 is preferable to 58), and the singer must of course sing *p*, but with rich sonority and perfect legato. The low C flat of the last line should not be too *p*, in order to allow the syllable 'co', an octave higher, to be more *pp*. The short cycle ends in an extremely poetic atmosphere.

*

BANALITÉS (BANALITIES)

A series of five mélodies, to poems by Guillaume Apollinaire. They do not constitute a cycle in the true sense of the word, for they have no connexion with one another either poetically or musically, and they vary greatly in character.

CHANSON D'ORKENISE	SONG OF ORKENISE
Par les portes d'Orkenise	Through the gates of Orkenise
Veut entrer | un charretier.	a carter wants to enter.
Par les portes d'Orkenise	Through the gates of Orkenise
Veut sortir un va-nu-pieds.	a tramp wants to leave.
Et les gardes de la ville	And the town guards
Courant sus au va-nu-pieds :	hasten up to the tramp :
' Qu'emportes-tu de la ville ? '	' What are you taking away from the town ? '
'J'y laisse mon cœur entier.'	'I leave my whole heart there.'
Et les gardes de la ville	And the town guards
Courant sus au charretier :	hasten up to the carter :
' Qu'apportes-tu dans la ville ? '	' What are you bringing into the town ? '
'Mon cœur pour me marier!'	'My heart to be married!'
Que de cœurs dans Orkenise !	What a lot of hearts in Orkenise !
Les gardes riaient, riaient.	The guards laughed, laughed.
Va-nu-pieds la route est grise,	Tramp, the road is hazy,
L'amour grisé, | ô charretier.	love makes the head hazy, O carter.
Les beaux gardes de la ville	The fine-looking town guards
Tricotaient superbement ;	knitted superbly ;
Puis les portes de la ville	then the gates of the town
Se fermèrent lentement.	slowly closed.

Guillaume Apollinaire

'Briskly and in the style of a folk-song' ♩ = 126, are the excellent indications. This means that the even pace of the song must not be affected by all the very important changes of dynamics, colours and expressions, which are numerous.

The beginning of the story is quite straightforward and *f*. The first change occurs when the guards of the town ('Orkenise' is an imaginary town) address the tramp bluntly: 'Qu'emportes-tu de la ville?' Second change: the poor man answers *p* with lassitude and sadness: 'J'y laisse mon cœur entier'. Then back to the straightforward *f*, and again comes the blunt question to the carter, who answers *mp* and very cheerfully: 'Mon cœur pour me marier!'. Both tramp and carter should be slightly coarse in their accent. After the little interlude: 'Que de cœurs dans Orkenise!' the ironical reaction of the guards laughing, laughing, must be expressed. Then again a sudden change: the poet seems to intervene and playing on the word 'grise', which as an adjective means 'grey' and as a verb 'intoxicate', suddenly creates a brief poetic climate *pp*. But *subito f* is the crazy evocation of the guards with their big moustaches—knitting! Then the heavy gates of the town begin to close, and the music, with its long notes, needs no *ritardando* to suggest how slowly they are closed.

HÔTEL	HOTEL
Ma chambre a la forme d'une cage	My room is shaped like a cage
Le soleil passe son bras par la fenêtre	the sun puts its arm through the window
Mais moi qui veut fumer	but I who would like to smoke
Pour faire des mirages	to make smoke pictures
J'allume au feu du jour ma cigarette	I light at the fire of day my cigarette
Je ne veux pas travailler	I do not want to work
Je veux fumer.	I want to smoke.

Guillaume Apollinaire

The laziest song ever written; but one must make no mistake, it is a song of happiness. The indolent poet is in his hotel room in Paris, and a bright ray of sunlight shines through the window; in a blissful mood, all he wants to do is to light his cigarette at the sun's fire.

From the beginning the piano part can suggest this idleness: ♩ = 50, *pp*, all the chords legato and very softly set. The voice is also 'very legato and expressive' (no sadness!), observing the dynamic indications, especially the crescendo on 'Pour faire des mirages', to prepare the *subito p*, as soft as possible, on 'J'allume' (only one 'l', please). A slothful *portamento* on 'cigarette'. 'Je ne veux pas tra<u>vailler</u>' with an exaggerated legato and a stress on 'tra'. 'Je veux <u>fu</u>mer' is *p*, with a little stress on 'fu' and a slight hesitation before the first beat, *pp*, on '-mer'. After a *ppp*, the piano should play the last two bars *mf*, as a happy conclusion to the mélodie.

FAGNES DE WALLONIE	WALLOON UPLANDS
Tant de tristesses plénières	Overwhelming sorrow
Prirent mon cœur aux fagnes désolées	seized my heart in the desolate uplands
Quand las j'ai reposé dans les sapinières	when tired I rested in the fir plantation
Le poids des kilomètres pendant que râlait	the weight of the kilometres while blustered
le vent d'ouest	the west wind
J'avais quitté le joli bois	I had left the pretty wood
Les_écureuils | y sont restés	the squirrels stayed there
Ma pipe essayait de faire des nuages Au ciel	my pipe tried to make clouds in the sky
Qui restait pur obstinément	which remained obstinately clear
Je n'ai confié aucun secret ✓ sinon une chanson | énigmatique	I did not confide any secret·except an enigmatic song
Aux tourbières_humides	to the damp peat bog
Les bruyères fleurant le miel	the heather fragrant with honey
Attiraient les_abeilles	attracted the bees
<u>Et</u> mes pieds_endoloris	and my aching feet
Foulaient les myrtilles_et les_ airelles	crushed the bilberries and the blaeberries
Tendrement mariée	tenderly united
Nord	north
Nord	north
La vie s'y tord	life twists itself there
En arbres forts_	in strong trees
Et tors	and twisted
La vie y mord	life bites there
La mort	death
A <u>belles</u> <u>dents</u>	ravenously
Quand <u>bruit</u> le vent	when the wind howls

Guillaume Apollinaire

'Wallonie' is a part of Belgium, in which Apollinaire lived for a time, and 'Fagnes' (a dialect word meaning peaty uplands) are a wild area of moors, fir woods, peat-bogs and gnarled trees twisted by the wind. Therefore this mélodie should be performed as though in one gust of north wind from beginning to end, even if the tempo ♩ = 88 seems better than ♩ = 92. All the beginning is *f*, and legato. There is a change of dynamics and of shading on 'J'avais quitté le joli bois', etc., but *f* again on 'Je n'ai confié', etc. There are three quaver rests in this line that may be disregarded: between 'confié' and 'aucun', between 'sinon' and 'une', between 'chanson' and 'énigmatique'. A sudden change of dynamics and shading on 'Les bruyères fleurant le miel', etc., which is *p*, bright and fresh. In certain editions there is a *p* instead of a *mf* on 'Et mes pieds', etc. This is quite permissible. (The word 'myrtilles' is pronounced: m[i]rt[i]l[ə].) All the end of the mélodie is *ff*, rhythmic, with *very strong* articulation. A *f* should be maintained throughout on 'A belles dents quand bruit le vent' especially as the voice comes down. Stress on 'bruit'. On the last *f* on the word 'vent' a big crescendo–decrescendo gives the impression of a last gust of wind. The piano coda should be *accelerando* rather than *rallentando*, especially the last chords.

VOYAGE A PARIS	TRIP TO PARIS
Ah! la charmante chose	Ah! how charming
Quitter un pays morose	to leave a dreary place
Pour Paris	for Paris
Paris joli	delightful Paris
Qu'un jour dut créer l'Amour	that once upon a time love must have
Guillaume Apollinaire	created

These doggerel verses are set to a 'valse-musette' as played in popular dance-halls in Paris or its suburbs. Both words and music must have a kind of 'Parisian accent', not without a certain coarseness. Thus on the word 'Paris' the stress should always be on the first syllable with a strong 'P'. The indicated tempo (♩. = 96) is just right (no slower, please!), *f*, mirthful, *cheerful*, with a sudden effect of charm, but witty charm, at the only *subito p*. The last two phrases are 'very simple' and 'very amiable' as indicated. The pianist should not fail to make the very big crescendo of his conclusion, with, of course, no *rallentando*.

<table>
<tr><td>

SANGLOTS

Notre amour est réglé par les
　calmes_étoiles
Or nous savons qu'en nous beaucoup
　d'hommes respirent
　　Qui vinrent de très loin | et
　　sont_un sous nos fronts
C'est la chanson des rêveurs
Qui s'étaient_arraché le cœur
Et le portaient dans la main droite
　　Souviens-t'en cher orgueil de
　　tous ces souvenirs
　　Des marins qui chantaient
　　comme des conquérants
　　Des gouffres de Thulé des
　　tendres cieux d'Ophir
　　Des malades maudits de ceux qui
　　fuient leur ombre
　　Et du retour joyeux des_
　　heureux_émigrants
De ce cœur il coulait du sang
Et le rêveur allait pensant
A sa blessure délicate
　　Tu ne briseras pas la chaîne de
　　ces causes
Et douloureuse | et nous disait
　　Qui sont les_effets d'autres
　　causes
Mon pauvre cœur mon cœur brisé
Pareil au cœur de tous les hommes
　　Voici voici nos mains que la vie
　　fit_esclaves
Est mort d'amour ou c'est tout
comme

Est mort d'amour et le voici
　Ainsi vont toutes choses

</td><td>

SOBS

Our love is ordered by the calm
　stars
now we know that in us many men
　have their being
　　who came from very far away
　　and are one under our brows
it is the song of the dreamers
who tore out their heart
and carried it in the right hand
　　(remember dear pride all these
　　memories
　　of the sailors who sang like
　　conquerors
　　of the chasms of Thule of the
　　gentle skies of Ophir
　　of the cursed sick people of those
　　who fled from their shadow
　　and of the joyous return of
　　happy emigrants)
this heart ran with blood
and the dreamer went on thinking
of his wound delicate
　　(You will not break the chain of
　　these causes)
and painful and said to us
　　(which are the effects of other
　　causes)
my poor heart my broken heart
resembling the heart of all men
　　(here here are our hands that
　　life enslaved)
has died of love or so it seems

has died of love and here it is
　such is the way of all things

</td></tr>
</table>

Arrachez donc le vôtre aussi   tear out yours also
   Et rien ne sera libre jusqu'à la   (and nothing will be free until
      fin des temps   the end of time)
Laissons tout_aux morts   let us leave all to the dead
Et cachons nos sanglots   and hide our sobs
        Guillaume Apollinaire

This great and beautiful poem, already almost 'surrealist', inspired Poulenc to write one of his best lyrical mélodies. It is certainly difficult to understand and to translate, the more so because it has no punctuation. But Poulenc's feeling for this poetry fortunately clarifies the text, giving it its correct rhythm and form; and the singer has no difficulty in agreeing with the composer's concept. Certain lines in the poem are in parentheses, as indicated in the translation; without these lines the sense of the poem is clear, and the lines in parentheses are linked in meaning.

♩ = 66 is a mistake, the very quiet initial tempo is ♩ = 56. The pianist should use a soft and transparent sonority, and the singer a floating *mezza voce*, with perfect legato. The modulation in E flat minor should immediately suggest much more warmth and richness of tone. Then a very progressive crescendo and *animato* begins. (The pianist must not hurry to play his arpeggio on the last beat of the bar in $\frac{4}{4}$, and the singer should follow him.) The *f* is important on 'Souviens-t'en', etc., to prepare a *mf* and always *accelerando* and crescendo from 'Des marins', etc., with a violent climax on 'Des malades maudits'. Then (Poulenc admitted that his indications were wrong) there is a *rallentando*, with the diminuendo on 'de ceux qui fuient leur ombre', which returns to a slower tempo *mf* on 'Et du retour joyeux' (stress on the B natural of 'joy'), and more *rallentando* brings back exactly the *tempo primo* (♩ = 56) with the E flat minor chord. This tempo must henceforth be maintained, in spite of all the peculiar difficulties due to the poem. The composer found the two following lines not easy to set:

'Tu ne briseras pas la chaîne de ces causes'
'Qui sont les effets d'autres causes'

It must be admitted that the interpreters find difficulties also. . . . From

'De ce cœur...' the first three lines should be kept *pp*. Then *subito f* on 'Tu ne briseras pas la chaîne de ces causes', with an immediate return to the dynamics of the preceding line, which is *p* and intense (the indication *mf* is a mistake) on 'Et douloureuse et nous disait'. Then *subito f* again on 'Qui sont les effets d'autres causes'. The same effect of contrast must be achieved on the parenthesis 'Voici voici nos mains que la vie fit esclaves', which is *subito mf* (and with no hurry) after the *p* of the preceding lines. There is a little *ritenuto* of one bar to introduce the big lyrical *f* 'Est mort d'amour ou c'est tout comme'; the second 'est mort d'amour' is *subito p*—echo. And the mélodie moves to its end, maintaining the same pace, observing the dynamics, but always with great lyricism and intense expression.

*

LA GRENOUILLÈRE	LA GRENOUILLÈRE (The Froggery)
Au bord de l'île on voit	By the shore of the isle one sees
Les canots vides | qui s'entre-cognent	the empty boats that bump against each other
Et maintenant	and now
Ni le dimanche ✓ ni les jours | de la semaine ✓	neither on Sunday nor on weekdays
Ni les peintres ni Maupassant ne se promènent	neither the painters nor Maupassant set out
Bras nus sur leurs canots avec des femmes‿à grosses poitrines	with bare arms in their boats with their women friends full-bosomed
Et bêtes comme chou	and stupid as a cabbage★
Petits bateaux vous me faites bien de la peine	little boats you make me very sad
Au bord de l'île	by the shore of the isle
Guillaume Apollinaire	★ sweetly silly

'La Grenouillère' (The Froggery) is the name of a little island in the Seine, in the suburbs of Paris, where writers and painters used to gather at the end of the nineteenth century. Poulenc said of this mélodie: 'It evokes the pleasures of years long past, Sundays which were happy and at ease, boatmen having lunch as Renoir painted them.' And his music suggests the rocking of the little boats now empty and unused.

♩ = 56 is the right tempo, with much pedal for the piano and much line for the voice, with a melancholy feeling. On the line 'Ni le dimanche ni les jours de la semaine' breath and break as indicated above. Very even triplets and with simplicity, no irony: 'avec des femmes à grosses poitrines'; then a little stress on the word 'bêtes'. 'Petits bateaux vous me faites bien de la peine' is *p* very soft, and 'Au bord de l'île' well-sustained *mf*. The pianist can display beautiful and transparent sonorities in his final bars.

LE PONT

Deux dames le long du fleuve
Elles se parlent par-dessus l'eau
Et sur le pont de leurs paroles
La foule passe et repasse en dansant

un dieu

    tu reviendras

        Hi! oh! Là-bas ✓

        Là-bas ✓

c'est
pour
toi
seule
que
le
sang
coule

Tous les enfants savent pourquoi

        Passe mais passe donc
        Ne te retourne pas

      Hi! oh! là-bas là-bas

Les jeunes filles qui passent sur le pont léger
        portent dans leurs mains
        le bouquet de demain
Et leurs regards s'écoulent
    Dans ce fleuve à tous étranger
Qui vient de loin qui va si loin
Et passe sous le pont léger de vos paroles
    Ô bavardes le long du fleuve
      Ô bavardes | ô folles le long du fleuve

Guillaume Apollinaire

THE BRIDGE

Two women along the river
they speak to each other across the water
and upon the bridge of their words
the crowd passes to and fro dancing

a god   it is
                                                         for
    you will come back   you
                                                         alone
        Hi! Oh! over there   that
                                                         the
            over there   blood
                                                         flows
all the children know why

            go on but go on then
            do not turn back

        Hi! Oh! over there over there

The young girls who cross over the airy bridge
                carry in their hands
                the bouquet of tomorrow
and their gaze pours
                into this river stranger to all
that comes from far away that goes so far away
and passes under the airy bridge of your words
        O chatterers along the river
        O chatterers O foolish ones along the river

Everything cannot be quite clear in this poem, in spite, or because of
its typographic arrangement, but once more the composer is of great
help. To give his own words: 'It was above all necessary to convey the
continuous flowing of the water, and the conversation across the water,
a conversation which becomes "the bridge of their words".' The impetus of the tempo: $\downarrow$. = 60 (which is fast but not 'very fast') must
launch the mélodie in one perfectly even flow. It is important to feel
it as one beat in the bar, to get the proper rhythm. The two breath
marks indicated after the two 'là-bas' must, however, be observed.

The dynamics are very well marked. For example the *f* on 'passe mais passe donc' with these indicated stresses; the crescendo–decrescendo on 'Qui vient de loin qui va si loin' with no change of tempo at all. (The liaison between 'Ô bavardes ô folles', indicated in certain editions, is ridiculous and impossible.) There is just a little *rallentando* on the last bars of the piano.

MONTPARNASSE	MONTPARNASSE
O porte de l'hôtel | avec deux plantes vertes	O door of the hotel with two green plants
Vertes qui jamais	green which never
Ne porteront de fleurs	will bear any flowers
Où sont mes fruits ? Où me planté-je ?	where are my fruits ? where do I plant myself ?
O porte de l'hôtel | un ange est devant toi	O door of the hotel an angel stands in front of you
Distribuant des prospectus	distributing prospectuses
On n'a jamais si bien défendu la vertu	virtue has never been so well defended
Donnez-moi pour toujours | une chambre à la semaine	give me for ever a room by the week
Ange barbu vous êtes en réalité	bearded angel you are really
Un poète lyrique d'Allemagne	a lyric poet from Germany
Qui voulez connaître | Paris	who wants to know Paris
Vous connaissez de son pavé	you know on its pavement
Ces raies sur lesquelles | il ne faut pas que l'on marche	these lines on which one must not step
Et vous rêvez	and you dream
D'aller passer votre Dimanche à Garches	of going to pass your Sunday at Garches
Il fait un peu lourd | et vos cheveux sont longs	it is rather sultry and your hair is long
O bon petit poète | un peu bête et trop blond	O good little poet a bit stupid and too blond
Vos yeux ressemblent tant | à ces deux grands ballons	your eyes so much resemble these two big balloons
Qui s'en vont dans l'air pur	that float away in the pure air
A l'aventure	at random

Guillaume Apollinaire

Montparnasse is a quarter of Paris where many artists used to live. Apollinaire is certainly speaking of himself in this poem. Garches is a little residential town in the suburbs of Paris. 'When the subject is Paris, I often approach it with a full heart and a mind full of music', said Poulenc. It inspired him to write this very vocal mélodie, to be sung with fluent legato and phrasing. The quiet tempo ($\bigcup$ = 58) is the maximum of speed. Again the dynamics are well indicated. The line 'On n'a jamais si bien défendu la vertu' is *pp* and without hurry; it should be almost *parlando* as a contrast. The big lyrical phrase 'Un poète lyrique d'Allemagne' (Apollinaire had been staying in Germany), with a little *rubato* on the syllable 'po' to give the pianist plenty of time, and no diminuendo coming down. The word 'Paris' in the following line can be emphasized with the 'P'. A little quick crescendo on 'Et vous rêvez D'aller passer', and a very soft *pp* on 'votre Dimanche à Garches'. The pianist should take a good breath before attacking the next phrase. All the end of the mélodie is sustained and played with lyricism, very poetic, with no sadness whatsoever, but a feeling of lazy contentment.

*

Paul Eluard, the second poet whose work was to be a great inspiration to Poulenc, is the most eminent poet of the surrealist movement which arose in France just after the First World War. Surrealism was an attempt to express (in writing, painting, etc.) thoughts arising directly from the subconscious, as opposed to the tangible and readily understandable creations of the conscious mind. A surrealist poem cannot be rationally explained, it must be intuitively felt. As it is from the subconscious mind that the words stem, may it not be that they are understood by the reader's subconscious? Poulenc without any doubt had genius in divining the meaning behind this poetry, and the interpreters are indeed fortunate that it is his conception of the poem that they are called upon to express.

These elusive poems are inimical to translation; the translations given here are more or less word for word. This, however, may be sufficient to suggest to the mind of the reader various images, atmospheres, poetic climates.

Poulenc first used Eluard's poems as late as 1935, but they provided the texts for thirty-three mélodies (plus several choral works). As for his settings of Apollinaire, Poulenc succeeds in clarifying the poems by his music, divining their correct movement, their punctuation (they have none on the printed page), their breaths, their inflexions; he catches their feeling, their emotion, often revealing their deepest and most hidden meaning, and giving them life.

TEL JOUR TELLE NUIT (SUCH A DAY SUCH A NIGHT)

These nine mélodies form a complete cycle, of which the songs are not intended to be sung in isolation. The value of each one is dependent upon the one before and after it, and upon its position in the cycle as a whole. Certain of them are really little more than linking passages to prepare the way for the mélodie they precede. The first and the last are in the same key and the same tempo, and establish the atmosphere of composed happiness, of calmness and serenity, which pervades the entire cycle.

BONNE JOURNÉE...

A GOOD DAY...

Bonne journée j'ai revu qui je
    n'oublie pas
Qui je n'oublierai jamais
Et des femmes fugaces dont les͜ yeux
Me faisaient͜ une haie d'honneur
Elles s'enveloppèrent dans leurs
    sourires

A good day I have again seen whom I
    do not forget
whom I shall never forget
and women fleeting by whose eyes
formed for me a hedge of honour
they wrapped themselves in their
    smiles

Bonne journée j'ai vu mes͜ amis sans
    soucis
Les hommes ne pesaient pas lourd
Un qui passait
Son͜ ombre changée en souris
Fuyait dans le ruisseau

a good day I have seen my friends
    carefree
the men were light in weight
one who passed by
his shadow changed into a mouse
fled into the gutter

J'ai vu le ciel très grand
Le beau regard des gens privés de tout

I have seen the great wide sky
the beautiful eyes of those deprived
    of everything

Plage distante | où personne n'aborde

distant shore where no one lands

Bonne journée qui commença mélancolique	a good day which began mournfully
Noire sous les‿arbres verts	dark under the green trees
Mais qui soudain trempée d'aurore	but which suddenly drenched with dawn
M'entra dans le cœur ✓ par surprise.	invaded my heart unawares.

Paul Eluard

A *mélodie* of peaceful happiness, of blissful gravity. With a beautiful legato, the whole first stanza should be sung ($\quarternote$ = 63) without any change of dynamics, keeping an even *mp*, with a rich timbre, and no 'involuntary nuances' on rising or descending phrases. (For instance, no crescendo on 'Elles s'enveloppèrent'.) The second stanza starts *mf*, and I suggest a diminuendo on the ascending scale 'J'ai vu mes amis sans soucis'. Then *mf subito* and the two lines 'Son ombre changée en souris Fuyait dans le ruisseau' well linked by their meaning. A crescendo, as indicated, on 'Le beau regard des gens privés de tout', breath for both performers, and *p subito*: 'Plage distante où personne n'aborde'. On the bar of piano solo there must be a little *ritenuto* to prepare the return to the initial theme for the last stanza. Poem and music naturally brighten for the end of the *mélodie*.

UNE RUINE COQUILLE VIDE...	A RUIN AN EMPTY SHELL...
Une ruine coquille vide	A ruin an empty shell
Pleure dans son tablier	weeps into its apron
Les enfants qui jouent | autour d'elle	the children who play around it
Font moins de bruit que des mouches	make less sound than flies
La ruine s'en va | à tâtons	the ruin goes groping
Chercher ses vaches dans‿un pré	to seek its cows in the meadow
J'ai vu le jour je vois cela	I have seen the day I see that
Sans‿en avoir | honte	without shame
Il est minuit comme‿une flèche	It is midnight like an arrow
Dans‿un cœur à la portée	in a heart within reach
Des folâtres lueurs nocturnes	of the sprightly nocturnal glimmerings
Qui contredisent le sommeil.	which gainsay sleep.

Paul Eluard

'Very quiet and unreal' ($\quarternote = 60$) are the indications. One could add 'mysterious', both for the wonderful atmosphere created by the music and for the meaning of the poem. Anyhow the ruin is certainly not an old woman! I have been asked this several times. I, personally, imagine that the apron into which the ruin cries is suggested by heavy masses of ivy tumbling down the old walls.

The pianist must achieve a subdued sonority in a haze of pedal, which he has to maintain *pp* during the *whole* mélodie in spite of the singer's changes of dynamics; these changes are made in contrasts, two lines by two lines, and it is important to note that there are no crescendi or diminuendi. The first two lines are whispered *pp*. The next two lines ('Les enfants', etc.) are *subito mf*. Then two lines ('La ruine s'en va', etc.) are *pp* again. And two lines ('J'ai vu le jour', etc.) *mf*. Then comes a strange and mysterious *pp* on 'Il est minuit comme une flèche Dans un cœur'; then *mf*: 'à la portée Des folâtres lueurs nocturnes', and the last line is *p*, with no crescendo for the top G. The mélodie ends as it began.

LE FRONT COMME UN DRAPEAU PERDU...

Le front comme un drapeau perdu
Je te traîne quand je suis seul
Dans des rues froides
Des chambres noires
En criant misère

Je ne veux pas les lâcher
Tes mains claires et compliquées
Nées dans le miroir clos des miennes

Tout le reste est parfait
Tout le reste est encore plus inutile
Que la vie

Creuse la terre sous ton ombre

THE BROW LIKE A LOST FLAG...

The brow like a lost flag
I drag you when I am alone
through the cold streets
the dark rooms
crying in misery

I do not want to let them go
your clear and complex hands
born in the enclosed mirror of my
     own

all the rest is perfect
all the rest is even more useless
than life

hollow the earth beneath your
     shadow

Une nappe d'eau près des seins	a sheet of water reaching the breasts
Où se noyer	wherein to drown oneself
Comme une pierre.	like a stone.

Paul Eluard

A mélodie of transition and contrast. It begins in violence and ends in a strange peacefulness. The indicated initial tempo, ♩ = 132, is a minimum of speed and after four bars there is an *accelerando* to at least ♩ = 144. All this first section is *non legato*, strongly articulated. In the three bars in $\frac{4}{4}$ for the piano, the left hand dominates with a crescendo and diminuendo. Then observe the dynamics carefully as they are indicated, and legato with contrasts of colours, and ♩ = 144 unvarying to the end.

UNE ROULOTTE COUVERTE EN TUILES...	A GYPSY WAGON ROOFED WITH TILES...
Une roulotte couverte en tuiles	A gypsy wagon roofed with tiles
Le cheval mort un enfant maître	the horse dead a child master
Pensant √ le front bleu de haine	thinking his brow blue with hatred
A deux seins √ s'abattant sur lui	of two breasts beating down upon him
Comme deux poings	like two fists
Ce mélodrame √ nous arrache √	this melodrama tears away from us
La raison √ du cœur.	the sanity of the heart.

Paul Eluard

A strange and striking mélodie. A picture of tragic slums in sordid suburbs. The scene might have been painted by Picasso during the period when he was painting youthful acrobats.

To create the 'sinister' atmosphere, ♪ = 72 seems more adequate than ♪ = 80. The first two bars are a kind of *parlando*, but well supported, and the marked stresses well emphasized. The following three bars are *p*, intense, and extremely legato. (It is hoped that the pianist has large hands!) Sudden *f* and *marcato* on 'Comme deux poings', after which singer and pianist must breathe exactly together. Short rest. And again a sinister *parlando*, *p*, precisely in tempo. The last note should be scooped and breathy.

A TOUTES BRIDES...

A toutes <u>brides</u> toi dont le fantôme
<u>Piaffe</u> la nuit sur un violon
Viens ré<u>gner</u> dans les <u>bois</u>

Les verges de l'ouragan
Cherchent leur chemin par chez toi
Tu n'es pas de celles
Dont on invente les désirs

Viens boire un baiser par ici
Cède au feu qui te désespère.

Paul Eluard

RIDING FULL TILT...

Riding full tilt you whose phantom
prances at night on a violin
come to reign in the woods

the lashings of the tempest
seek their path by way of you
you are not of those
whose desires one imagines

come drink a kiss here
surrender to the fire which drives
    you to despair.

A typical *mélodie* of transition to highlight the following one. *Prestissimo* ♩ = 112 is excellent. There is still an *accelerando* for the four bars of piano; but a return to ♩ = 112 is better for the legato of the following stanza, the final one being violent and rather *accelerando* to the end. (For the left hand in the sixth bar a bass clef is obviously forgotten.) There is a long silence before:

UNE HERBE PAUVRE...

Une herbe pauvre
Sauvage
Apparut dans la neige
C'était la santé
Ma bouche fut émerveillée
Du goût d'air pur qu'elle avait
Elle était fanée.

Paul Eluard

SCANTY GRASS...

Scanty grass
wild
appeared in the snow
it was health
my mouth marvelled
at the savour of pure air it had
it was withered.

When spring comes, high in the mountains, the first blades of grass, piercing the melting snow, give such an impression of purity, of health-fulness that one cannot resist tasting their refreshing bitterness. This transparent atmosphere is wonderfully expressed musically in this *mélodie*, and the performers must succeed in capturing it with a soft and clear sonority, a perfect legato and a quiet immutable tempo (♩ = 60). In the line 'Du goût d'air pur qu'elle avait', make a little crescendo coming down, and a diminuendo going up. The line 'Elle était fanée' should not be too *p*, in order to reserve a *pp* for the repeat of the first line, with, of course, not the slightest crescendo going up to the top G. No *rallentando* towards the end.

JE N'AI ENVIE QUE DE T'AIMER...

Je n'ai envie que de t'aimer
Un orage emplit la vallée
Un poisson la rivière

Je t'ai faite à la taille de ma solitude

Le monde entier pour se cacher ✓
Des jours des nuits pour se comprendre ✓

Pour ne plus rien voir dans tes yeux
Que ce que je pense de toi
Et d'un monde à ton image

Et des jours et des nuits réglés par
tes paupières.

Paul Eluard

I LONG ONLY TO LOVE YOU...

I long only to love you
a storm fills the valley
a fish the river

I have formed you to the pattern of
my solitude

the whole world to hide in
days and nights to understand one
another

to see nothing more in your eyes
but what I think of you
and of a world in your likeness

and of days and nights ordered by
your eyelids.

A song of happy love. In a rather fast tempo ($\bullet$. = 100) it flows uninterruptedly from beginning to end, but should not give the slightest impression of agitation. The dynamics are clearly indicated. After the crescendo on 'Des jours des nuits pour se comprendre', there is a breath before attacking *p subito*: 'Pour ne plus rien voir dans tes yeux'. On the last line, 'Et des jours et des nuits réglés par tes paupières', it is preferable to make a little *accelerando*, rather than to drag. There is a *rallentando* only on the final beats of piano.

FIGURE DE FORCE BRULANTE ET FAROUCHE...

Figure de force brûlante et farouche
Cheveux noirs | où l'or coule vers
le sud
Aux nuits corrompues

IMAGE OF FIERY WILD FORCEFULNESS...

Image of fiery wild forcefulness
black hair wherein the gold flows
towards the south
on corrupt nights

Or englouti étoile impure	engulfed gold tainted star
Dans_un lit jamais partagé	in a bed never shared
Aux veines des tempes	to the veins of the temples
Comme_au bout des seins	as to the tips of the breasts
La vie se refuse	life denies itself
Les_yeux nul ne peut les crever	no one can blind the eyes
Boire leur éclat ni leurs larmes	drink their brilliance or their tears
Le sang | au dessus d'eux triomphe pour lui seul	the blood above them triumphs for itself alone
Intraitable démesurée	intractable unbounded
Inutile	useless
Cette santé bâtit_une prison.	this health builds a prison.

Paul Eluard

With its contrasts of vehemence and calm, this is again a mélodie of transition. The violent ♩ = 138, with a biting articulation, gets faster and faster from 'Aux nuits corrompues', etc. to 'jamais partagé'. Then the gloomy ♩ = 66 is maintained *p* and dismal up to the sudden *ff*: 'Intraitable', etc. which is in the same tempo, using the whole intensity of the voice. This terrific climax, in Poulenc's words, 'makes more keenly perceptible the kind of silence that is the beginning of':

NOUS AVONS FAIT LA NUIT...	WE HAVE MADE NIGHT*...
Nous_avons fait la nuit je tiens ta main je veille	We have made night I hold your hand I watch over you
Je te soutiens de toutes mes forces	I sustain you with all my strength
Je grave sur un roc l'étoile de tes forces	I engrave on a rock the star of your strength
Sillons profonds | où la bonté de ton corps germera	deep furrows where the goodness of your body will germinate
Je me répète ta voix cachée ta voix publique	I repeat to myself your secret voice your public voice
Je ris_encore de l'orgueilleuse	I laugh still at the haughty woman
Que tu traites comme_une mendiante	whom you treat like a beggar
Des fous que tu respectes des simples_ où tu te baignes	at the fools whom you respect the simple folk in whom you immerse yourself

* We have turned out the light

Et dans ma tête qui se met doucement
   d'accord
	avec <u>la</u> tienne avec <u>la</u>
	   nuit
		and in my head which gently begins
		   to harmonize with yours with the
		   night

Je m'émerveille de l'inconnue que tu
   deviens
	I marvel at the stranger that you
	   become

Une inconnue semblable à toi
   semblable à <u>tout</u> ce que j'aime
	a stranger resembling you resembling
	   all that I love

Qui est toujours <u>nou</u>veau.	which is ever new.

Paul Eluard

To get the 'kind of silence' suggested by the composer at the beginning of this mélodie, the interpreters should try to obtain the most perfect legato in the *p*, with total relaxation. Poulenc says, à propos of this mélodie: 'It is only calmness that can give a love poem its intensity'. The quiet tempo ($\quarternote$ = 60) must go on its even pace up to the very end of the piano coda, with a steadiness which will exclude any cheap sentimentality, but will confer a solid and virile profundity to the feelings expressed by both poet and musician with such a wonderful lyricism.

The initial *p* should not, in my opinion, be a *pp* because of the low tessitura and because the voice must be warm and full. Thus the higher tessitura of the fifth bar and of the following ones can continue in the same *p* to make the sudden contrast of 'Sillons profonds', etc., which should be *pp* as soft as possible and clear, with no crescendo whatsoever on 'germera'. After a breath, for both performers, 'Je me répète ta voix cachée ta voix publique' is only *p*. From this last bar the piano continues to sustain its own melodic line *p* or *mp*, while the singer attacks *f* 'Je ris encore', etc., and maintains the *mf* on the lines that follow.

Then at the change of key, the big lyrical section of the mélodie begins, quite unique in its impetus. It is better to attack 'Et dans ma tête' only *mf* with no diminuendo as indicated on 'qui se met doucement d'accord' and to maintain the *mf* on 'avec <u>la</u> tienne avec <u>la</u> nuit' emphasizing the B and the A on the two words 'la'. Thus one reserves a real *f* for 'Je m'émerveille', returning to a *mf* to permit another crescendo on 'Une inconnue semblable à toi' which is *ff*. The following 'semblable à tout ce que j'aime' should not have too much diminuendo, and 'qui est toujours <u>nouveau</u>' is *mf* and intense.

All this lyrical section should give the impression of complete wonderment; and the piano coda prolongs this feeling, becoming more serene in its peaceful happiness.

*

TU VOIS LE FEU DU SOIR...

Tu vois le feu du soir qui sort de sa
    coquille
Et tu vois la forêt | enfouie dans sa
    fraîcheur

Tu vois la plaine nue aux flancs du
    ciel traînard
La neige haute comme la mer
Et la mer | haute dans l'azur

Pierres parfaites‿et bois doux secours
    voilés
Tu vois des villes teintes de mélancolie

Dorée des trottoirs pleins d'excuses
Une place‿où la solitude‿a sa statue
Souriante ✓ et l'amour | une seule
    maison

Tu vois les‿animaux
Sosies malins sacrifiés l'un‿à l'autre

Frères‿immaculés | aux‿ombres
    confondues
Dans‿un désert de sang

Tu vois‿un bel enfant quand‿il
    joue quand‿il rit
Il est bien plus petit
Que le petit‿oiseau du bout des
    branches

YOU SEE THE FIRE OF EVENING

You see the fire of evening emerging
    from its shell
and you see the forest buried in its
    coolness

you see the bare plain at the edges of
    the straggling sky
the snow high like the sea
and the sea high in the azure

perfect stones and sweet woods
    veiled succour
you see cities tinged with gilded
    melancholy
pavements full of excuses
a square where solitude has its statue
smiling and love a single house

you see animals
malign doubles sacrificed one to
    another
immaculate brothers with inter-
    mingled shadows
in a wilderness of blood

you see a beautiful child when he
    plays when he laughs
he is smaller
than the little bird on the tip of the
    branches

Tu vois_un paysage | aux saveurs
    d'huile et d'eau
D'où la roche est_exclue où la
    terre abandonne
Sa verdure √ à l'été qui la couvre de
    fruits

Des femmes descendant de leur
    miroir ancien
T'apportent leur jeunesse √ et leur
    foi en la tienne
Et l'une √ sa clarté la voile √ qui
    t'entraîne
Te fait secrètement voir le monde
    sans toi.

you see a countryside with its savour
    of oil and of water
where the rock is excluded where the
    earth abandons
her greenness to the summer which
    covers her with fruit

women descending from their ancient
    mirror
bring you their youth and their faith
    in yours
and one of them veiled by her clarity
    who allures you
secretly makes you see the world
    without yourself.

Paul Eluard

This song is from a series of two mélodies called *Miroirs Brûlants*. One of the purest and most profound of Poulenc's mélodies, it is the one which he himself liked best. The beautiful poem is a long enumeration in litany form, a form Eluard used often with great inspiration. (*See also La Fraîcheur et le Feu*: 'Homme au sourire tendre'.) The composer chose a quiet pace (♩ = 60) and kept it unchanged throughout the whole mélodie, without any pause, without even the distraction that a semiquaver would create; and yet this long mélodie does not give the least impression of monotony. Poulenc avoids this by the extreme refinement of his writing for the piano, by the simplicity of the vocal line and the subtle interplay of modulations which must continually suggest to the singer fresh shades of tone-colour.

The first three lines of the poem should be sung *mezza voce pp* (the first line in one breath), with a floating quality; the following two lines are crescendo to *f*. The ⁵⁄₄ bar of the piano is diminuendo. Then *pp* for one line, with a sudden warm and mellow quality in the voice. The following two lines are rather *mp* and with a rich timbre in the low tessitura. 'Une place où la solitude', etc. begins a very lyrical section, *mf* with crescendo. 'Tu vois les animaux', etc., is *mf*, the piano part being the melodic part, and a really intense *f* is required on the two lines 'Frères immaculés aux ombres confondues Dans un désert de sang'. Breath for both performers; then attack *pp* with the clearest and most transparent voice 'Tu vois un bel enfant', etc. A sudden contrast for the following two lines 'Tu vois un paysage', etc., another very lyrical section *mf* to *f*. There is an optional C sharp instead of G sharp on 'l'été'. (In certain editions there is a misprint. The text is: 'qui *la* couvre de fruits'.) The line 'Des femmes descendant de leur miroir ancien' is *mp*, the piano having the melodic line, but there is a quick crescendo and *marcato* on 'T'apportent leur jeunesse et leur foi en la tienne'. Then 'Et l'une' and 'qui t'entraîne' are *f*, with the parenthesis in between of 'sa clarté la voile' which is *p*. The last line is *p* and diminuendo to the end.

This mélodie can be a display of vocal effects, masterly changes of dynamics and vocal colours, but all this must be achieved without the slightest *rubato* or alteration of the initial tempo; this is the only possible way of releasing all its poetic atmosphere.

*

'La Fraîcheur et le Feu' is not really a cycle but a single poem set to music in separate sections, exactly as the poem is printed in the literary edition. Poulenc said: 'They are the most carefully thought out of all my mélodies'. They are also those in which he best reveals the mastery which he had attained in expressive writing for the piano as well as for the voice. Two contrasted tempi, one fast: ♩ = 132 (♩ = 120 for the last section), and one slow: ♩ = 66/69 (♩ = 50 for the last but one section) give a unity to the work in spite of the diversity of its sections.

LA FRAÎCHEUR ET LE FEU

THE COOLNESS AND THE FIRE

I

Rayons des_yeux et des soleils
Des ramures_et des fontaines
Lumière du sol et du ciel
De l'homme_et de l'oubli de l'homme
Un nuage couvre le sol
Un nuage couvre le ciel
Soudain la lumière m'oublie

I

Beams of eyes and of suns
of branches and of fountains
light of earth and of sky
of man and man's oblivion
a cloud covers the earth
a cloud covers the sky
suddenly the light is unmindful of me

La mort seule demeure entière
Je suis_une ombre je ne vois plus
Le soleil jaune le soleil rouge
Le soleil blanc le ciel changeant
Je ne sais plus
La place du bonheur vivant
Au bord de l'ombre sans ciel ni terre.

death alone remains complete
I am a shadow I see no longer
the yellow sun the red sun
the white sun the changing sky
I know no longer
the place of living happiness
at the edge of the shadow with
    neither sky nor earth.

II

Le matin les branches_attisent
Le bouillonnement des_oiseaux
Le soir les arbres sont tranquilles
Le jour frémissant se repose.

In the morning the branches stir up
the effervescence of the birds
at evening the trees are peaceful
the rustling day is resting.

III

Tout disparut même les toits même le
    ciel
Même l'ombre tombée des branches

Sur les cimes des mousses tendres
Même les mots_et les regards bien_
    accordés

Sœurs miroitières de mes larmes
Les_étoiles brillaient | autour de ma
    fenêtre
Et mes_yeux refermant leurs_ailes
    pour la nuit
Vivaient d'un_univers sans bornes.

All disappeared even the roofs even
    the sky
even the shade fallen from the
    branches
upon the tips of the soft mosses
even the words and the concordant
    looks

sisters mirroring my tears
the stars shone around my window

and my eyes closing their wings
    again for the night
lived in a boundless universe.

IV

Dans les ténèbres du jardin
Viennent des filles_invisibles
Plus fines qu'à midi l'ondée

Mon sommeil les_a pour amies
Elles m'enivrent_en secret
De leurs complaisances_aveugles.

In the darkness of the garden
come some invisible girls
more delicate than the shower at
    midday

my sleep has them for friends
they elate me secretly
with their blind complaisance.

V

Unis la fraîcheur et le feu
Unis tes lèvres et tes yeux
De ta folie attends sagesse
Fais image de femme et d'homme.

Unite the coolness and the fire
unite your lips and your eyes
await wisdom from your folly
make a likeness of woman and of
man.

VI

Homme au sourire tendre
Femme aux tendres paupières
Homme aux joues rafraîchies
Femme aux bras doux et frais
Homme aux prunelles calmes
Femme aux lèvres ardentes
Homme aux paroles pleines
Femme aux yeux partagés
Homme aux deux mains utiles
Femme aux mains de raison
Homme aux astres constants
Femme aux seins de durée

Il n'est rien qui vous retient
Mes maîtres √ de m'éprouver.

Man of the tender smile
woman of the tender eyelids
man of the freshened cheeks
woman of the sweet fresh arms
man of the calm eyes
woman of the ardent lips
man of the plenitude of speech
woman of the shared eyes
man of the useful hands
woman of the sensible hands
man of the steadfast stars
woman of the enduring breasts

there is nothing that prevents you
my masters from testing me.

VII

La grande rivière qui va
Grande au soleil et petite à la lune

Par tous chemins | à l'aventure
Ne m'aura pas pour la montrer du
doigt

Je sais le sort de la lumière
J'en ai assez pour jouer son éclat

Pour me parfaire au dos de mes
paupières
Pour que rien ne vive sans moi.

The great river that flows
big under the sun and small under the
moon
in all directions at random
will not have me to point it out

I know the spell of the light
I have enough of it to feign its
brilliance
so that I may perfect myself behind
my eyelids
so that nothing lives without me.

Paul Eluard

I. This vehement mélodie does not ask for much subtlety of interpretation; a few contrasts which are well indicated must be made, but without breaking the general impetus. A sharp articulation is indispensable. *N.B.* In the seventh bar, first beat, of voice part, it is an A flat. In the ninth bar, third beat, it is an A natural.

II. The twittering and the agitation of the birds in the bright morning light is admirably suggested by the first two lines of this quatrain, and by the music. There should be no diminuendo with the slowing down of 'Le bouillonnement des oiseaux'. The last quaver must have its precise value, and a good breath prepares the contrasted last two lines, the words and the music evoking so well the quietness of the evening. The slower tempo is about ♩ = 104 and it slows gradually to the end.

III. The poet falls asleep, a tranquil nocturne to be sung with a floating voice and a peaceful legato. The dynamics, very well indicated, imply no crescendo at all in the first three lines, a definite *mf* on the fourth line, a good breath and a contrast of *pp* for the two following lines; then a crescendo, with its climax on 'pour la nuit' which is *f* (of course a relative *f*), prepares the striking *subito pp* of the last line. In the sixteenth bar, second beat, it is a D flat in the piano part.

IV. This is a happy dream. A long breath can be taken between the two tercets, and the last four chords of the piano can be slightly *rallentando* with the diminuendo.

V. Marked with gravity, this mélodie should be performed with intensity. The piano prelude is *marcato molto* and the voice must sing with a tense legato. (Carefully observe the evenness of the quavers 'De ta folie', and the semiquaver 'attends sagesse').

VI. A long silence must precede this mélodie, to enhance the beautiful and unexpected change of colour from C major to F sharp major, and the attack must be as *pp* as possible. Very soft, very slow (♩ = 50). The poem, in Eluard's favourite form of a litany, has rightly suggested to the composer a mélodie built in groups of two lines. The first two remain *pp*, the next two are *mf* crescendo, *f* diminuendo. I suggest that this diminuendo goes only to a *p*, to make it possible to attack *pp* the following two lines which are crescendo. Then, in a tempo just a little less slow, the following two lines are *f*, and the next two *f* crescendo to the big climax *ff* followed by *molto diminuendo*. The last two lines must be a complete contrast expressively: here is the conclusion to all the foregoing invocations to those who are the poet's masters, in his profound humanity. A *p* seems more adequate than a *pp* as well as broad declamation. An expressive breath should be taken between 'Mes maîtres' and 'de m'éprouver'.

VII. This last mélodie must flow as the river of the poem; and in the second quatrain it recalls the vehemence of the first mélodie—its biting articulation and its impelling impetus.

*

Most of Poulenc's mélodies composed on poems by Apollinaire and Eluard are best suited to male voices, though several of them are quite possible for female voices. But when he wished to write typically feminine songs he liked to set really feminine poems, and he found them in the charming and elegant works of Louise de Vilmorin.

FIANÇAILLES POUR RIRE (WHIMSICAL BETROTHAL)

This is a series of six mélodies which does not, as *Tel jour telle nuit*, constitute a real cycle, but is a well-balanced group of mélodies.

LA DAME D'ANDRÉ	ANDRÉ'S WOMAN FRIEND
André ne connaît pas la dame	André does not know the woman
Qu'il prend aujourd'hui par la main.	whom he took by the hand today.
A-t-elle un cœur à lendemains,	Has she a heart for the tomorrows,
Et pour le soir a-t-elle une âme ?	and for the evening has she a soul ?
Au retour d'un bal campagnard	On returning from a country ball
S'en allait-elle en robe vague	did she go in her flowing dress
Chercher dans les meules la bague	to seek in the hay stacks the ring
Des fiançailles du hasard ?	for the random betrothal ?
A-t-elle eu peur, la nuit venue,	Was she afraid, when night fell,
Guettée par les ombres d'hier,	haunted by the ghosts of the past,
Dans son jardin, lorsque l'hiver	in her garden, when winter
Entrait par la grande avenue ?	entered by the wide avenue ?

Il l'a aimée pour sa couleur,
Pour sa bonne humeur de Dimanche.
Pâlira-t-elle aux feuilles blanches
De son album des temps meilleurs?

     Louise de Vilmorin

He loved her for her colour,
for her Sunday good humour.
Will she fade on the white leaves
of his album of better days?

Each quatrain of this charming, light poem ends with a question mark. Will 'la dame d'André' be really important in his life, or just the passing fancy of a day? The question is put by the musician with equal lightness and charm. The gently moving tempo ($\quarternote = 126$) is excellent, with a slowing down at the end of the little piano prelude. The dynamics are well indicated (but a *mf* is omitted on 'Pâlira-t-elle', etc.), and are on contrasted plains which must be observed, and which are perfectly suited to the words of which they emphasize the meaning. There is no *rallentando* for the voice at the end of the mélodie, but a definite one for the piano conclusion.

DANS L'HERBE

Je ne peux plus rien dire
Ni rien faire pour lui.
Il est mort de sa belle
Il est mort de sa mort belle
Dehors
Sous l'arbre de la Loi
En plein silence
En plein paysage
Dans l'herbe.
Il est mort inaperçu
En criant son passage
En appelant
En m'appelant.
Mais comme j'étais loin de lui
Et que sa voix ne portait plus

Il est mort seul dans les bois
Sous son arbre d'enfance.
Et je ne peux plus rien dire
Ni rien faire pour lui.

     Louise de Vilmorin

IN THE GRASS

I can say nothing more
nor do anything for him.
He died for his beautiful one
he died a beautiful death★
outside
under the tree of the Law
in deep silence
in open countryside
in the grass.
He died unnoticed
crying out in his passing
calling
calling me.
But as I was far from him
and because his voice no longer
  carried
he died alone in the woods
beneath the tree of his childhood.
And I can say nothing more
nor do anything for him.

★ He died a natural death

There is much more profundity in this poem and this music, which must be sung with complete sincerity. The quiet tempo ($\quarternote = 56$) should be maintained very evenly with a flawless legato, and as usual, carefully observed dynamics markings. A beautiful vocal effect can be achieved, after the big crescendo and a breath, with the *subito pp* on 'Mais comme j'étais loin de lui'. Several important stresses are indicated in the above text. There is no *ritardando* at the end.

IL VOLE	HE FLIES
En allant se coucher le soleil Se reflète au vernis de ma table	As the sun is setting it is reflected in the polished surface 　　of my table
C'est le fromage rond de la fable Au bec de mes ciseaux de vermeil.	it is the round cheese of the fable in the beak of my silver scissors.
Mais où est le corbeau? Il vole.	But where is the crow? It flies.
Je voudrais coudre mais un aimant Attire à lui toutes mes aiguilles. Sur la place les joueurs de quilles De belle en belle passent le temps.	I should like to sew but a magnet attracts all my needles. On the square the skittle players pass the time with game after game.
Mais où est mon amant? Il vole.	But where is my lover? He flies.
C'est un voleur que j'ai pour amant, Le corbeau vole et mon amant vole, Voleur de cœur manque à sa parole Et voleur de fromage est absent.	I have a thief for a lover, the crow flies and my lover steals, the thief of my heart breaks his word and the thief of the cheese is not here.
Mais où est le bonheur? Il vole.	But where is happiness? It flies.
Je pleure sous le saule pleureur Je mêle mes larmes à ses feuilles. Je pleure car je veux qu'on me veuille Et je ne plais pas à mon voleur.	I weep under the weeping willow I mingle my tears with its leaves. I weep because I want to be desired and I am not pleasing to my thief.
Mais où donc est l'amour? Il vole.	But where then is love? It flies.
Trouvez la rime à ma déraison Et par les routes du paysage	Find the rhyme for my lack of reason and by the roads of the countryside

Ramenez-moi mon_amant volage	bring me back my flighty lover
Qui prend les cœurs ǀ et perd ma raison.	who takes hearts and drives me mad.
Je veux que mon voleur me vole.	I wish that my thief would steal me.
Louise de Vilmorin	

This poem plays on the words 'Il vole' which mean both 'he flies' and 'he steals'; thus the line 'The crow flies (vole) and my lover steals (vole)'. There are also hints of a well-known fable by the seventeenth-century fabulist, La Fontaine, 'The crow and the fox'; the latter being the thief of the crow's round cheese. There are other lines which are also a play on words, on gallicisms: 'jouer la belle' means to play the deciding game; 'sans rime ni raison' without rhyme or reason. All this does not make the word-for-word translation of the poem quite clear. However, it reaches a clear conclusion: Bring me back my fickle lover thief.

This sparkling mélodie requires virtuosity from the pianist ('in the style of a piano study' is Poulenc's indication), and from the singer, who must have the most precise articulation, as well as great lyricism. The indicated tempo ($\quad$ = 120) is certainly on the slow side and a minimum of speed; it should be inflexible, and more rhythmic than legato, with sudden contrasts of melodic and legato phrasing on the lines 'Sur la place les joueurs de quilles De belle en belle passent le temps'. Also on the lines 'C'est un voleur que j'ai pour amant' and 'Et voleur de fromage est absent'. And also in all the fourth quatrain: 'Je pleure', etc. at the end of which there is a big *ritenuto*, before starting again in tempo and rhythmically: 'Mais où donc est l'amour?', etc. All the last part of the mélodie should give an impression of breathlessness; 'haletant' means 'panting'. There is no *rallentando* up to the end. The indication *dans un souffle* means rather 'in one expiration'.

MON CADAVRE EST DOUX COMME UN GANT	MY CORPSE IS AS LIMP AS A GLOVE
Mon cadavre est doux comme un gant	My corpse is as limp as a glove
Doux comme un gant de peau glacée	limp as a glove of glacé kid

Et mes prunelles_effacées
Font de mes_yeux des cailloux blancs.

and my two hidden pupils
make two white pebbles of my eyes.

Deux cailloux blancs dans mon visage
Dans le silence deux muets
Ombrés_encore d'un secret
Et lourds du poids mort des_images.

Two white pebbles in my face
two mutes in the silence
still shadowed by a secret
and heavy with the burden of things
    seen.

Mes doigts tant de fois_égarés
Sont joints_en_attitude sainte
Appuyées_au creux de mes plaintes
Au nœud de mon cœur arrêté.

My fingers so often straying
are joined in a saintly pose
resting on the hollow of my groans
at the centre of my arrested heart.

Et mes deux pieds sont les montagnes
Les deux derniers monts que j'ai vus
A la minute_où j'ai perdu
La course que les_années gagnent.

And my two feet are the mountains
the last two hills I saw
at the moment when I lost
the race that the years win.

Mon souvenir est ressemblant,
Enfants | emportez-le bien vite,

I still resemble myself
children bear away the memory
    quickly,

Allez, | allez ma vie est dite.
Mon cadavre_est doux comme_un
  gant.

go, go, my life is done.
My corpse is as limp as a glove.

Louise de Vilmorin

A pendant to 'Dans l'herbe' after the preceding mélodie, and marked with a gravity which does not exclude great lyricism. The quiet tempo ($\downarrow$ = 60) must not drag, but must move with an even pace. The vocal line is very legato and intense. There are many dynamics markings to be observed with care. On the two descending phrases 'Et lourds du poids mort des images' and 'La course que les années gagnent' there should be no diminuendo coming down and an almost exaggerated legato. 'Mon souvenir est ressemblant' is *pp*, like an already remote voice. The first 'Allez' is *mp*, break, and the second one is *pp*: but the last phrase for the voice should not be too *p* in the low register. There is a misprint in the seventh bar, third beat: it is a C natural for the voice and the piano.

VIOLON	VIOLIN
Couple amoureux aux accents méconnus	Enamoured couple with the misprized accents
Le violon | et son joueur me plaisent.	the violin and its player please me.
Ah! j'aime ces gémissements tendus	Ah! I love these wailings long drawn out
Sur la corde des malaises.	on the cord of uneasiness.
Aux accords sur les cordes des pendus	In chords on the cords of the hanged
A l'heure où les Lois se taisent	at the hour when the Laws are silent
Le cœur, | en forme de fraise, √	the heart, formed like a strawberry,
S'offre à l'amour comme un fruit | inconnu.	offers itself to love like an unknown fruit.

Louise de Vilmorin

An elegant lady in a Hungarian nightclub is very moved indeed by a
violin and a violinist. This sensuous mélodie demands from both its
performers a style of almost excessive expression, remaining of course
within the limits of good taste. It should not itself sound like a night-
club song, but should only evoke this atmosphere.

The tempo (♩ = 63) seems rather on the slow side, but in any case
it must be very supple; the pianist should do his best to imitate the
languorous and scooping playing of a gipsy violinist.

A little *ritenuto* can be made to prepare the entrance of the voice,
which starts *f* extremely legato, even *portando*. In this bar:

'Le' and 'vi' are extremely staccato, but 'iolon' is legato with a stress
on 'io'. (The 'i' has to be repeated.) On the line 'Ah! j'aime ces gémis-
sements tendus', an expressive breath can be taken before 'tendus';
the whole should be phrased with *portamenti* and a long D on the
syllable 'se'. 'Le cœur' and 'S'offre à l'amour' are *mf* and legato, but
the parenthesis 'en forme de fraise' must be truly *p* with a diminuendo

going up and *quasi parlando*. This effect is not easy to achieve but should not be neglected. The last phrases for the voice are again with *portamenti* and rather *f*. The piano ending is strictly in tempo, concluding with the imitation of a violin staccato.

FLEURS	FLOWERS
Fleurs promises, fleurs tenues dans tes bras,	Promised flowers, flowers held in your arms,
Fleurs sorties des parenthèses d'un pas,	flowers sprung from the parenthesis★ of a step,
Qui t'apportait ces fleurs l'hiver	who brought you these flowers in winter
Saupoudrées du sable des mers?	powdered with the sand of the seas?
Sable de tes baisers, fleurs des‿ amours fanées	Sand of your kisses, flowers of faded loves
Les beaux‿yeux sont de cendre et dans la cheminée	the beautiful eyes are ashes and in the fireplace
Un cœur enrubanné de plaintes	a heart beribboned with sighs
<u>Brûle</u> | avec ses images √ saintes.	burns with its treasured pictures.
Louise de Vilmorin	★ The shape made by a footprint in the sand

The melancholy poem of a lady burning the souvenirs of a faded love. A long silence must precede this *mélodie*, when it is sung after 'Violon', in order to emphasize the modulation from A minor to the surprise of a beautiful attack *p* in D flat major, with a floating voice and a pure line, perfectly legato, but now with no *portamento* whatever and carefully even quavers ($\bullet = 56$). The chords of the piano must also be as legato as possible (in a haze of pedals) with the upper melodic line clear and transparent.

The climax of intensity is the line 'Brûle avec ses images saintes', with a break between 'brûle' and 'avec', an expressive breath before 'saintes' and no diminuendo at all, to achieve the contrast of a *pp subito* on the repeated 'Fleurs promises' which should be as *p* as possible, like a remembrance. From 'Qui t'apportait', etc. to the end, it is better to sing only *mf*. There is no *rallentando*.

MÉTAMORPHOSES (METAMORPHOSES)

This is another series of three mélodies to poems by Louise de Vilmorin, but these poems can also be sung by a man. They constitute a nice group, but can be separated, the idea of metamorphosis linking them being rather vague.

REINE DES MOUETTES	QUEEN OF THE SEAGULLS
Reine des mouettes, mon orpheline,	Queen of the seagulls, my orphan,
Je t'ai vue rose, je m'en souviens,	I have seen you pink, I remember it,
Sous les brumes mousselines	under the misty muslins
De ton deuil ancien.	of your bygone mourning.
Rose d'aimer le baiser qui chagrine	Pink that you liked the kiss which
	vexes you
Tu te laissais accorder à mes mains	you surrendered to my hands
Sous les brumes mousselines	under the misty muslins
Voiles de nos liens.	veils of our bond.
Rougis, rougis, mon baiser te devine	Blush, blush, my kiss divines you
Mouette prise aux nœuds des grands	seagull captured at the meeting of the
chemins.	great highways.
Reine des mouettes, mon orpheline,	Queen of the seagulls, my orphan,
Tu étais rose accordée à mes mains	you were pink surrendered to my
	hands
Rose sous les mousselines	pink under the muslins
Et je m'en souviens.	and I remember it.

Louise de Vilmorin

The queen of the seagulls is undoubtedly a delicate and charming lady, blushing under her grey muslin veils. Her poetic image is well suggested by the poet and the musician in this mélodie of a palpitating elegance.

The tempo ($\downarrow$ = 108) is very fast but *just right*. (It cannot be perfectly achieved immediately!) There are constant and important contrasts of rhythmic and legato phrases which could be better indicated. In the first two quatrains, the first two lines are rhythmic, and the last two lines are melodic and legato. The two following lines, 'Rougis', etc. are *f* and lyrical; then 'Reine des mouettes, mon orpheline' is *p* and slightly *parlando*; 'Tu étais rose accordée à mes mains' is *mf*, the triplets being very even and legato. A little breath for both performers can be taken before 'Rose sous les mousselines', which is *pp* and supple, and 'Et je m'en souviens' is *mf*, rather *accelerando* to launch the brilliant and fast piano coda, which has only a *very* slight *rallentando* at the end.

C'EST AINSI QUE TU ES	IT IS THUS THAT YOU ARE
Ta chair, d'âme mêlée,	Your body imbued with soul,
Chevelure emmêlée,	your tangled hair,
Ton pied courant le temps,	your foot pursuing time,
Ton ombre qui s'étend	your shadow which stretches
Et murmure à ma tempe.	and whispers close to my temples.
Voilà, c'est ton portrait,	There, that is your portrait,
C'est ainsi que tu es,	it is thus that you are,
Et je veux te l'écrire	and I want to write it to you
Pour que la nuit venue,	so that when night comes,
Tu puisses croire et dire,	you may believe and say,
Que t'ai bien connue.	that I knew you well.

Louise de Vilmorin

There is a 'Chopinesque' lyrical flavour in this *mélodie*, rightly demanded by the lyrical gravity of the poem. The tempo (♩ = 60) is very quiet and supple, at ease. The important piano part requires expressive, legato and fluid playing (the appoggiaturas without haste), and the voice part requires a rich low register to get the warmth of the first part of the *mélodie*, which is *mf* and very well phrased. Then there is a sudden *p*, bright and 'with tender melancholy' on 'Voilà, c'est ton portrait, C'est ainsi que tu es'. *Subito mf* and crescendo on 'Et je veux te l'écrire' to be able to achieve the big diminuendo going from the low D sharp *f*, to the top G *pp*. The last line is less *p* and intense. Poulenc has indicated important fingering and precise pedalling to achieve the legato of the piano coda.

PAGANINI	PAGANINI
Violon hippocampe et sirène	Violin sea-horse and siren
Berceau des cœurs cœur et berceau	cradle of hearts heart and cradle
Larmes de Marie Madeleine	tears of Mary Magdalen
Soupir d'une Reine	sigh of a queen
Echo	echo
Violon | orgueil des mains légères	Violin pride of agile hands
Départ à cheval sur les eaux	departure on horseback on the water
Amour chevauchant le mystère	love astride mystery
Voleur en prière	thief at prayer
Oiseau	bird
Violon femme morganatique	violin morganatic woman
Chat botté courant la forêt	puss-in-boots ranging the forest
Puit des vérités lunatiques	well of insane truths
Confession publique	public confession
Corset	corset
Violon alcool de l'âme en peine	violin alcohol of the troubled soul
Préférence muscle du soir	preference muscle of the evening
Épaules des saisons soudaines	shoulder of sudden seasons
Feuille de chêne	leaf of the oak
Miroir	mirror
Violon chevalier du silence	violin knight of silence
Jouet | évadé du bonheur	plaything escaped from happiness
Poitrine des mille présences	bosom of a thousand presences
Bateau de plaisance	boat of pleasure
Chasseur.	hunter.

Louise de Vilmorin

This is only a piece of virtuosity for both singer and pianist, as is suggested by the title of the poem and by the poem itself which is a kaleidoscope of images suggested to the poet by a violin.

The *tempo prestissimo* ($\downarrow$. = 100) must be inflexible from beginning to end, with breaths only from time to time.

15 | Other Composers

Several other composers must at least be mentioned, although the size of this book does not permit a study in detail of some of their mélodies.

DÉODAT DE SÉVERAC (1842–1912). There is a book published by Salabert, which contains twelve mélodies, often picturesque and rewarding for the interpreters. Among them are: 'Chanson de la nuit durable', 'Chanson pour le petit cheval', 'Les hiboux' and 'Ma poupée chérie'.

ALEXANDRE GEORGES (1850–1938) has composed a series of fourteen mélodies called 'Les chansons de Miarka' (publisher: Enoch). They are gipsy songs on poems by Jean Richepin.

VINCENT D'INDY (1851–1931). A pupil of César Franck, important for his influence on French music at the beginning of the century. He wrote only a few mélodies, among them 'Lied Maritime' (publisher: Salabert).

CHARLES BORDES (1851–1931). Also a pupil of César Franck, founder with Vincent d'Indy of an important school. He wrote about twenty-five mélodies. Among them are 'Paysages tristes' (4 mélodies), 'O triste était mon âme', 'Dansons la gigue', 'La poussière des tamis', 'Sur un vieil air' (publisher: Salabert).

GABRIEL PIERNÉ (1863–1937). Fine musician and great conductor. The 'Six Ballades Françaises de Paul Fort' form a varied group of mélodies (publisher: Hamelle).

ALFRED BACHELET (1864–1944) is well known for a very lyrical mélodie, 'Chére nuit', for a lyric soprano, which is better in the orchestral version.

REYNALDO HAHN (1874–1947) was a composer with a charming musical gift, who wrote about sixty mélodies (publisher: Heugel). Several of them are very well known, but, not always the best ones. I recommend 'Études latines' (7 mélodies), 'L'heure exquise', 'Quand je fus pris au pavillon', 'Le rossignol des lilas', etc.

GABRIEL DUPONT (1878–1914). 'Mandoline', 'Chanson des noisettes' (publisher: Heugel).

JACQUES IBERT (1890–1962). 'La verdure dorée' (4 mélodies), 'Chansons de Don Quichotte' (4 mélodies) (publisher: Leduc).

ARTHUR HONEGGER (1892–1955), who was chiefly a symphonist, wrote about thirty mélodies. 'Six poèmes d'Apollinaire', 'Six poèmes de Jean Cocteau', 'Trois poèmes de Paul Claudel' (publisher: Salabert).

MARCEL DELANNOY (1898–1962) wrote about forty mélodies. 'Deux chansons de Clarin' (publisher: Heugel), 'Quatre regrets de Joachim du Bellay' (publisher: Durand), 'Cinq quatrains de Francis Jammes' (publisher: Heugel).

*

Living composers, fortunately, are adding more mélodies to the French vocal repertoire:

DARIUS MILHAUD has already written nearly two hundred mélodies of very varied character, among them: 'Poèmes juifs' (8) (publisher: Eschig). 'Chants populaires hébraïques' (6) (publisher:

Heugel), 'Quatre poèmes de Léo Latil' (publisher: Durand), 'Catalogue de fleurs' (7) (publisher: Durand), 'Les soirées de Petrograd' (12) (publisher: Durand), 'Chansons de négresse' (mezzo) (3) (publisher: Salabert), 'Petites légendes' (15) (publisher: Heugel), 'Chants de misère (baritone-mezzo-soprano) (4) (publisher: Heugel), 'Chansons de Ronsard' (4) (high soprano) originally with orchestra (publishers: Boosey and Hawkes).

GEORGES AURIC has already written about thirty mélodies. 'Six poèmes de Paul Eluard' (publisher: Heugel), 'Trois poèmes de Léon-Paul Fargue' (publisher: Eschig), 'Trois poèmes de Louise de Vilmorin' (publisher: Eschig), 'Trois poèmes de Max Jacob' (publisher: Heugel).

HENRI SAUGUET has already composed more than one hundred mélodies: 'Six mélodies symboliques' (Amphion-Ricordi), 'Les pénitents en maillots roses' (5) (publisher: Heugel), 'Visions infernales' (6) (for bass) (publisher: Heugel).

JACQUES LEGUERNEY has written more than fifty mélodies, mostly to verses by sixteenth-century French poets: 'Vingt poèmes de la Pleiade', 'La nuit' (3) 'Le carnaval' (3) (publisher: Salabert).

OLIVIER MESSIAEN. The mélodies are not numerous in the important catalogue of this musician: 'Trois mélodies', 'Poèmes pour Mi' (9), 'Chants de la terre et du ciel' (6) (publisher: Durand).

ANDRÉ JOLIVET has also composed relatively few mélodies: 'Trois Complaintes du Soldat' (publisher: Durand), 'Poèmes intimes' (5) (publisher: Heugel). Both series were originally written with orchestral accompaniment.

JEAN FRANÇAIX. 'L'Adolescence Clémentine' (5) (publisher: Eschig), 'Cinq poèmes de Charles d'Orléans' (publisher: Schott), 'Huit anecdotes de Chamfort' (publisher: Eschig).

DANIEL LESUR. 'Trois poèmes de Cécile Sauvage' (publisher: Amphion-Ricordi), 'Clair comme le jour' (3) (publisher: Amphion-Ricordi), 'L'enfance de l'art' (publisher: Amphion-Ricordi), 'Berceuses à tenir éveillé' (publisher: Durand).

Several other composers should be mentioned who are at present composing mélodies: JEAN RIVIER, GEORGES MIGOT, CLAUDE ARRIEU, PIERRE PETIT, JEAN-MICHEL DAMASE, HENRI DUTILLEUX.

*

This short chapter, which is merely an enumeration, may, however, give an idea of the importance of the present repertoire of French mélodies. I hope that young singers will be sufficiently interested to become familiar with this repertoire, since there are many works of great poetical and musical value still remaining for them to discover.

Index of Titles

Indexes © Cassell and Co Ltd 1970

Index of First Lines

Index of Composers